# Michael Wilding and the Fiction of Instant Experience

# Michael Wilding and the Fiction of Instant Experience

Stories, Novels, and Memoirs, 1963–2012

Don Graham

AMHERST, NEW YORK

Copyright 2013 Don Graham

All rights reserved.
Printed in the United States of America

No part of this publication may be reproduced, stored in or introduced into a retrieval system, or transmitted, in any form, or by any means (electronic, mechanical, photocopying, recording, or otherwise), without the prior permission of the publisher.

Requests for permission should be directed to:
webmaster@teneopress.com, or mailed to:
Teneo Press
PO Box 349
Youngstown, NY 14174

Library of Congress Control Number: 2013944185

p. cm.
ISBN 978-1-93484-495-3 (alk. paper)

The cover image is copyright Deborah Adamson.

Teneo Press thanks Deborah Adamson
for permission to use the cover image.

*For Betsy Berry*

# Table of Contents

Acknowledgments ................................................................. ix

Introduction ....................................................................... xi

Chapter 1: The Undergrowth of Literary Production ..................... 1

Chapter 2: Varieties of Jamesian Experience ............................. 13

Chapter 3: Varieties of Kerouacian Experience .......................... 81

Chapter 4: Writers Living Together ....................................... 115

Chapter 5: Post-Modernism in High Gear ............................... 141

Chapter 6: Sex and the Single Male ...................................... 179

Chapter 7: Renovated Realism ............................................. 213

References ....................................................................... 235

Index .............................................................................. 253

# Acknowledgments

I would like to thank Dean Randy L. Diehl of the College of Liberal Arts at the University of Texas for a College Research Fellowship that allowed me time to begin work in earnest on this book. I also want to thank Elizabeth Cullingford, Chair of the Department of English, for her enthusiastic support, as always.

For my professional interest in Australian literature, I owe a huge debt to Professor John Higley, a widely published expert on elites in government, and longtime head of the Edward A. Clark Center for Australian Studies at the University of Texas. John put together a multi-year exchange program between the University of Texas and the University of Sydney in the late 1980s, and my exchange semester Down Under in 1991 proved to be a career-enhancing experience. In the years since, John has supported numerous travel and research trips for me to attend academic and literary conferences in Australia and the U.S. Fran Cushing at the Clark Center has been a big help as well.

Four of my colleagues in the English Department—John Rumrich, Mary Blockley, Phillip Barrish, and Matt Cohen respectively—helped me out with information on Renaissance poetry, Anglo-Saxon Chronicles, and a Henry James allusion.

I also want to thank Jessica Pierce, Andrea Golden, and especially Chad Vredingburgh of the staff of the Department of English for their expert help with digital technology beyond my ken.

Anyone reading this book will see my deep indebtedness to Michael Wilding for his immensely helpful sharing of information on his life and works. It has been a great pleasure to read those incoming emails going on a decade or more.

And as always, I am deeply grateful to my wife, Betsy Berry, for her constant support and love.

# INTRODUCTION

### WATER GLIMPSES

The artist has this advantage over the rest of the world, that his friends offer not only their appearance and their character to his satire, but also their work.

Somerset Maugham,
*The Moon and Sixpence*

Memoir disguised as fiction, of course, but that has always been the way of the best fiction.

Michael Wilding,
*Wild Amazement*

In 1991, my wife, Betsy Berry, and I went to Australia where I was to teach the spring semester on exchange at the University of Sydney. Among the paperbacks in the Leichhardt household that we rented were several by Michael Wilding who, as I soon learned, was a well-known author and a professor in the English Department at the University. He and his wife, Lyndy Abraham, were still in Greece when classes began, and in fact did not arrive back in Sydney until a month later. In the meantime Betsy, a poet and short story writer, was invited to teach Wilding's creative writing class until he returned. When we finally met Michael and Lyndy, we all four hit it off immediately and spent a lot of time together during that wonderful semester in Sydney.

I went back to Sydney several times to attend conferences and deliver papers on Wilding's works—both there and in the states. Throughout these years we kept in touch through postal mail, then by email. Finally, in 2009 I decided to write a full-length study of Wilding's fiction. The present book is the result of that decision. A crucial part of this study is an extensive exchange of emails, and in a sense I have "interviewed" Wilding many times regarding particular questions that his work provoked in my attempts to understand and elucidate his fiction. The whole literary scene in Sydney in the sixties and seventies has been of constant interest to me.

Through a close analysis of short stories and novels, I seek to underscore Wilding's artistry and his importance as a craftsman and cultural commentator unmatched in Australian literature. Several key elements of his fiction are evident: (1) an intensely literary background revealing itself in a wide-ranging allusiveness; (2) an early dialectic between the controlled craftsmanship of Henry James (an early Wilding favorite) and the looser, racier vernacular of Jack Kerouac (also an early favorite); (3) an intense interest in urban experience in Australia rather than the wide brown land; (4) an intense interest in sexual experience in the era of women's liberation; (5) a post-modern turn in the mid 70s; and (6) a quest for what I call the aesthetic of instant experience. In addition, throughout his career Wilding has worked assiduously in editing, publishing, and championing writers of all types.

Another primary aim of this study is to restore Wilding to the forefront of Australian literature.

Ian Syson has remarked upon Wilding's anomalous situation: "In Mark Davis's *Gangland* (1997), a contemporary who's who of Australia's cultural elites, Wilding does not rate a mention; while his one-time fellow *enfant terrible*, Frank Moorhouse, is firmly situated (at six references) within the dominant cultural gatekeepers—alongside a number of other ex-members of Sydney's libertarian Push" (270). Syson further states, "Given that Wilding has worked as a writer, academic, critic and publisher/publicist in Australia for more than thirty years since his arrival here from England in 1963, and that his work in each field has often been ground-breaking and exemplary, this absence is astounding" (270). Syson concludes, however, that Davis's omission of Wilding in 1997 pointed to another puzzling fact: "It appears that Australian critical schools, whether they gather around traditional, conservative, progressive or radical positions, find Wilding easier to ignore than accommodate" (270). In an attempt to explain the silence surrounding Wilding, Syson quotes from Laurie Hergenhan's review of Wilding's *Studies in Classic Australian Fiction* (1997) to suggest one reason—Wilding's emphasis upon the political in literature. Writes Hergenhan, "In fact, an important and unfashionable part of Wilding's argument throughout is that institutionalized criticism brought with it the repressive and narrowing view that the discussion of ideas is improper in considering the novel as an art form" (205). Syson agrees that Wilding's interest in "explicitly socialist ideas . . . usually seen as quaint and irrelevant," makes many academic critics uncomfortable (271).

Viewed today, fifteen years later, Davis's book seems so outdated that it is almost a mark of integrity not to be included. In one passage he lists various "icons" who "embody the national cultural consciousness": David Williamson, Helen Garner, Frank Moorhouse, Germaine Greer, Robert Hughes, Les Murray, and a few others (29). Davis recites a roll call of the reactionary views of such figures, among others, as Barry Oakley, Les Murray, Frank Moorhouse, and Richard Neville: "None looks forward except with gloom. They all seem to long for the good old days when feminists burned bras, queer meant strange, literature meant Shakespeare, when divisions between high culture and low, critic and object were unambiguous, and ethnicity meant nothing more complex than eating out. Since their heyday the world has become a strange, fearful place" (31).

Perhaps it should be noted that for the last twenty years Richard Neville has defined himself as a futurist. Davis concludes that "What these figures have tended to offer lately isn't so much creative energy as backlash politics" (31). As for Moorhouse, Davis reports that in a 1996 Warana Writers' Week in Brisbane the author "gave vent to a...diatribe against 'postmodern terrorists,' 'gender supremacists' and 'Asianists'" (36). Again Moorhouse comes in for it, as Davis states of another public pronouncement by the author: "I'm not a fan of arguments about art for art's sake—when Frank Moorhouse starts talking about the free rein of the 'feral imagination', I switch right off" (225). As I said, it seems better *not* to be mentioned in that mob of old fogies as lampooned by Davis.

But still, the current tendency to overlook Wilding is depressingly evident in the fact that the recent 1,000 plus page anthology, *The Literature of Australia*, edited by Nicholas Jose and published by W.W. Norton in 2010, contains nothing by Wilding. His absence is troubling and in my view indefensible. Jose's omission of Wilding makes no sense at all in the light of what the editor himself states. In his introduction to Moorhouse, Jose declares him to be "one of the foremost young Australian writers of the 1970s; with Peter Carey, Murray Bail and Michael Wilding" (913). So, according to Jose, although Wilding was "one of the foremost young Australian writers of the 1970s," he is not included in the volume while the other "foremost young Australian writers of the 1970s"—Moorhouse Carey, and Bail—are included. Des Houghton, in the Brisbane *Courier-Mail*, called attention to Wilding's absence: "And how could they leave out literary lion Michael Wilding, the long-time professor of English at the University of Sydney?" He continued: "Wilding's omission is baffling. He has 16 works of fiction and more than 20 works of non fiction under his belt and is a respected publisher and critic." Don Anderson, a keen observer of the literary scene, said, "In my opinion, this omission is just disgraceful" (Email "Re: from Des," April 13, 2010).

Since his retirement from the University of Sydney in 2000, Wilding has authored two memoirs; five novels; dozens of essays, many of which are autobiographical in nature; several essays on Australian literary history; and a scholarly book in press titled *Wild Bleak Bohemia: Marcus Clarke, Adam Lindsay Gordon and Henry Kendall*. He has also been very active in publishing and editing, including starting a new press, Press On. Indeed the Wilding who turned seventy in 2012 seems to be as energetic in his three fields of activity—writing, publishing, editing—as he was in his twenties. And novels like *Academia Nuts* (2002/2003) have begun to garner significant critical attention both in Australia and abroad.

Wilding's latest autobiographical work, *Wild & Woolley: A Publishing Memoir* (2011), has generated renewed interest in the 1970s. David Williamson, Australia's foremost playwright, has pointed to Wilding's accomplishments in a recent book launch:

> Michael has made a huge contribution to Australian culture in all three of his chosen areas. A body of creative writing that just keeps getting better and better, a body of critical work in which his keen intellect informs and illuminates the literary landscape, and the legacy of Wild and Woolley and his other publishing ventures that literally changed our cultural expectations and landscape. (4)

In a laudatory review of the book, Peter Pierce concludes, "Time, too, to honour the long service that Wilding has done for the state (well, to its literary health)" ("Just Wild about the Book Business" 28). In another review Owen Richardson points to the importance of Wilding's long career: "Wilding was on the town, and how, but he stayed a man of the gown and Wild & Woolley contributed to the growth in Australian studies, now unfortunately so diminished..." (30).

The present book, I hope, will be part of an ongoing effort to revive Australian literary studies by looking closely at one of the most innovative, energetic, and influential figures in Australian literature for the past fifty years.

# Michael Wilding and the Fiction of Instant Experience

## Chapter 1

# The Undergrowth of Literary Production

## England, Editing, Early Stories

Born in Worcester in the Midlands of England in 1942, Michael Wilding grew up in "a small, landlocked country town" as he has recently described it ("Writing Humour" 172). His father, Richard, was an iron-moulder, and his mother, Dorothy Mary (Bull) Wilding, came from a "family of servants to the aristocracy" (Syson 280). Like many Englishmen, Wilding was made keenly aware of class and its invidious privileges and exclusions. He was a scholarship student at the Royal Grammar School in Worcester and then went on to Oxford. He has described his first-rate schooling in these terms: "It was a privileged education but you …always felt conscious of being on the outside of that world of privilege" (Syson 280).

Perhaps not surprisingly, Wilding's interest in writing stories evidenced itself early in his childhood. At age seven he wrote his first story, in a spiral bound notebook that now resides in the Wilding papers at the Mitchell Library in Sydney ("Writing Humour" 172). He also kept some diaries as a teenager. Looking back on them many years later, he pronounced it "all teenage despair, even less interesting than the mature aged despair I had ready access to" ("Education, Location and Creativity" 10). Another story he remembers writing as a youth came about when a physics teacher at his Grammar School told him to write something about "nothing" because he had been looking out the window during class and upon being interrogated by the teacher as to what he was looking at, replied "Nothing" ("Humour" 172). The punishment proved exhilarating. He wrote about authority and the subversive power of humor. At nineteen he wrote a story, "Frrrried Potatoes," that was broadcast on the regular BBC radio programme, "Morning Story." It dealt with sexual fantasy and humiliation, the longing for a waitress at a new coffee bar that had opened in the town. Although the story was read on the BBC, the author, who was working at the time delivering bread, did not hear it, only catching the sign-off at the end from a customer's radio where he was making a stop. The typescript has not survived ("Humour" 173). Those early subjects—authority, humor, and a waitress at a coffee bar—are quintessential Wilding material.

When Wilding graduated from Oxford in 1963, no doors of privilege swung open. He didn't want to do postgraduate work because the stipend was so small, and there were no attractive jobs in the offing in the UK. Many years later he recalled the dim prospects of those years and the powerful drag of class:

> The future looked bleak in England. Three years at Oxford had made it clear to me that if you came from the working class, you were never going to be accepted by the ruling elite. And the ruling elite ran the cultural show. Oh, you might find yourself a niche, as long as your politics were conformist, as long as you basically accepted the order of things and said so. But you'd always be a sort of upper-servant. ("Expatriation, Location and Creativity" 9.)

When Wallace Robson, his tutor at Lincoln College, Oxford, mentioned that there was a lecturer position available in the English Department at the University of Sydney, Wilding was receptive to the idea for many reasons. Both his grandfather and his father had been to Australia, though briefly. (Syson 280) For the iron moulder's son who wanted to be a writer, Australia offered employment and the romance of expatriation. As Wilding explained years later, going expat sounded like a great idea: "What I wanted to do was write. I didn't want to be an academic. I didn't want to do a postgraduate degree. The models for me as a writer were Lawrence, Isherwood, Durrell, people who'd gone into exile. You know, expatriation, travel around the world" (Syson 280).

So Wilding found himself in Sydney amidst all the freedom and splendor that the great city had to offer. In an autobiographical essay published in 2008, Wilding recalled that moment with images that bespoke his proletarian beginnings: "I had arrived in Sydney aged twenty-one to take up a lectureship—my first job, apart from being a bread roundsman with an electric delivery truck, and a milk roundsman, and a casual farm labourer, picking apples and beans and dabbing sheep with iodine solution to deter some fungus or fluke" ("Cars in My Life" 75). For the first time in his life he had money, he owned a car, and he gravitated naturally into that loose confederation of libertarians, bohemians, journalists, academics, artists, writers, pub crawlers, chicks, birds, sheilas (all overlapping with budding feminists), leftists, anarchists, the whole lot known as the Push. I think it is safe to say that he fell in love with Sydney.

Yet Wilding was not to commit finally, fully, to Australia until 1969. He taught at the University of Sydney from 1963 to 1966, then returned to England in 1967, taking up an Assistant Lectureship in English at the University of Birmingham, and the next year, a Lectureship at Birmingham, before rejoining the University of Sydney as Senior Lecturer in English, 1969-1972, followed by an appointment as Reader, 1973-1992, Professor in English and Australian Literature, 1993-2000, and Emeritus Professor in English and Australian Literature, 2001 to the present. In the late 90s he applied for and received dual citizenship in Australia and Great Britain.

Prior to 1972, Wilding published several academic studies, including a major study of Milton, *Milton's Paradise Lost*, in 1969; *Cultural Policy in Great Britain* (1970), co-written with Michael Green; and *Marvell: Modern Judgements* (1969), which he edited. He was also very active in editing fiction and poetry. In 1967 he edited *Three Tales* by Henry James. An edition of *Julius Caesar* and *Marcus Brutus* by John Sheffield appeared in 1970. Wilding later characterized such work in anthology-making for the educational market as "part of the undergrowth of literary production" (*Wildest Dreams* 49).

Two other early editing projects deserve some attention. One is *Australians Abroad* (1967), which he edited with Charles Higham, an Englishman, a poet, and the book editor of *The Bulletin* in the 1960s. Working on this book gave Wilding an excellent grounding in the works of many important Australian writers. And in 1971 Wilding co-edited with David Malouf, Shirley Cass, and Ros Cheney the important anti-Vietnam War volume, *We Took Their Orders and Are Dead: An Anti-war Anthology*, published by Ure Smith in Sydney. It brought together work by seventy-seven writers, including stories by Frank Moorhouse, David Malouf, Christina Stead, Jack Lindsay, Randolph Stow, Patrick White, Thomas Keneally, and Michael Wilding, and poems by Robert Adamson, Charles Higham, A. D. Hope, John Tranter, Nigel Roberts, Vicki Viidikas, and Judith Wright. In addition to his editing duties, Wilding's contribution was "The Silence of the Seer," a Borges-like fable which he later collected in his 1975 volume, *The West Midland Underground*. Wilding was also an energetic reviewer of both current fiction and scholarly books.

During the nine-year run up from his arrival in Australia to the publication of *Aspects of the Dying Process* in 1972, Wilding wrote 25 stories that were eventually collected and 7 that were not. This is an estimate since Wilding's CV cites publication dates but not dates of original composition. Still, we are talking about a minimum of 32 stories in nine years, for an average of just under 4 per year.

Many of these stories drew upon Wilding's pre-Australian experience. That is, they were stories set in Great Britain in the main. These included such early pieces as "Jealous of Ali," "Canal Run," "Reading the Signs," and "Class Feeling," each of which dealt with Wilding's school days in Worcester, and each of which, though written early, was not collected until much later. Robert Yeo has usefully suggested that these early stories offer the best point of entry into Wilding's oeuvre (193). Bruce Bennett in his book *Australian Short Fiction: A History* makes the same point: "Wilding's short fictional oeuvre is often at its most engaging in the autobiographical mode" (191).

As an example of Wilding's precociousness in the short story form, there is no better example than "Class Feeling." Yeo suggests its importance as well: "Already experimental concerns, intrusive, process-oriented, as well as the obvious, developing 'general leftist position' (in his own words), had begun to appear" (193). But there is more to be said about the story's originality and form. In this story Wilding utilizes an approach that seems to be unique—the technique of personal address. A close analysis shows the rhetoric of personal address in its richest form, though there are other stories that display partial deployments of such a strategy.

Wilding wrote "Class Feeling" in 1963, the year he first came to Australia. Although it deals with his English experience, there is a definite Australian perspective at one juncture in the story, making it different from other entirely English-based stories written at about the same time. "Class Feeling" was not published, however, until twenty-one years later, in the collection *Reading the Signs* (1984). Then two years later it appeared in the literary periodical *Stand,* published in England. The story was re-collected in Wilding's *Somewhere New,* 1996, and afterwards translated into Chinese and Punjabi.

For those who have not read it in English, Chinese, or Punjabi, a brief plot summary is helpful. A boy in an English grammar school leaves school one day to catch the bus home. Nearing the bus stop, he sees his father riding a bicycle home from work, dressed in clothes made grimy by his job at the local iron works. Aware that a prefect of the school is standing nearby, the boy pretends that he does not see his father in order not to disclose his class background. The father sees what has happened and though he never says anything about the denial and betrayal to his son, he knows and the boy knows. It is not a thing one forgets. The story ends with the detail that years later, at Oxford, upon filling out the entrance forms, in the place of father's occupation, the boy wrote "iron-moulder," but he is fully aware that this act is too late to repair that early betrayal. Thus we can see, and feel, the full force of "class feeling"—one of the central themes of Wilding's English upbringing and probably the most determinative fact in British history and culture: Class.

The autobiographical roots of "Class Feeling" are apparent, and the experience must have been one of the most searing and troubling of Wilding's youth. He restages the episode in two other stories. In "Reading the Signs," published in the *New Yorker* and collected in *Reading the Signs* (1984), the narrator, named Michael (no disguising here) recounts an incident that embarrassed his mother. The family had seen what they believed to be a flying saucer, and Michael's father had written a letter to the local newspaper. Michael then retells the iron moulder story:

> Mum was mortified. On the forms at school we wrote "Engineer," not "Iron-moulder." Filling in the forms for university, I went off to a private place and my stomach wrenched for a long time and for "Father's Professon or Occupation" I crossed out "Profession" and wrote "Iron-moulder." (10-11).

The next paragraph completes the circle of class-consciousness: "The man at the appointments board, just before I left, congratulated me. "Well, well," he said, "you're tipped for a first, you edited the university paper, you've done very well for an iron-moulder's son" (11).

In "Canal Run," an early autobiographical story first published in *Overland* in 1967, Wilding briefly describes his feelings about his father's occupation: "When in German conversation I was asked what job my father did, I blushed furiously. In the A stream everybody's father was vaguely white collar" (*The West Midland Underground* 26). These three early stories form the basis for an interesting documentary film titled *Reading the Signs*, made in 1988, featuring Wilding on camera amid scenes of his Grammar School and Worcester.

One literary source for "Class Feeling" may well be a passage in *Lady Chatterley's Lover*. Early in the novel Connie Chatterley is having a conversation with an intellectual with whom she has a brief affair. Here is the pertinent passage: "Now she and Michaelis sat on opposite sides of the fire and talked. She asked him about himself, his mother and father, his brothers...other people were always something of a wonder to her, and when her sympathy was awakened she was quite devoid of class feeling" (26). The context and phrasing are highly relevant to Wilding's story, but almost everything in British literature is centrally about "class feeling."

The plot summary, which hews closely to the basic facts of Wilding's education and his father's working-class job, only accounts for half of the story, however. The story begins with the narrator talking about what kind of story he is going to tell. The first sentence indicates a delaying/deferral tactic: "I've been intending to write you a story for a long time now, D" (47). The reader of this sentence realizes that "D" must refer to Deborah Thompson, to whom the story is dedicated just below the title: "For Deborah Thompson." The authorial voice—clearly autobiographical or meant to be read thus—continues to address "D" for six pages of a story that is only twelve pages long; therefore, as much of the story is this back and forth between the narrator and the absent D as it is one of conventional narration. The story's narrative content does not begin until halfway through the story, with this situational narrative sentence: "I used to catch the bus from the stop opposite the school from where, if I had looked across the road from the stop to the school itself, I could have seen that statue of Queen Elizabeth" (52-53). The sentence immediately before this one indicates the narrator's full consciousness of the deferrals that we are treated to at the outset: "And if I could just begin to tell the story, all this would be unnecessary, surely, as you would be able to make your own decision" (52).

So who is Deborah Thompson? I taught the story for several years before it occurred to me to ask Wilding directly. His reply explained much:

> Deborah Thompson was a close friend of my Oxford girlfriend, both upper middle class, private school (Cheltenham Ladies College, like Kristin Scott Thomas—I watched her with Jeff Goldblum in *Framed* last night, her accent reminded me of those Oxford years). Her father was a psychiatrist who had gone to Trinity College, Dublin with Samuel Beckett; Beckett was godfather to her brother. She is one of the girls, the other girl, in my story "Europe"... about a trip to Greece we made in 1962. She, her boy friend, my girl friend and myself. I rather fancied her, but various taboos intervened. I haven't kept in touch with any of these people—I did for a year or two" (Email "Re: a couple of quick items," December 5, 2004).

Later, Wilding commented further on the significance of Deborah Thompson as a muse for this story: "I wanted to explain to her, a girl from a vastly more privileged background than myself . . .what some of the stresses and tensions of being working class at that time were like. A corrective to all that talk of the new classless society" (Email "Re: repairing documentation..." February10, 2010).

In terms of narrative procedure, the story "Europe" is a more conventional one than "Class Feeling." It was also published earlier, in *The West Midland Underground*, in 1975. In "Europe" Deborah Thompson appears as "Deb," and the story is quite explicit in setting forth the terms of desire that the Wilding protagonist holds for her. On one occasion during the shared journey of the two couples in Greece, we are told: "He had walked into Deb's room once and she was dressing there, her breasts bare, and she had let out some cry of surprise and raised her hands and whatever it was that was in them, a shirt may be, up to cover herself, and he had said sorry and backed out; but as he was backing out she had said, oh sorry it's you, come in, sorry I didn't know who it was, and he had come back in and she had lowered her arms and the covering and whatever it was she was putting on, and she smiled at him all very matter of fact and uncomplicated, clear and clean and uncluttered, unworried" (147). Throughout the story, the protagonist is with his girl friend and at the same time desirous of being with Deb, but it never happens. Wilding's stories are replete with narratives of unrequited desire.

Wilding's technique of writing a story with a very specific audience in mind—in this instance, one person—suggests a new way of thinking about short stories in general. Perhaps far more of them than we know are written to very specific audiences, whether the writer discloses that fact or not, either in the text and "address" of the story, or in private. In a way, it's a letter that's not a letter. But it is certainly not an "epistolary" story. An epistolary story consists of narration by means of letters written by the main character (or characters in the story). This method clearly seems to be an abbreviated version of epistolary novels such as *Pamela* from the 18$^{th}$ century, the period of the "rise of the novel." But Wilding's "letter" is something different. It is not a letter but a personal address to a potential real reader. Another point to make here is that the story and the dedication mimic the usual practice of books "dedicated" to someone.

Wilding's story is extremely interesting in many ways. In the address to "D," to Deborah Thompson, Wilding's narrator creates an autobiographical context that "frames" the story proper. So in a way it is something like a prologue to a story. In the address to D., Wilding recounts how once at a party, when they were talking, D. asked him to write a story for her. Such a request has many functions, as we may well guess. First, it is a way of flattering the author; it signals that the author holds some special significance for the one asking, either as an author, a possible suitor, a friend, or some multilayered combination of these and further combinations, muse, mentor, mentee, patron, subject, etc. A Renaissance courtier's book would offer further permutations of supplicant and superior, female and male, lord and liege.

The spark set off by D's request that he write a story for her leads Wilding's narrator into a catalogue of possible narratives that he could produce to satisfy her request. The process is very interesting because it calls attention to the range of choices facing a fictionist facing a real one-on-one audience. (The unspoken anxiety, of course, is that no one reads one's story and one has no audience. This uncertainty hardly inhibits the interior buzz, the excitement, of being asked to write a story for a pretty girl who might or might not ever see it or who, upon seeing it, might not like it.)

The narrator recalls how D. had asked him, casually, over a drink at a party, to write a story for her, and how later, when she asked him again, he began to take her request seriously. The possibilities for such a story always came down to one group of subjects, he says: "and that was of writing something that would shock you" (48). His first thought, soon rejected, is to write something about one of the "nastier incidents" of his life, something that would shock her (48). He describes such narratives only to discard them: "And so the pick-ups of barmaids or the midnight drunkenness on motorways, the criminal fringe and the bohemian fornications of the provinces, I don't think they would have been very shocking, and I think to have told them in this way would have been to have missed their significance, spoilt their images" (49).

Then he recalls how he always, in their conversations, introduced a hostile tone. As he puts it, "...I loved to come and talk to you, but there was always that hostility, covering inefficiently I suppose a shyness, and it came from the old business of different backgrounds, different childhoods, different, I think, futures" (49). Here he hits at the heart of the difference between himself and D: the class system. In Britain it always comes down to class. He decides that the most shocking and truest thing he can tell her about himself, in a story, is to draw upon something so true and painful and embarrassing that he could never have told it to her in person, and that is the story that follows, of a boy's betrayal of his working class father, on the basis of class, indeed of class feeling. He tells her that the hostility towards her is rooted in their very different backgrounds. And in this passage he lays out a major difference between the two of them and between their two countries, because he has a new country now, Australia: "Perhaps, so geographically far away now I don't feel the need to shock you any more—getting older or communicating only, and irregularly, by airmail; or again may be the conditions of life in this democratic country—and though we use the phrase ironically we know it refers to a real quality—remove the pressures I used to feel" (50).

So among Wilding's contributions to the art of the short story must be added the story of personal address. Wilding defines the form as "partly epistolary, partly confessional, an outpouring to a specific audience" (Email "Re: a couple of quick items," December 12, 2004). Wilding also notes a distinction between a story written "for" someone as opposed to a story written "at" someone: "Other stories are written with people in mind but are more in the way of a provocation than a plea for sympathy—poking a stick with a horse's head handle into the lion's cage (to recall the old song about Alfred) to see what happened" (Email "Re: repairing documentation…," February 10, 2010). The story written "at" someone is the kind directed at a recurring figure in some of his best stories. Stories directed at his friend and rival Frank Moorhouse would liven up the Sydney literary scene, as would those Moorhouse wrote in rebuttal directed at Wilding. Individually and together, they made the short story personal in a way that one does not ordinarily think of short stories. The same was true of the stories Wilding wrote about Vicki Viidikas and the stories she wrote about him.

A natural question is whether Deborah Thompson ever responded to the story. Wilding says that as far as he knows, she never saw it. This certainly seems likely, as twenty-one years passed between the writing of the story and the "sending" of it via publication. So in a way the story has a kind of dead letter provenance, a story written both "for" and "to" Deborah Thompson but unreceived and unread, by the "addressee."

In the long view, "Class Feeling" signaled Wilding's embrace of his expatriate status as a burgeoning "Australian" writer, a designation he would expand upon in his first collection, *Aspects of the Dying Process*.

# Chapter 2

# Varieties of Jamesian Experience

## Aspects of the Dying Process

Somewhere along the line Wilding decided to remain in Australia and not return to England on any permanent basis. England was the past, Australia the immanent present—and future. For someone of Wilding's intellect and ability, the University of Sydney offered inviting opportunities: "The syllabus at Oxford ended in 1872. So everything afterwards was discovery—either self-discovery (like Kerouac) or the Goldberg syllabus at Sydney when I arrived—with Faulkner, Conrad, Lawrence, James &c, which made the work of preparing lectures and seminars new and exciting. Fun, in those days" (Email "Re: Bukowski," November 28, 2009).

Fun but challenging too, for the literary world that Wilding encountered in Sydney in the late 60s and early 70s offered just as many obstacles as those he would have found had he remained in England. In an assessment of the Australian scene, Owen Webster wrote in 1970:

> The literary life of Australia is a turmoil of old love-hates, of unburied hatchets and unextinguishable torches, of unconfessed prejudices and indiscreet gossip. Withal, it is unhealthy, and we

> cannot expect a healthy literature to emerge from it. Unless some therapeutic or cathartic stimuli come from somewhere and foster, inter alia, a conviction among Australians that the centre of the universe is here, we may find ourselves with the literature we deserve. None. Which will mean that as a nation we shall drift where we deserve. Nowhere. "I am Down Under, Therefore I am not." (32)

Nonetheless Wilding and his fellow writers forged ahead. Their immediate goal was to open up Australian fiction to new locales, new discourses, and new material. As his friend and co-editor Frank Moorhouse put it, the aim was to take Australian fiction beyond the traditional formula which he described in these terms: "They were humanistic. They were kind to the working class. They were sympathetic to kangaroos" ("There's No Such Thing as a Gay Novel" 19). In their search for venues for the New Writing, Wilding and Moorhouse ran headlong into a conservative publishing environment.

In 1972, in an attempt to find new venues, Wilding and Moorhouse started the lively and innovative *Tabloid Stories*, a locally famous breaker of taboos and smasher of genteel prohibitions. They discovered a lot of new talent and generated a lot of literary energy.

As for Wilding himself, the most important career event of 1972 was the publication of his first volume of short stories, *Aspects of the Dying Process*. One way of showing his newfound identity was to bring out a collection of Australian stories intended, in part, to authenticate his standing in the new writing in his new country. "Sidestepping Englishness was important I think," Wilding has stated (Email "Re: Bukowski," November 28, 2009). According to Wilding, *Aspects* "was published towards the end of the era of portentously lugubrious titles" ("Writing Humour" 173). In its author profile on the back cover, the University of Queensland Press described Wilding as "an Englishman, at present a Senior Lecturer in English at the University of Sydney. His stories have been appearing in England and Australia over the last half dozen years, and this first volume collects those with an Australian setting." Wilding was irritated at the insistence upon his identity as an Englishman: "I excluded anything non-Australian. The White Australia immigration policy was repealed that same year, 1972, but the literary culture remained, remains indeed, staunchly nationalistic. I tried to conform. Then they went and described me as an Englishman on the back cover" (Email "Re-: send-out," February 15, 2011).

The stories in *Aspects* are arranged to suggest thematic continuities and to position Wilding's career within an Australian literary context. In several stories, the ghost of Henry James hovers over the subject matter and manner. But those come later in the collection. In "Somewhere New," the first story, Wilding puts forward a quest for the new, for the rejection of England, and for the advancement of Australia and, tangentially, America as fields of literary ambition. Wilding recalls having written the story probably in 1969 after returning to Australia "that second time" (Email, July 13, 2009). It was published in England originally and has been republished several times, including translations in Chinese and Punjabi.

The story offers a sketch of an Englishman named Gavin Mulgrave who lives in Sydney where he pursues a career in the arts on radio. The character is based on Charles Higham, an Englishman born in 1931, who moved to Sydney in 1954 and pursued a career in book and film criticism. He had already published two volumes of verse back in England and published three more while living in Australia. In 1964 he became literary editor of the *Bulletin*, the legendary newspaper that published Henry Lawson, Banjo Paterson, and virtually every other writer of significance since the 1890s. (The *Bulletin* closed down in 2008). It was inevitable that two ambitious and gifted Englishmen like Higham and Wilding would meet, and soon Higham was assigning Wilding reviews. In 1967 the two writers co-edited *Australians Abroad*. In "Somewhere New" Wilding changes some details to camouflage Higham's identity. In the story

Mulgrave solicits radio reviews from the narrator instead of newspaper reviews. Nor do they collaborate on anything.

Mulgrave is a rather dodgy character in the story and dominates many of the scenes. A single man in his thirties, he likes to control social occasions in which he can hold forth on whatever ideas he wishes to espouse at the moment. Much of his extensive discourse to the auditor-narrator has to do with the idea of "somewhere new." In this discourse England is the dead land, the old decaying empire, a place of boredom and rotting bones. In one of their first discussions, Gavin says, "I think Australia's a young person's country. There's a lot of young talent in Australia" (2). On other occasions he turns directly to the wasteland that is England. "A lot of old witches sitting round at a funeral," he says (4). England is a "corpse," and he says that he hasn't been back in ten years (4). Wilding has stated that "some of the characterization [of Gavin] is projections of my own thoughts about the UK, developing on from conversations, but getting more extreme" (Email, April 28, 2011).

In contrast, the "somewhere new" that Gavin is searching for appears to be where he is, in Australia. But England, he continues on, has nothing culturally alive. "What are the magazines? You can list them on one finger. In the States every tin-pot university has its quarterly review." The narrator, who is also an Englishman living in Sydney, defends England: "*London Magazine, Stand, Transatlantic*" (4). What's interesting about this is the inside reference. For several years Wilding was Australian editor for *Stand,* which was edited by Jon Silkin, a poet, man of letters, and friend of Wilding. Indeed, "Somewhere New" appeared in *Stand* in 1972. Wilding also published stories in *London Magazine.*

After listening to Gavin rail against England's cultural malaise, the narrator asks him whether he publishes in Australia. This question sets Gavin off, "It would be suicide...Apart from the petty jealousies and the rivalries and ratbaggery here which makes it absolutely essential to keep well clear if one wants to preserve one's skin, who would ever *read* anything one published here? You might as well put it in a bottle and throw it into the harbour. No one in England or America has ever heard of the Australian magazines " (4). He goes on, calling Australian writers "minnows" and Australia one of those places that are "utter graveyards for one's reputation" (5). The dismissal of Australian literary culture sounds very much like the long-standing British view of colonial inferiority, the kind of dismissal that gave rise to the Cultural Cringe label famously identified and defined by A.A. Phillips in the *Meanjin Quarterly* in 1951. In a later interview, Phillips boiled his thesis down to a very simple proposition: "Essentially, the tendency to tag along dutifully behind England instead of doing our own thing" (Davidson 286). Wilding's narrator does not rise to the bait but simply listens to Gavin's opinions. One of Wilding's points about Gavin is his bland inconsistency—he happily contradicts himself or totally forgets previous utterances.

On another social outing, Gavin renews his analysis of England vs. Australia. He denounces English weather, intrusiveness, and regimentation. It is clear that in coming to Australia, Gavin is looking for "somewhere new," but it is also clear that Australia cannot, in his view, supply the kind of literary environment that he seeks. Turning away from his pejorative assessment of Australia's provincial and minor literary scene, he now focuses on other attributes which make Australia superior to England. Which of course leads him to the obvious, but Gavin is quite eloquent in elaborating that obviousness. He seizes upon the climate and the beaches as prime indicators of Australia's superiority over England: "I think the hedonism of the beaches is one of the truly unique qualities of Australia. It's so utterly healthy. There's none of the English neurosis. They don't sit around in damp basements and drafty pubs" (6). Then he cites two prominent British writers of that era, Kingsley Amis and Brigid Brophy, and scoffs at the very idea of imagining two such authors in Australia. It's not possible, he says, because "The beaches are the *centre* of life here instead of those dreadful damp churches" (6). He goes on, "The body is culture and religion here...The sun here destroys any of that unhealthy introversion, it drys it out like mould. Everything's vitalist and sinewy here" (6).

Then he connects the weather/health/beach culture with the literary (or lack of) culture. The one is the reason the other need not even exist. Again, here is Gavin holding forth: "It's an utterly healthy culture. Nobody bothers with theatre or books...It's absurd writing books in Australia. Who would ever want to read them? The glare's too strong on the beaches" (6). Moreover, the only audience for books in Australia, he says, are "a few neurotic housewives and ... university intellectuals who've got a vested interest in print culture to keep their jobs" (6).

After extolling Australia's anti-intellectual culture, he once more expatiates upon the freshness and health of Australia compared with their lack in England. The fishing boats that bring in fresh catches every day lead Gavin into a new metaphorical tack: "You can tell the vitality of a culture by the amount of fresh meat eaten." In London, he says, nobody ever eats or sees fresh meat, living as they do on sausages and such. He uses a timely literary allusion to drive the point home: "They probably wouldn't have known what it was. Something out of *Portnoy*. They all had congenital rickets and scurvy" (7). The evocation of the raw liver masturbation scene from Philip Roth's famous 60's novel is a nice touch—raw protein and sex equal Australia; stale meat and illness equal England.

At the end of this scene Gavin and the narrator leave the waterside restaurant and walk along the beach. The last paragraph comes from the consciousness of the narrator: "The firmness of the flesh, the taut stomachs, the just covered nipples on the full breasts, the clean undulant lines of throat and breast, belly and crutch, the mascara'd eyes and open mouths, the emanations of warmth and content" (7). This passage lingers in the mind of the reader who is attentive to the second story in the collection, "The Sybarites." For that story is in many ways an elaboration of the analysis of hedonistic beach culture set forth in "Somewhere New."

Later, after a broken engagement, when Gavin failed to attend a dinner invitation from the narrator and his girlfriend Barbara, Gavin telephones and offers gratis, as usual, one of those obsessive analyses on the impoverishment of Australia's literary culture. The passage is worth observing: "You get howled out of town if you so much as mention culture or poetry here. It must be the convict settlement. There's a resistance to anything cultural or new" (8-9). He continues, "But there must be lots of young people starved of literary culture here. Where would you ever buy any of the magazines? There's not a decent bookshop in the whole continent. At least in Europe people are aware of literature even if they don't read it. But there must be millions of Australians who go to the grave never knowing any other poetry than I love a sunburnt country. Imagine it" (9). The allusion, of course, is to Dorothea McKellar's poem "My Country," published originally in Sydney in 1908 and destined to become one of Australia's best-known poems, especially the lines "I love a sunburnt country" and "The wide brown land for me." (Across the water from where Wilding now lives on the island in Pittwater, he can see the house that Dorothea McKellar once lived in.) The poem is not well known in America, though Bill Bryson's mediocre book on his "travels" in Australia was titled *In a Sunburnt Country.*

Accepting an invitation to dine at Gavin's flat, the narrator and Barbara find themselves at the top of a ten-story building near King's Cross, with water glimpses of the Harbour Bridge. The narrator is frightened of the heights and of the balcony and of the fact that the building sways in high winds. All of this amuses Gavin, who tells him, "You'd probably pass out before you hit the bottom." The fear of falling reminds Gavin of "James Dickey's poem about the air hostess" (9). The poem in question, titled "Falling," appeared in the *New Yorker* on April 18, 1967. Gavin thinks even reading it would make the narrator "nauseous" (9).

The evening consists almost entirely of Gavin talking about such disparate topics as the lions in the zoo across the harbor. At one point the narrator asks him about plans for the "late-night underground poetry programme," but Gavin is completely dismissive and asks, "Who reads poetry now anyway?" (11). Then Gavin turns to the subject of food, of the many exotic dishes he has eaten. The comedy here resides in the fact that Gavin never brings forth anything for his little dinner party to eat. The narrator grows so hungry that he becomes dizzy. At one point he thinks to himself, "Perhaps like the chameleon he lived on air. Alone he never feeds, save only when he tryes with gristly tongue to dart the passing flyes." Here Wilding appears to have blended quotations from two sources. The first sentence seems be a paraphrase of Dryden's translation of Ovid, and the second part of this unspoken, internalized quotation, beginning with "Alone," comes from Andrew Marvell's poem "MacFlecknoe." Many of Wilding's stories contain lines from Renaissance or other English poetry, some very well-known, others like this rather complicated one from Dryden and Marvell. Wilding's intensely literary sensibility informs much of his work, and it must be remembered that among his non-fiction books are *Milton's Paradise Lost* (1969) and *Dragons Teeth: Literature in the English Revolution* (1987), and two edited books on Renaissance literature: *Marvell: Modern Judgements* (1969) and *Julius Caesar and Marcus Brutus* by John Sheffield (1970). Wilding's expansive literary reach deepens and extends the thematic implications of his body of work.

When Gavin finally does go to dinner at the flat of the narrator and Barbara in Paddington, he finds new material in his ongoing monologue on England vs. Australia. In this instance it is the old house that the narrator and Barbara have rented. He says it reminds him of England too much, where every house bears an historical marker, where "There's not one inch of England that hasn't been trampled over time and time again. That's why Australia's so refreshing. It's untouched, it's forward looking, it's alive and vital" (12).

The narrator's response to this familiar riff on Gavin's part is a line from Yeats' "Sailing to Byzantium": "Caught in that sensual music all neglect monuments of unageing intellect" (12). Sensual music might stand as a two-word summary of Australia's meaning for the narrator, in this and in other Wilding stories.

In a funny reversal, Gavin announces his latest scheme. He has been asked to participate in a symposium on Australian intellectual life, a phrase that previously one would expect him to denounce as an oxymoron. But Gavin surprises the narrator by saying that he sees an opportunity for a book and a TV documentary coming out of materials he has put together for his radio show, "Today's Writing." He also mentions that *The London Magazine* (which he had earlier dismissed) would be a good venue in which to place an article, as would "a Texan review" which has requested an article on the Sydney scene from him. (Perhaps the reference is to the *Texas Quarterly*, a rather splashy arts periodical from that era, published at the University of Texas.)

The narrator in the meantime continues to supply content for Gavin's radio program, and it is interesting that he is requested to use American spellings though how would that matter on the radio (it must be for the book that Gavin has planned). Among Gavin's other strategies is to snag visiting writers from overseas, ones that the narrator notes are usually propped up by either the British Council or the Congress for Cultural Freedom, a notorious CIA-funded organization of the period. In any event such writers as Iris Murdoch, Anthony Burgess (both English, obviously) and the American, Kenneth Rexroth, are specifically mentioned.Wilding's story acts as a kind of primer for getting ahead in the writing game. Gavin is a great schemer and an adept student of literary networking. He knows all the inside gossip, who publishes whom and why, and values the reciprocity that comes from publishing only writers who are also editors. To Gavin, Norman Podhoretz's *Making It*, a famous insider literary how-to memoir of the era, is a kind of manual of manipulation and self-promotion. Wilding himself purchased a copy of Podhoretz's book during a trip to New York in 1969. He was "fascinated," he has stated, by "that naked desire for Fame and Success—very unEnglish, un Australian in those days" (Email, July 13, 2009).

On one occasion Gavin and the narrator attend a musical performance held at the Cell Block Theater, site of a former convict prison. While Gavin goes on about how awful it is to listen to music in a place where men were hanged, the narrator, unspokenly, thinks, "And see the final ejaculation, the posthumous seed shot over the inheriting culture" (15). The narrator's ability to see into and absorb the historical ironies and complexities of Australian culture is subtly set against Gavin's facile and contradictory observations. Gavin, it seems, is having an external debate with himself about the place where he must make his mark, the somewhere new: Is it to be Australia, or not? Certainly it cannot be dead, dying, washed-up old England. Always free with advice, Gavin urges the narrator to write for the "big American magazines" like *The Atlantic* or *The New Yorker*. And he has strong opinions about everything. He goes on about a horror film that reminds him of Sunday afternoons in England. The premise of the film is that a pair of disembodied hands kills people and plays a piano. Upon hearing this the narrator whimsically recalls Kurtz's famous words from *Heart of Darkness*: "The horror, the horror" (17).

Then suddenly Gavin has seized upon "somewhere new." It's America, to which he has been trending all along. He is going over to make some documentaries, and upon learning that the narrator is preparing to leave Australia as well, naturally assumes that his destination is America. Gavin is shocked to hear that the narrator is going to England for a year and simply cannot believe that the narrator, if something turned up there, might stay in England.

A year passes and the narrator returns to Australia where Gavin still is, though he is currently planning to immigrate to Canada before moving to the U.S. The narrator notices that Gavin has changed his appearance somewhat and now wears a "wavy Dylanesque mop" (19), an obvious reference to Bob Dylan but one, Wilding says, that led a translator to think the allusion was to Dylan Thomas (Email, July 13, 2009). Gavin also has a flat mate, and their relationship is somewhat ambiguous. Gavin may be gay or asexual, it is hard to say. In any event he is noticeably cold towards the narrator's girl friend, Barbara (based on Margaret Clancy, Wilding's girl friend with whom he lived from 1963 to 1972) [Email, June 10, 2009]. *Aspects of the Dying Process* is dedicated to "Margaret."

Now that Gavin has made a decision to go to the New World, he is more than ever preaching the cultural supremacy of America. He repeats his denigration of England, "There's absolutely no life at all there..." (20). He tells the narrator, "You should go there [that is, America]. It makes Australia seem like an undeveloped country" (20). He goes on, ecstatic about America's wealth, energy, its newness in everything from media to drugs. At story's end Gavin is gone. To where, the narrator asks the flat-mate: "Oh, America" is the answer (21).

In real life Charles Higham, the prototype for Gavin, did move to America, where he enjoyed considerable success writing Hollywood biographies in the land that the fictional character in "Somewhere New" dreams of. Higham died in 2012.

"Somewhere New" was in many ways the perfect story to initiate Wilding's career in Australia. It defined a lively cultural debate positing three sites of possible artistic creativity: England, America, and Australia. The story shows the narrator's choice, which was Wilding's choice. Wilding, it should be noted, has a strong claim to being regarded as an internationalist writer. Besides stories set in England and Australia, he has written fiction set in Europe, America, North Africa, and South America, and his works have been translated into many languages, including Punjabi, Bengali, Kannada, Japanese, Chinese, Serbo-Croatian, German, Danish, Norwegian, Czech, Hungarian, Spanish, Italian, and Vietnamese. Wilding's literary presence in America includes the collection *Her Most Bizarre Sexual Experience*, published by W.W. Norton in 1991 (*Great Climate* in Britain), and individual stories published in American venues such as *New Yorker, Harpers, Bachy, Cimarron Review, Gargoyle, Nimrod, Antique Children, Review of Contemporary Fiction,*

*Antipodes*, and *Assembling*. Reviews and criticism of Wilding's oeuvre reveal a widespread, multi-national dimension as well.

Still, in the main, Australia has been the primary ground of his literary being, and the continuing importance of "Somewhere New" for its author is evident in a couple of facts. One, this was the story that he chose to represent his work in *The Oxford Book of Australian Short Stories*, which he edited for Oxford University Press in 1994. Two, a collection of his short fiction published in 1998 bore the title *Somewhere New: New & Selected Stories*. (That book, incidentally, is dedicated to Don Graham and Betsy Berry.)

The second story in *Aspects of the Dying Process*, "The Sybarites," published in *Transition*, ed. Nancy Keesing, in 1970, has been often reprinted, including translations in Serbian and Vietnamese. Thematically related to "Somewhere New," it explores "instant Sydney" and its sun-saturated, beach-and-pub loving culture of youth and sexuality. The title derives from the name for the inhabitants of Sybarus, a $6^{th}$ century B.C. Greek city whose inhabitants became known for opulent luxury and extravagant pleasure seeking. The almost Biblical sound of the word "sybarite" carries a judgment, while at the same time redefining the meaning in a hip, avant-garde manner.

The story opens on a Sydney beach where four young people are sunbathing. One, Ian, is new to Australia; the others are Andrew and two women, Helen and Pat. Each of these characters is based upon people Wilding hung out with during his early years in Australia in the 1960s. Ian, of course, is Wilding, and Wilding reports that the name was chosen because the first letter is *I*, thus indicating a first person observer-participant though the narration is third person (Email, July 25, 2009). Andrew is based on Stephen Knight, at that time a lecturer in English at Sydney University. Knight and Wilding edited *The Radical Reader* together, published in 1977. Knight later became a professor at Melbourne University, and in the UK he taught at Simon de Monfort University and Cardiff University. He became an authority on Robin Hood and crime fiction and currently is retired, living in Melbourne. Helen, based upon Alison Ferraro, née Cunningham, worked in the Department of English as a tutor. She was married to a Hungarian medical academic, but left him and became pregnant in a relationship with David Ferraro, "an old libertarian figure"' (Email, July 25, 2009). They moved to England, their son lodged with Germaine Greer at Cambridge, and about fifteen years ago both Alison and her husband died. Pat was Lee Sonnino, like Alison a graduate student in the Department of English. Wilding recalled, "I had sat as an invigilator in the Muniment Room beneath the clock tower when she and Germaine Greer had taken their entrance exams for Oxford and Cambridge. My first official task" (*Wild & Woolley*, pp. 54-55). Sonnino later married an Italian named Cataldi, but they soon separated. She lectured at Bristol University for a time, where she wrote *A Handbook of Renaissance Rhetoric*. She later returned to Sydney where she taught high school. Wilding's Wild & Woolley published her first book of poems, *Invitation to a Marxist Lesbian Party*. As for Germaine Greer, she turns up as the outlandish character Gretel Mann in Wilding's novel *Living Together*.

Of course none of these correspondences with actual people are necessary for an understanding of the story, but they are facts and they are inherently interesting in and of themselves. Stephen, Alison, and Lee took Wilding about, showed him "instant Sydney," and in the process provided him with the material that would eventuate in this story.

It's Ian the newcomer who launches the story with an observation, "I suppose what's so marvelous in fact is that you can just get out to the beach all the time...You're not trapped in a city all the time or anything" (22). The remark is met with silence as the bathers gaze at the sea amidst all the other people on the beach, "all the various colours of trunks and bikinis" (22).

Then Pat says from out of nowhere: "It creates a democratic hedonism" (22), thus announcing the dominant interpretation of life on the beaches and in the pubs, evident in later scenes. Her phrase also reminds us of Gavin's "hedonism of the beaches" from "Somewhere New." A few passages later, the rather mindless hedonism of heat, sweat, and lassitude is emphasized: "...most people simply lay there, saying nothing, doing nothing, reading nothing, and idly moving. It was too hot to talk: it was too bright to read..." (23). Again, one can imagine Gavin making similar observations: Australia as a land of physical hedonism without the need or desire for culture, for literature. But this story focuses instead on hedonism and its handmaiden, eroticism. The broader literary discourse of "Somewhere New" is left behind in the pursuit of the moment.

Along with the foursome's mutual pleasure on the beach, a sexual tension develops from Ian's fascination with Helen. At one point Pat questions Helen about another man, Mark, and his behavior at a recent party. The exchange is sexually explicit, with references to Mark's having disappeared from the party and jibes about whether he might have masturbated or not. The conversation heats up Ian's interest in Helen, and the scene ends with Pat musing, "It's beaut lying in the sun," and Helen observing, "Our range is narrow but consistent. We're terribly sybaritic here" (25).

The next section begins, "Sybaritically they took him to drink with them one later afternoon in a pub on the harbour's edge" (25). The pub in the harbor setting was at Watson's Bay (the area where one of Wilding's favorite Australian authors, Christina Stead, grew up). As Wilding has pointed out, there are very few pubs on the harbour (Email, July 25, 2009). This makes Watson's Bay even more iconic, a defining site of Australian urban culture, of Sydney in particular, and this is very much a story of Sydney. There is even a reference to the "opera house," which comes as a bit of a surprise. It's Helen who says, "Like the opera house," as she observes the sails of yachts plying the harbour (25). This is certainly prescient on her part, considering the fact that in 1968 when Wilding wrote this story the Opera House was still under construction and would not open until several years later, in 1973 (Email "Re: opera house," July 23, 2009.) Wilding remembers: "Checking with an architect at the ferry wharf, it seems the opera house construction began in 1966. I was still in Australia in 1966—then in Birmingham 1967-8—back in Sydney 1969. It took a long time to build, especially with all the disputes about costs and design and the architect leaving" (Email "opera house," July 24, 2009). In the story it's as though the Opera House is already an emblematic site of the Sydney urban scene, with Helen as its resident homegrown goddess.

With all the beauty of Sydney spread before them, Ian's main attention is focused on Helen, but one thing she says leads him to look at her in a new light. They watch a huge ship in the harbor and she says its name, *The Marconi*. Ian is surprised that she knows its name and questions her as to how she would know that. To him such knowledge bespeaks "how incurably provincial it was to know the names, how colonially dependent on Europe" (26). Here Ian's Englishness manifests itself in a reflex assumption of the Empire's superiority over its far-flung former colony. But entranced by Helen's laconic provinciality, Ian begins a journey of entering fully into Australian reality that provides an important motif in the story: the embrace of "somewhere new," to borrow that phrase from the first story.

At the pub Ian is left alone with Helen for a short time during which he tries to imagine what kind of life she has led. He offers a view: "I suppose," he said, "growing up in these sort of surroundings makes you sort of more relaxed" (27). Her answer is predictably ironic: "The climactic theory of climatic zones" (27). Then Ian follows up with another remark suggesting "that people here do get a different sort of attitude to life" (27). Helen again offers an ironic response: "I wouldn't know... I'm just a poor provincial, I've been nowhere else" (27). It is as though she were reading Ian's private thoughts and mocking his Anglo-Saxon attitudes.

But Helen is also a critic of the provincial world she seems both to represent, in her ironic responses to Ian's questions, and to stand apart from as a hip avant-garde observer of Australian culture. This sense of cultural superiority comes across in her remarks about the common folk, as she imagines them: "And everyone in his light pink with plum feature panel two-toned Holden Special De Luxe just sitting looking at nothing and listening to 2UW and chewing meat pies" (28-29). 2UW is a reference to a popular Sydney AM radio station that played pop music. Helen's set would never listen to that or drive the big bulky Holdens, which were a marker of a certain level of bourgeois values and smug nationalism. Sophisticated connoisseurs like the sybarites could only do such things ironically. The sight of two Aussie males sets her off again: "Look at those two, the short back and sides, the ginger freckled legs. God knows why they all wear shorts, and that sort of look, the way they—" (29).

In retrospect, Wilding says today that Helen's riff against Australian ugliness was probably influenced by a popular book of the period, Robin Boyd's *The Australian Ugliness*, published in 1960. Boyd, an architect, attacked bad taste as exemplified by bourgeois material culture, and Helen seems to be echoing those sentiments. Wilding says he found Boyd's book "rather snobbish" and points out that it was "out of phase with the new hyper realism and pop art and Warhol approach that soon commemorated all that commercial kitsch" (Email, July 25, 2009),

The foursome continue to enjoy the pub, the grog, the sun, the view of the harbor; and at the end of the scene the narrative voice, reflecting Ian's perspective, encapsulates the experience into "a warm uniformity, an apathy of acceptance" (28). But there is more of the afternoon left and they all repair to Pat's terrace house in "arty Paddington" (where Wilding lived from time to time). From a height on the balcony Ian, standing on a couch, can see the iconic harbour bridge (though there is no mention here of the opera house). They drink flagons of wine, and the dialogue begins to sound a bit like *The Sun Also Rises:* "But it gets you drunk quicker," said Pat to Andrew. "By God it does" (29). Helen tells Pat to call Mark, and Mark comes over, "smooth and suited from his office" (29). Mark has a job, a career, unlike the sybarites, who seem to have nothing to do except indolently pursue pleasure. And Mark is Helen's husband, which comes as a shock to Ian: "...Ian blushed, because he had not realized that Helen was married, and because, perhaps, he felt that his fantasies could be read" (29).

On another evening the four of them go out for dinner and get "very drunk" (p. 30). Helen, sounding more and more like an Australian Brett Ashley, starts relating stories of drunken sprees, of jumping into fountains, throwing Mark's shaving gear out of a window, "chukking at important dinner parties" (30). Emboldened by the liberties of libertine drinking, Ian begins telling sexual jokes, and Helen, clearly the leader, proposes that they go back to the flat and "grog on" (30). On the way there, Andrew and Pat speak of Mark's having slept with another girl, and Helen does not comment. Once at her flat, Helen startles everybody by announcing that she hasn't a key to get onto the roof. The owners have taken it away because of "parties, things" (30). So Andrew has to break down the door to gain access to the roof.

From there Ian watches the lighted ferries on the dark waters of the harbour and the night sky and embraces the word "enchantment," realizing that "He suddenly loved the place at night, its stillness, its lights, its easy beauty" (31). But Helen introduces a note of danger by sitting on the edge of the roof, eight stories from death, her legs over the side. The height and obvious danger make Ian feel nauseous (just as the narrator in "Somewhere New" felt in Gavin's flat). Andrew joins Helen, sitting beside her, both still drunk.

Once everybody descends into the flat, Mark is there, eating oysters and listening to Vivaldi. The party is over, and Ian is returned to his own flat.

But there will be future gatherings, Ian hopes. He imagines himself being taken to "the pubs where everyone drank" and they "would find way-out parties they would grog on all night at, that would lead to dawn swimming, naked in the harbour menaced by sharks and vice squad prowlers" (32). One afternoon the girls promise to show him "instant Sydney" (32), and Ian is delighted at the indolent, bohemian, sybaritic pleasure of an afternoon drinking in random pubs before joining the afternoon mob at the Newcastle, a favorite watering hole of artists and intellectuals, located in downtown Sydney. The cover of *Aspects of the Dying Process* features a photograph of the interior of the Newcastle. Wilding can just barely be discerned standing at the bar.

The phrase "instant Sydney" is suggestive but undefined. According to Wilding, the phrase "instant something" was part of the idiom of the period (MW email, July 31, 2009). Instant coffee might have been the starting point of the phrase's popularity. In any event just about anything could be instant. But instant Sydney is, I believe, particularly important in the Wilding aesthetic. It is one of the earliest manifestations of the artistic and cultural view that Wilding was developing, of writing in such a way as to create a sense of instant experience. (By receiving this email from Wilding on July 31, 2009, and writing this passage on July 31, 2009, I am in a manner practicing instant criticism.)

At the Newcastle, the scene becomes increasingly sybaritic, with a surging crowd of drinkers pressed close together and Ian still preoccupied with Helen's nearness and erotic appeal. Into the pub comes Mark, wearing a suit and expressing a sense of "distaste" and "determination" (32), thoroughly "contrasting with the beery apathy" of the drinkers. He buys beers for Helen's group and says, "God knows how you stand it" (32). Feeling the effect of the beer, the party moves outside where Ian feels dizzy and Helen says, "So much for instant Sydney," adding that they should have eaten something, and then she throws up four times on the pavement. Pat points out that before Helen's marriage she "used to be able to go on all night" (33). Mark drives her away from the pub, and Pat drives Ian back to the flat he has recently moved into, and because it's in her neighborhood she proposes that now they're neighbors, they can hold a party. The story ends with a perception of Ian's assimilation into the new culture: "That'd be beaut," he said, cautiously trying out for the first time the idioms that he felt he had caught" (p. 33).

Reading his story for the first time in forty years, Wilding summed up his feelings about it this way: "I recently read Jay McInerney's *Story of My Life* which is much more, indeed totally, into substance abuse. But that flip, blasé attitude the girl there [Helen] has is the sort of thing I was trying to capture here, some 20 years earlier. The Australian milieu was less wealthy, less extreme—but to me, just arrived from UK proletarianism, it seemed all very exotic & weird. I guess I was, as the young girls say these days, conflicted" (Email, July 25, 2009).

The third story in the collection, "The Altar of the Family," published in *Southerly,* 30 (1970), 301-305, should be paired with the seventh story, "As Boys to Wanton Flies," published originally in *Thor* in 1971. Both are stories about children and have enjoyed widespread anthologizing. According to Wilding, "they were popular because stories about sex and drugs were not suitable for the substantial Catholic school system here and the residual Australian censorship. And the fact that they were about children, and about features of Australian life, meant they could be discussed on school syllabuses" (Email "Re: childrens' stories," February 23, 2012).

The fourth story in the collection, "Joe's Absence," is one of Wilding's signal accomplishments in the short story form. It was published in *Southerly* in 1968, while Wilding was in England. He had submitted stories to the editor of *Southerly,* Gerald Wilkes, before, during his years at Sydney from 1963-66, but they were all set in England and none were accepted. As he recalls, Wilkes, a distinguished professor in the English Department at Sydney University, invited him to submit a story. Since Wilding was to return to Sydney for good in 1969, he thinks the Wilkes invitation might have been a gesture welcoming him back. That issue also contained a story by Patrick White, and over the years Wilkes published innovative work by Vicki Viidikas, Frank Moorhouse, and Robert Adamson, all friends of Wilding and all part of the new wave in Australian writing.

The story is a very important one in the Wilding canon. It deals centrally with the question of writing—a major theme in many of his stories—and it introduces us to Joe, who is based on Wilding's friendship with Frank Moorhouse. Their relationship is a long and vexed one, and this is the opening gambit in what would become a decades-long fictional back-and-forth, almost a war really. According to Wilding, "It is I think the first I wrote about Frank. I called him Joe as in 'Honest Joe'—as a version of 'frank.' Not that he was ever either" (Email "copy of cover" August 4, 2009). Another time Wilding gave a complete rundown of the naming of the Moorhouse-based figure:

> First of all he was called Joe, then in the S S Embassy he was Wendel (after Oliver Wendel Holmes, with whom Marcus Clarke corresponded & to whom Clarke dedicated his book of stories "Holiday Peak"; I was working on Clarke at the time. The pun is on MoorHOUSE and Holmes/Homes). Later, in Scenic Drive, I end up calling the character by all 3 names, Joseph Wendel Holmes. I called him Joe originally as a play upon Frank—Frank meaning honest in England, so by analogy "Honest Joe." Irony pertaining to this aspect of the nomenclature entered later in the course of our relationship. (Email "Re: catching up," April 18, 2005).

On still another occasion he recalled that "'Joe's Absence' was…an attempt to capture an updated version of the literary life à la Henry James, and to prod a contemporary of mine, a now forgotten minor writer, Whoremouse, Moorhouse, some such name, who later became frenchified as Francois de Maison Close" (Email "Re: repairing documentation..." February 10, 2010).

The story opens with Graham, Wilding's viewpoint character, driving in the bush, headed to a beach where his friend Joe is living and writing. Graham, incidentally, is a name that Wilding has used in other stories and the memoir *Wildest Dreams* (2006). The Graham of "Joe's Absence" is more overtly a writer than the implied viewpoint figures in "Somewhere New" and "The Sybarites." Immediately Graham wonders why he doesn't live out here himself, away from the scattered, sybaritic, rather frenetic life in the city, a whirlwind of drinking at the pubs or parties, going to movies, and "writing too little." On the previous Friday Joe had come into the pub looking tanned and "with the peace of a beachcomber" (39). When Joe informs Graham that he has written a dozen stories in two weeks, all of Graham's writer anxieties kick in. Graham reminds himself that he hasn't written a dozen stories in two years and thinks also of an abortive novel that he hasn't been able to finish. Then, as usual in the pub scenes, girls make their presence felt. One of them, Pat, is miffed at Joe for having "dropped her" and at Graham for not reciprocating her interest in the first place. The other is named Helen, but they are not the same characters that appear in "The Sybarites." The Pat and Helen of "Joe's Absence" are based on two of Moorhouse's girlfriends of that era, Gillian Burnett and Sandra Grimes" (Email "Comments and Corrections," November 28, 2011).

Graham keeps asking Joe about his productivity, and Joe invites him to come visit at the shack on the beach. Joe says he is holding back the stories from magazines, planning to publish them together in a book. Everything about the way Joe looks, his confidence, his bush isolation, his remarks about his work—everything increases Graham's envious anxiety. The scene ends with Joe mentioning, "And then there's Margot" (39). Margot keeps him company, he says. So Joe has it all, a calm life, productive work, and a girl friend.

Wilding devotes a brief but powerfully poetic paragraph to Graham's thoughts as he drives through the bush. The first few sentences capture the "huge stretching silence" by focusing on the apparent absence of birds: "The gums were high and never seemed to have any birds in them, no movement, no rustling; yet they must have done; perhaps if he stopped the car and got out and watched, he would notice some" (40). In this passage Wilding was consciously echoing the following passage from Marcus Clarke's preface to the poems of Adam Lindsay Gordon: "Some see no beauty in our trees without shade, our flowers without perfume, our birds who cannot fly, our beasts who have not yet learned to walk on all fours" (Email, August 29, 2009). At that time Wilding had not yet read Marcus Clarke's fiction, but he had read the preface cited above. Gordon came from Wilding's old school, the Royal Grammar School Worcester, and because of that and other sympathetic connections with Gordon (and later Clarke) as Englishmen living in and writing about Australia, Wilding had begun to collect Gordon's works. The preface was reprinted in Wilding's edition of the *Portable Marcus Clarke* of some years later.

The passage continues: "It was frightening when you thought of all that emptiness reaching right out into the centre, it was frightening like looking at the stars was frightening, the terror of those inconceivable distances. It was the terror that made you cluster in the cities, clinging like ants on a dead lizard's sore, sucking sustenance from the skin's small crack" (39). Here, though Wilding has not mentioned it, he seems to be echoing a stanza from A.D. Hope's famous poem, "Australia":

And her five cities, like five teeming sores

Each drains her: a vast parasite robber-state

Where second hand Europeans pullulate

Timidly on the edge of alien shores.

Just after this bush reverie, Graham ponders Joe's life away from the city, "stabbing reams of white paper with black characters" for part of the day, then enjoying the beach and "sleeping at night between the immense silence of the sea, and the mute stillness of the bush" (40). Wilding has commented in an email that the phrase "silence of the sea" came from a French book that he had read in the school library titled *Le Silence du Mer* by Vercors (Email, August 29, 2009).

There is one more pub scene in the story. As Graham is driving, a flashback encapsulates pub life very effectively. Margot comes into the pub and Joe introduces her to Graham but she pays him no attention; instead she talks very quietly to Joe, who talks louder as though he doesn't approve of her intimate manner. Finally he tells her to go have dinner with her friend and she leaves. Then he tells Graham, "We have a free relationship. She's gone off to screw some old friend" (40). Joe and Graham have some more beer and just as Helen and Pat are leaving the pub, Joe "intercepts" them, and the foursome go out for a meal together, return to the pub till it closes, and then go out to a party. Thus Joe is in a sense vacationing in the city, but the round of pub drinking and parties is Graham's life, and Joe's newfound sense of artistic dedication makes Graham curious and envious at the same time. Hence the trip down the coast to visit Joe.

The actual site where Moorhouse was living at that time was Bundeena (Email, August 29, 2009). Bundeena is located in the northeast corner of the Royal National Park, on the southern edge of Port Hacking. A 2009 Total.Travel website describes it as a "perfect place to spend a quiet day away from the city of Sydney." Bundeena is only a twenty minute ferry ride from Cronulla. In 1966 or so when Moorhouse was there, Bundeena would have been even more isolated, though still close, a ferry ride to all the splendors of Sydney. Wilding believes that his visit to see Moorhouse must have been in 1966.

There is another interesting subtext to the story's origins. In an article written nearly forty years later, "Faulty Memory or Phantom Editor?" Wilding recalled listening, the previous year, to a new jazz album by Australian jazz saxophonist Bernie McGann titled "Bundeena," and was struck by its liner notes, which he thinks must have been read on the radio: "It is, fittingly, a golden album, named for the sunlit place where McGann once worked as a postman and practiced daily in seaside heath and gum forest" (*Newswrite* 3). Hearing that made Wilding recall a girl telling him about the jazz sax player that she heard on the beach during mornings and evenings. Wilding thinks that perhaps he himself heard McGann during his visit to Bundeena. Wilding was also certain that he had put the musician into the story about Joe and Margot, but when he reread the story it wasn't there. He thinks it might have been in an early draft and was later excised. Or maybe it was never there at all.

Graham, following Joe's directions, finds the shack, which is made of crude stone construction, and peers through the window where he sees a typewriter with a sheet of paper in the carriage, but he is unable to read it. This detail prefigures the central preoccupation of the visit, which unfolds through the rest of the story. Graham then turns his attention to the beach. Joe had told him that it looked like Big Sur, but Wilding who later saw Big Sur for himself, during a trip to California in 1974 with his publishing partner Pat Woolley, realized then that the beach at Bundeena didn't look anything like Big Sur. The reason Joe made the comparison originally is suggested by Wilding's recollection of a literary context from that era: "But the Kerouac myth—and the Henry Miller *Big Sur & the Oranges of Hieronymus Bosch*—were names to conjure with in those days" (Email, August 29, 2009). It was on this same trip that Wilding and Woolley met the Beat poet Lawrence Ferlinghetti (who owned a shack on Big Sur where he sometimes hung out).

As Graham surveys the beach, his eyes fall upon a girl in a yellow bikini. As he draws closer to her, he realizes it's Margot, Joe's girl to whom he was briefly introduced at the pub. They reintroduce themselves, and Graham learns that Joe is not there (hence, "Joe's Absence"). Margot says he stayed overnight in town and has not returned yet. "He had to see someone or something," she reports (42). Joe's absence seems to hint at some aspect of the "free relationship" that he had made a point of telling Graham about in the pub. And, given Margot's later statements in the story, Joe might have been lying about what she was going to do with her friend. But the point remains ambiguous. There was, of course, a real Margot. She was a girl friend of a film producer, who at the time was a pharmacy student, named Erroll Sullivan. Sullivan is now a successful film producer with Southern Cross, an Australian film production company. Ironically, he owns the rights to Moorhouse's late novels (Email, August 29, 2009).

Margot invites Graham to join her sunbathing on the beach, and he does so while she resumes reading her book. In the quietness of the sun and surf Graham goes into a reverie about Joe's last "bird," Lydia, who Graham believes is better looking than Margot. Graham thinks that he ought to ask Joe for Lydia's address, as he, Graham, had not seen her since the conference. It was at the conference where he and Joe had given talks and Graham had met Lydia. The conference alluded to here was one on adult education, held c. 1965-66, and Wilding gave a paper on "Mass Media and Literary Criticism," later published in the Australian magazine *Dissent* (Email, August 29, 2009). The conference was held at Newport, on Pittwater where Wilding lived on Scotland Island for a number of years).

In the story Joe, Graham, and Lydia went to lunch together and had several beers, and afterward, Graham and Lydia, sitting side by side, had helped keep each other from nodding off when the afternoon speaker came on. Joe, meanwhile, had chosen a seat on the front row so that he could attack the speaker. At another conference, Joe had spoken on the subject of new directions in literature, and Graham thought to himself, "Funny how no one else had noticed it sounded like nude erections" (42). This joke was a quip made by a member of the audience, Richard Neville, famous for his editorship of the satirical magazine *Oz* in London. (Neville appears as King Zog in the Wilding story "I am Monarch of All I Survey," collected in *This Is For You*.)

The conference was held at the Hunters Hill Festival and organized by Grace Perry, a poet who was also a medical doctor and who ran *Poetry Australia*. It was also at this conference that Wilding met Andrew Fabinyi, the publisher who commissioned Wilding to do a book. This eventuated in the anthology *Australians Abroad*, which Wilding co-edited with Charles Higham (Email, August 29, 2009).

For their talks Joe received a bottle of whiskey and Graham a bottle of brandy, and later, after the pub has closed, Graham shared his brandy with Lydia and told her she should "relax more, be less frigid, more swinging" (42). "Swinging," that signature Sixties word, appears in a number of the stories in *Aspects of the Dying Process*.

"It's a beaut place," says Margot (recalling the significance of that idiom in "The Sybarites"), and bringing the story back to the present with her and Graham on the beach. While Graham notices every move, every nuance of her body, especially her breasts, she describes the landscape and how healthy being there has made her feel, the long walks, the benefits of sea and sand. Then she starts talking about Joe and his stories, how they're better, in her opinion, than his earlier ones. Seeing the small ferry approaching the bay, she says Joe will probably be on it if he's going to return in time for lunch. Graham asks her the burning question in his mind: "'What are Joe's stories about? The same themes?' Restraining a pejorative old" (43). She answers, "Joe, of course" (44). Then she asks Graham what he does, a question that makes him wonder why Joe has never mentioned it to her. "I write, a bit, not so prolifically as Joe seems to be doing" (44). When she asks him what kinds of things he writes, all he says is stories.

When Joe does not arrive on the ferry, Margot walks to a pay phone and then, before returning to Graham, takes a swim in the bay. Graham focuses now entirely on her physical presence, both while she is in the water, and especially when she comes back wet, the dripping water emphasizing every curve and feature of her body. The news she brings is that Joe isn't coming back until the next day, to which Graham responds, "He must have got so pissed [drunk] he didn't bother to remember, the bastard" (45). Still, she says, it's a "beaut day" but Graham points out that he could have been writing another story. Then he wonders whether he had really wanted to talk to Joe "and be competitive about acceptances and women" (45). So the two of them embrace the fact of Joe's absence and go forward from there.

After grabbing some snacks at a shop, Margot suggests that they go to another beach that is always deserted. Walking along that beach, Graham is attuned to her every movement and at the same time, to the cosmic emptiness of the setting: "Alone on this stretch of beach he felt naked with her, unwatched, unhampered, unprotected by the smallest of societies" (45). Walking along, he tries to determine whether she is sexy or not. The question is given an Einsteinian dimension: "Space's infinity turns back on itself" (45), an observation reminiscent of e. e. cummings' line "unwish through curving wherewhen till unwish/return on its unself" in his poem "[pity this busy monster, manunkind,]." He looks at her intensely, which gaze she says reminds her of Joe. She tells him, "When Joe looks like that I know there's going to be trouble," and Graham replies, "Like he's going to rape you?" to which she replies, "That wouldn't be a trouble" (46). There will be a rape in this story but not of a woman, as we shall see.

And Margot points out that Joe is sexy. She persuades Graham to doff his clothes, and she removes her bikini, and they both swim naked in the surf. The sexual tension increases sentence by sentence until, returned to lying on the sand, Graham feels an erection coming on. He observes her nakedness close up; they grip hands, and as a quick rain storm blows in, she says, "We could do a Lady Chatterley in the storm" (47). And Graham responds, "The shack might be better. Besides, I haven't got any flowers handy" (47). (Here I cannot help but point out that few English majors in the first decade of the 21$^{st}$ century have any knowledge at all of the allusion to Lawrence's lovers.)

On the walk back Graham has time to think about the situation with regard to Joe. Noting that Joe might return early, he decides that the real question has to do with having sex with Margot in and of itself. He reasons, "He pondered his loyalties to Joe, which needed only to be few. He had Joe's comment that it was a free relationship, and Joe's absence as support. Why wait till Joe dumped her?" (47). Then he thinks about Joe some more and concludes that neither has two-timed the other, so far as he knows, with the comical exception of Graham's having encroached upon Joe's allotted time to speak at a conference, "And rubbishing his stories privately, but Joe probably reciprocated that" (47). Here is one of those writerly insights that makes this story hum with truth. Here there is no brotherhood of writers; all is envy and competition.

With the rain increasing they reach the shack and embrace and the moment seems imminent, but Margot hesitates and asks, "What...what about Joe?" (47). In the ensuing discussion, she says that she knows that Joe will eventually dump her and that such a betrayal would also be harder for Graham than for her. Graham suggests that they have something to eat first because he's not sure yet. Margot says she's always sure but is also hungry and turns away to prepare "an orgiastic meal" (48).

As they get comfortable on an old mattress, drinking wine, he points to the typewriter and asks her "What's the masterpiece?" (48). She tells him he should have a look, and Graham replies, "I don't like anyone looking at what I'm working on. I don't even like them reading it in typescript when it's finished. It's a sort of intrusion. It makes me feel exposed and vulnerable" (48). Then they eat some of the canned delicacies and talk further about Joe's writing, and Margot admits that when he's out, she reads Joe's stories, saying, "I sneak a look now and then when they're finished" (49). But the talk quickly turns back to the question of fidelity. Although Graham's sexually drawn to her even more now, the way she looks, he thinks it's not a "brilliant idea" and tells her that it might not even bother Joe, to which she says "Thanks," and goes ahead to argue the same point, saying that Joe "cares more about his stories than almost anyone—even himself" (49). She argues that essentially Joe's life consists of material for his stories, that he's "almost anaesthetized" (49). She goes on to say that she really doesn't want to sleep with anybody else and that she loves Joe. But then she gets to the heart of her problem with Joe: "I couldn't 'betray' him because I don't think there's anything he cares about; I can't do anything, he's not involved with me, all he's involved with is his stories" (50).

There is more erotic touching and more introspective reverie on Graham's part about the complexities of "betraying Joe" and the general messiness of a dalliance with Joe's girl. In the interim he mentions that in any event they should eat first. While she prepares the canned soup, she tells Graham that he should take a look at the finished stories. When Graham asks wouldn't Joe mind, she says he wouldn't know. Graham approaches her and touches her again, erotically, and she shrugs him off, irritated because of the arousal that will not come to anything. So Graham goes over to Joe's desk on which are arranged a dozen stories or more, all immaculately typed and bound in folders: "Before he took out those unsmutched white sheets from their manila folders, before his fingers probed the collection, fumbling along the edges of the pages, easing off paper clips, he knew that Joe would mind" (51).

In lush Lawrentian imagery Wilding presents the reading of Joe's manuscripts as a seduction, a sexual act complete with foreplay and consummation. Forcing open the folders is analogized to bees forcing "open the petals of flowers" (51). Human sexual imagery is used as well: "He unclothed the stories, taking them from their covers as if he were prizing open oysters" (51). Continuing: "His fingers turned the pages gently. He was not rough. They were the same fingers that had stroked Margot's buttocks, that had held off from fondling her nipples. But they did not hold off here" (51). Graham is lying on a mattress throughout this foreplay, and is happy to arise and have soup with Margot before returning to the mattress to continue his erotic conquest of Joe's stories.

Graham reads slowly at the outset because he wants to see if Joe's work is improving, if it's developing: "He read to see if Joe was on to anything new, in case a new richness had thickened or there had been a blaze of metaphorical efflorescence" (51). Graham is not interested in Joe's real-life sources, the way Margot is. Margot reads every story as autobiography. She wants to know if he has read the story about Lydia, and Graham thinks to himself that he's not sure and thinks that all he knows about Lydia is "the finely marked face and the small breasts" (51); otherwise he knows nothing about her. And he also thinks, "Why need he care, as Margot did, about Joe's past life, his past loves, his past betrayals, his current infidelities?" (51). But Margot cares, and cares deeply, "That bitch in that story, the one he goes over the mountains with" (51). Graham's interest in the story, however, is entirely in its technical mastery: "but it wasn't that bitch that interested him, but Joe's lyrical treatment of the mountain trip and the swim in the cool clear sea, their early morning bathing in the sharp translucence. That and the ending, and the framework he had set the story in that so enhanced it" (51-52).

When Margot points out that the "bitch" in question is Helen, Graham is quick to agree, "Oh yes, she is a bitch" (52). But what interests Graham more is "Joe's new control...the bitch of assurance that was in Joe"(52). Margot goes on, reading the story personally, from the viewpoint of her own vexed relationship with Joe. She asks Graham if he doesn't agree that it's a "waste of a good story on her" (52). She judges Helen, thinking her a "rat" the way she treats Joe at the end of the story (52). But Graham's response is purely that of a writer interested in technique; instead he thinks that Helen's existence in the story is "like one of the drops of clear water beading on her breasts, or the striped pebbles at the sea's edge" (52). Here it becomes clear that Helen's function in Joe's story is the same as Margot's in "Joe's Absence." The nakedness/beach imagery clearly links both stories, and both girls are merely props in the imaginations of both Joe (Moorhouse) and Wilding (Graham). Graham's reading of Joe's story ends on this note of praise: "He wondered how Joe had achieved that ending with its fine balance, the irresolvable ambivalence of attitude between the two figures, the complexities of involvement and repudiation, the final frozen tableau that represented the whole action and like a pedestal supported and sustained it" (52).

The story that Graham praises is Moorhouse's "Across the Plains, Over the Mountains, and Down to the Sea." It appeared in his first collection, *Futility and Other Animals*, published in 1969 by Gareth Powell Associates. In 2009 Wilding remembered this story as the best one in Moorhouse's first book, saying "One of the few of his stories in which I found some lyrical notes to appreciate—otherwise I did find his writing flat" (Email, August 29, 2009).

Having recognized an artistic advance in this story, Graham is relieved at what he finds in some of Joe's other stories. In this expansive commentary Graham thinks: "But the old flatness was still there. He could find traces of it, of the old over explicitness, the clumsiness: gold amongst the dross, the silt, the rubble" (52). This perception makes him feel good that Joe has not achieved an artistry greater than his own. Graham goes on, recording the technical flaws: "He registered the redundancies, the spelled out endings, the unrealized and untransmuted autobiography, and said nothing" (52). But he also registers Joe's "new control" and attributes it to his "bush exile" and "not just Margot" (52).

Margot asks him if he has read the story about the abortion and identifies the girl in that one as Pat. Margot joins Graham on the mattress and as she flicks through the stories, leaves grease stains on the pristine pages. She doesn't care; he'll just have to type those despoiled stories again. She asks Graham whether he had read the "gang bang one" (52), and they read that one together, joined as one in the invasion of Joe's artistic privacy, his unpublished stories. She comments upon reading a story about Joe's wife walking out on him, "And I don't blame her" (52).

Exhausted from the sun, the food, from reading in the bad light, Graham enjoys a kind of camaraderie with Helen based on mutual comfort, not sex, and she rejoins him once again on the mattress with a new bottle of wine. The only thing of Joe's left to read is the unfinished story on his desk, and they read those pages, and Margot spills wine on them, and Graham reaches for the last page, left in the typewriter, and tears it in the process. This sequence ends: "Between them they completed the rape of the stories" (52).

Graham leaves the stories "roughly together" and the wine uncorked and, because Margot doesn't want to stay there alone, they drive through the rain and stars on the way to Sydney. The story ends: "He dropped her off in town at a friend of hers and refused coffee. When he got back to his own place, he went straight to bed and flaked" (53). "Flaked" is another instance of Wilding's embrace of the idiom of the era.

Wilding's retrospective commentary on this story, from a distance of over forty years, is fascinating:

> It's hard to remember what was true and what was fiction. I honestly cannot remember whether we actually looked at the MSS. I know she suggested we should. But did we? Maybe I was inhibited. Maybe I didn't want to read them—quite likely, who wants to read someone else's MSS. Certainly the ravaging of them is fiction—a development of whatever the germ of actuality was there. I guess I could go under hypnosis if you really want to know. I suspect in fact I didn't look at them—but the enormity of the idea gave me the germ of the story. (Email, August 4, 2009)

Another factor in the story's genesis, apart from the experience, ambiguous as that might be in memory, was the influence of Henry James. According to Wilding, "I'd been very taken by Henry James' stories of writers and writing and I think it was his influence from those stories that enabled me to see the possibilities in this episode for a story of writers' envies and jealousies. To see the literary potential, that is, for producing a story." And he added, "The feelings themselves I needed no encouragement for" (Email, August 4, 2009).

The brilliance of "Joe's Absence" resides in many elements of the story, but perhaps its greatest accomplishment is the fact that by making of Joe's absence a story, Wilding transcends Moorhouse's stories as contained, described, analyzed, and defined in "Joe's Absence."

"Odour of Eucalyptus," originally scheduled to be published in *London Magazine* but somehow lost in production, appeared in the meantime in *Coast to Coast*, ed. Clement Semmler (Sydney: Angus & Robertson, 1966; London, 1967), 243-57. The second longest story in *Aspects of the Dying Process*, it has not been anthologized except in the collection *The Man of Slow Feeling* (Angus and Robertson, 1985). An extremely interesting work that bears rich thematic connections with the main themes of *Aspects of the Dying Process*, it is also one of Wilding's earliest stories set entirely in Australia. In fact, he says, "it may have been the first" (Email, November 7, 2009).

Its title would seem to echo D. H. Lawrence's "Odour of Chrysanthemums," a story set in Lawrence's home area of Eastwood, a colliery town in northern England. Lawrence's story, which revolves around the death of a collier and his wife's coming to terms with their marriage, has no relation to Wilding's (beyond the title). But the figure of Lawrence certainly does. Indeed Lawrence hovers over the story in the characterization of Peter, a young Englishman who, like Lawrence, is from northern England. The other major literary influence is Henry James. In fact, the story can be read as James crossed with Lawrence.

But the title comes from Borges, as Wilding himself has indicated (Email, November 7, 2009). In "Death and the Compass," from *Ficciones*, the following phrase seems to confirm Wilding's statement: "amid the boundless odour of the eucalypti" (102). Curiously, the Borges story also has a dedication, in this instance "To Mandie Molina Vedia." (Perhaps Borges' practice was another influence on such stories as "Class Feeling.")

Peter is based on a contemporary of Wilding's, John Wiltshire, who came from northern England. Wiltshire studied at Cambridge under F.R. Leavis and joined the English Department at the University of Sydney the same year as Wilding, in 1963. The two Englishmen shared a house together in Paddington for a year or so. Later Wiltshire left Sydney for a position at La Trobe University. Eventually he published a book on Dr. Johnson's illnesses. Wiltshire came by ship to England, but Wilding came by air. The story's plot line derives from Wiltshire's account of meeting an English girl on the voyage (Email, November 7, 2009).

The story opens onboard a ship sailing from England to Australia in the early 1960s, a four-week voyage during which time Peter, in his "very early twenties," and another young man, Ralph, both on "contracts," are journeying to "the full sun" (56) where they will pursue their careers. The only other young person on the ship is a woman who is not so young, approaching thirty, named Miss Thorn. Because everybody else on the ship is old, and because the strictly enforced class distinctions on the ship compel the "first-class" passengers not to go below deck to mingle with the lower or tourist classes, the threesome spend a great deal of time together at dinner and in the evening during the long voyage. The whole set-up feels a good deal like a James novel, with two young bachelors seeking to entertain a youngish woman who comes from a different background. Miss Thorn (a Jamesian name if there ever was one) grew up in southeastern England and attended an all girls' Church of England school. Although she has been brave enough to launch herself alone on a journey to "discover" Australia, the young men find her stiff, formal, unable to bend. In a key paragraph the two characters of Miss Thorn and Peter are brought out:

> She was attracted to his stubby northernness, a sort of blunt clumsiness. It reminded her, perhaps, of Lawrence, but though she had read Lawrence—indeed at the time of their getting to know each other was sitting in a deckchair reading *Kangaroo*, which she didn't like—she would not have liked to have seen her interest in Peter as that, as belonging at all to that area of literature. Rather he existed in her consciousness as a character from some English television series, new and provincial and colloquial, with speech rhythms difficult quite to catch. She liked the way he liked the Beatles, and associated him with them, though not liking the Beatles herself. Indeed, when they came to Sydney she refused his invitation to go see them. She could not face the mass of screaming teenagers in the Stadium. But she knew he would not have thought of that. (55)

Here Wilding captures, stylistically, a kind of Jamesian syntactical complexity while at the same time placing Miss Thorn as fussily removed from both the radicalized literary context of Lawrence and the pop cult phenomenon of the Beatles. Miss Thorn is exactly that sort of fastidious Jamesian female who is frightened of the physical and enamored of polite manners and "good" conduct. All through the story spinsterhood seems her certain destiny, but we never know whether that is the case. It will either be that or marriage to a highly conventional, unimaginative man that she can control. At the same time that Peter is taking her measure, she is taking his: "She knew his lack of assurance, and felt assured, as she sat in the soft silk dress, her back erect and her elbows in her hands held calmly in her lap" (55).

Miss Thorn is very content not to visit amongst the other classes onboard: "She was glad, though, in an unexamined way, that they now couldn't go and wander amongst the noisiness of the tourists, the large families of unpatriotic cockneys or northerners who had only dislike for Britain..." (57). And in the exclusive company of the two intelligent, well-educated young men, she "felt that she was moving in something of the sophisticated world, not the formal and elegant sophistication of the dull diners at the table, but the new dynamic, dogged sophistication, the technology of English quality Sundays" (57).

Once in Sydney, Peter and Miss Thorne see a good deal of each other as they jointly set out to "discover" the city. Miss Thorne, "stepping on the alien shore" (58), takes lodgings in a hotel, while Peter shares a flat with another Brit, Derek, who came by airplane instead of by ship. Derek is based on Wilding himself. Derek's flat is in King's Cross, an obvious site for a young man embracing Sydney's culture at its most un-English entry level. Derek finds the girls in Australia "prettier, browner, easier" (58).

On one weekend Peter and Miss Thorn visit Bilgola, a suburb 33 k. north of Sydney's business district, near Pittwater. There is a lovely beach there. Another time they go to a theatrical review in the city, but this is not what she really wants; it is not her idea of seeing Sydney. In Miss Thorne the tourist resolve to take in everything of a special scenic value is very strong (as it is in many of James' travelers abroad), and so she implores Peter to "encounter the distinctively Australian, to breathe in the air of the harbours whose names she did not know, to see the surf of the beaches of which she had heard, to get the feel of the city" (60).

One Saturday they visit the botanical gardens in the heart of the city and, walking further, they reach the edge of the harbour and look "across at the skinless frame of the opera house, a model of brontosaurus under construction, and at the molluscal crouching of Pinchgut." The emergent opera house would of course become the single greatest constructed icon of Australia—high culture vs. the greatest natural icon, Uluru/Ayers Rock. Pinchgut is a stony island in the middle of Sydney Harbor, originally used for recalcitrant prisoners, left there without much if any food —hence its name. Later it became a fortress, but by 1857 Ft. Denison, as it was called, was obsolete. It is now the site of a museum. Though there is no odour of eucalyptus in this story, there is the odour of Miss Thorne's perfume and "rare scents from the trees," among which would be eucalyptus (60-61).

Derek is very interested in what is not happening between Peter and Miss Thorn. He tries to puzzle it out with no help from Peter. One day Peter takes her to The Cross, but she doesn't like it: It "wasn't pleasant, wasn't, except for this once, a place she really wanted to see except for her duty of discovering Sydney. Repute and that brief visit were enough for her" (61). The Cross, with its sex shops, massage parlor girls, and transvestites, is more than Miss Thorn can countenance.

Derek's imaginings run to the explicit demotic; he envisions Peter trying to "race her (Miss Thorn) off. He relished the phrase, race off. He had not heard it in England" (62). "Race off" is now somewhat dated slang meaning to leave a place, party, etc., for sexual intercourse. Wilding remembers it to mean "have sex with" (Email, November 5, 2009). But sex with Miss Thorn is not going to be easily accomplished, if at all.

Miss Thorn also stiffens at being taken to Derek and Peter's flat, where evidence of Derek's bohemian existence is on view, at least in her imagination. She recoils fastidiously from the "activities that go on here" (62). Peter's hopes of "loosening" her and of "broadening the horizons she had traveled so far towards" are meeting resolute resistance (62). A headline from a paper brought back to the flat by Derek catches Peter's attention: RAPE PACK STRIKES AGAIN (62). Derek's interest in such cultural phenomena is another marker of his assimilation into Sydney contrasted with the onlooker/avoidance syndrome of the tourist mentality.

The fact of Miss Throne's maiden virginity is becoming the central feature of her identity. She wants no more of the "vicious Cross" (62), but continues her round of sight-seeing with Peter. One weekend they visit the Domain, one of Sydney's oldest pieces of open space, consisting of 34 hectares that were set aside for a farm by Arthur Phillip, Commander of the First Fleet, in the summer of 1788. Phillip Domain, as it was called, eventually became just the Domain, where cricket matches were held, along with many other public events including celebrations and political rallies of the kind held in December, 1975, following the dissolution of Gough Whitlam's Labor government. Another feature of the site is Speakers Corner. In the story Miss Thorn resists that full experience: "Even the speakers at the Domain she insisted only on watching out of earshot, there for the visual and pictorial interest only" (62). But Peter doesn't seem to mind, and they both continue their tourist tour of "their new found land" (62). The narrative voice summarizes: "So the weekends went as they discovered Sydney" (63).

One excursion carries them to the Sydney Zoo. Here the muted sexual subtext receives a jolt of energy from the animal kingdom. They see chimpanzees "with their legs wide apart, dangling like priapic puppets" (63). They see snakes twining. But Peter and Miss Thorn remain as before: "They walked, in that heat, all round the zoo, safe amongst the rampant animals, side by side" (63).

Derek, who never meets Miss Thorn, remains intrigued with the relationship between his friend Peter and Miss Thorn. According to Wilding, he himself never met the English girl, but created her character from what Wiltshire told him and from his own "observations of girls in England." Wilding avows that the story "has something of an agenda about my feelings about English girls and English prudishness in those days" (MW email, November 7, 2009).

Derek wonders aloud to his current live-in girl friend, "I can't work out whether he is or whether he isn't" (63), a bit of ambiguity that may refer to whether Peter is sleeping with Miss Thorn or whether Peter himself is a virgin. The narrative voice complicates Derek's interest: "...but Derek, curious about Peter's possible methodistical decency, northern prudery, satisfied those qualities in himself by his speculative voyeurism" (63).

On still another excursion, the question of Miss Thorn's virginity is played out in a fascinating symbolic sequence. Walking together, Peter follows "the straight and gravelly path" (echoing obviously the "straight and narrow" of the Bible), but strays occasionally, playfully kicking a stone or two, and he imagines one of them slamming into her. This imaginary outcome leads to an analysis of her physical qualities: "She was built for stability—some sad aberration on the part of nature, like giving limpets such staying power. Who would want to aim the blows she was built to resist? But resist them, whenever they might come, she would, resist anything she would, so that the stability might be almost a simply deterrent device" (64). Continuing, the narrative voice develops two themes: the Lawrence figure and the symbolism of limpets: "As for him, he might have been more Lawrentian; or even simply more curious. Like the people who prize limpets off just to have a look at them underneath and poke their fingers in them. It was a subject for curiosity, as Derek kept explaining defensively to the girl, who didn't care either way" (64). Lawrence of course represents the rampant male who will push through to achieve a connection with the female, and limpets are a type of snails—true limpets as they are called—that cling to rocks and, as a survival strategy, will not relinquish the attachment short of destruction. The image of clinging limpets has become a metaphor for stubbornness and obstinacy—exactly the meaning of Wilding's employment of

## Varieties of Jamesian Experience    51

the imagery, but with an added sexual charge: "But he poked his fingers nowhere, not even to her hands" (64). The closest the two come to intimacy is a "tête à tête," which is only a meeting, as it were, of minds. After evenings at restaurants, she won't invite him up for coffee because "you know what people might think" (64).

A summary analysis of the English girl and the erstwhile English suitor concludes this sequence: "He might bluntly have wanted this girl from the soft southeast of England, the girl with the elocuted voice and the straight back, the obviously unplucked rose. Her name was actually Mary, but at first he'd not mentioned this to Derek, and so Rose was the name that Derek vicariously fed on, the budded, full, and slightly mildewed Rose, amongst her patronymic briars" (64). These metaphors could scarcely be more Lawrentian.

Throughout this story, one is reminded of the typical tropes of English fiction, the conflict between North and South, the eternal obstacles of class. In *Burnt Diaries* Emma Tennant described England as " this country, so long mired in novels about class or north-south divisions" (88-89). Australia in a way provided an escape hatch for Wilding. Tennant, incidentally, published one of Wilding's stories, "Sex in Australia From the Man's Point of View," in her magazine *Bananas* in 1978.

Miss Thorn, who has taken a teaching job, lives in a hotel, and it is there that she hosts a small party of acquaintances from work, and of course Peter. Much is made of manners in this scene, as in a Henry James story. Peter, instructed to pass peanuts around, starts eating them instead in his "northerly" way (65). Miss Thorn tut-tuts him, and he extends the bowl of peanuts to a guest: "And they laughed, and she [Miss Thorn] liked him for his gaucheness, that never exceeded its limits and became boorishness" (65). He strikes up a conversation with a young girl in attendance, and after a bit Miss Thorn breaks it up and insists he meet some other people. The signs of possessiveness on her part are clear.

The next section is a trip to Manly, roughly six kilometers across the harbor from Circular Quay. On this day Peter is suffering from having drunk too much at one of Derek's parties the night before, but still he accompanies Miss Thorn in their dedicated common purpose "to discover Sydney" (66). At Manly they encounter Australian urban beach culture in ways that disturb both of them. They see bikies and surfies, two sub-cultures that are unsettling to the proper English sensibilities possessed in full by Miss Thorn and by Peter to a lesser degree. Miss Thorn remains the tourist, looking on at the alien forms: "For Miss Thorn it was discovering Sydney, and she looked at the surfies with white zinc coated on their noses, or their backs peeling, the skin coming away, cancerous multicolor patches speckled like the underbelly of some fish, looked at all this with interest" (67). The passage goes on to include her and Peter's reaction: "She didn't like it, but discovering Sydney was what she had come to do, whereas for Peter it was where he had come to live; and this was somewhere he would rather have not known existed." Here Peter's fastidiousness links him with Miss Thorn; they both take an English view of the scene: "Their dislike of the vulgarity and ugliness they both saw, the newspaper posters and headlines, the fibro shacks, the corrugated iron and rusted shop awnings, had bonded them together" (67).

They make one more trip together, to Camp Cove Beach, located in Watsons Bay. To this day Camp Cove Beach is one favored by Sydney insiders who wish to avoid the mobs at Bondi Beach or at Manly. But on this occasion the relationship, such as it is, is breaking up. In a key analytical passage the narrative voice draws upon imagery that echoes the most famous seduction poem in the English language, Andrew Marvell's "To His Coy Mistress." Sensing a keen lack of attraction to her physically, Peter wonders why he has continued to escort her for so long: "Perhaps the friendship remained, perhaps the trouble was that he feared to encroach on that long untouched virginity, that grew each day longer untouched and less attracting plucking, a buttonhole he would not want to wear" (67). The relevant line from Marvell's poem is: "...then worms shall try/That long preserv'd virginity..." Peter is both Prufrockian and Marvellian, concluding: "Perhaps touching nothing and forcing nothing they were both happier" (67). But being with her on those "weekends of discovery" does not make him happy, though ironically he does discover places and sites that Derek does not know. Derek, however, is happy with his Australia, "with the delicate soon faded flowers that Derek ravaged" (68). At the parties Derek throws, Peter continues his acts of discovery: [he] "ploughed through the new continent in his own way, finding a different sort of knowledge, gaining a different acquaintance" (68).

Peter never satisfies Derek's curiosity about Miss Thorne, who, as the story nears its end, has moved on to Melbourne from where she keeps up a correspondence with Peter. The letters keep coming, from Canberra, then Brisbane, "as she discovered Australia"' (68). Peter visits her in Brisbane, and in a letter to Derek he suggests that "he was not getting on too well with his English friend who kept expecting him to be an English gentleman" (68).

After his visit the correspondence from her falls off but on occasion a letter comes. A passage of analysis explores the possible reasons for a slackening of interest on both sides:

> Perhaps she had become bored with the Lawrentian hero, the colloquial northerner, and tried to make him wear a dinner jacket in the Brisbane hotels. Or perhaps he had tired of treating her as the English lady, pure, unmolested, untouched by human hand, and scattering the rocks and pebbles of morality aside, had lowered his head and charged. Perhaps he had tired of the stiff back and deportment on the Queensland sands, or perhaps she had wanted to go out discovering in the hot midday sun." (69)

The only thing Peter ever tells Derek about the English lady is that she "had wanted things done for her all the time" (69).

Letters continue to arrive in Sydney as Miss Thorn travels over the continent "with that solid independence that he had first admired in her, moving from hotel to hotel and place to place and in her own way, perhaps the only way possible for her getting to know the land and taking photographs of it" (69). The story ends with one last letter of impressions, from Perth where, a year after entering the country, "she boarded the liner that would take her back home on her boomerang ticket" (69). With the last sentence, Wilding had in mind another Jamesian gesture: "I think 'boomerang ticket' was some marketing term at the time. I don't think I would have made that up. What I was trying to do was incorporate some of the current idioms into the Jamesian rhythms, the way the Master used to" (Email, November 8, 2009).

This story could easily have been placed first in the collection. In retrospect, Wilding has stated, "If I had been more sensible I would have set up a chronological sequence and had some consistency of names in the different stories and made it a sort of novel—but I didn't think of that at the time!" (Email, November 8, 2009). As Wilding remembers that period, "Somehow I must have felt each story should be a self contained work in itself" (Email, November 7, 2009). Placing "Odour of Eucalyptus" first would have formed a sequential narrative of arrival and immersion and choice as seen in "Somewhere New" and "The Sybarites." In any event Wilding placed it right in the middle, in the number five slot.

"The Watertight VW" was first published in *Westerly* in 1971. Twenty years later it appeared in a Serbian translation, published in *Ovdje* (Titograd, Montenegro). Otherwise it has neither been anthologized by others or in Wilding's own short story collections. Hence it would have to be considered one of the lesser known stories in *Aspects of the Dying Process*.

Yet to the reader of this volume, it will seem very familiar, as the four anxiety-ridden characters of "The Sybarites" are brought together again, in much closer proximity than in the Sydney beach and pub story. Carl Harrison-Ford sees parallels with "Joe's Absence" in the theme of

## Varieties of Jamesian Experience

"sexual indecisiveness" (176). Here Ian, Andrew, Helen, and Pat are on a road trip to the northeastern tropical climes of Queensland. Wilding and friends from the English Department at the University (Stephen Knight, Lee Cataldi, and Alison Cunningham) made such a trip to Cairns during Christmas break in 1963. Wilding remembers that both Stephen and Lee were in love with Alison, and, he adds, "I rather fancied her too" (Email, October 28, 2009). Wilding was quite new to Australia at the time, having arrived in October of that year. Thus this story, like several others in the collection, is about coming into the country.

The situation in the story is very familiar from the earlier portraits of the foursome. Ian is tormented by desire for Helen, while Andrew appears to be having some kind of covert sexual relationship with the siren of Ian's dreams. Pat, as usual, is of little interest to Ian. Everything in this story is more claustrophobic than in the Sydney story; the closeness of Helen's flesh and yet its distance from Ian creates an anxiety he can hardly bear.

The story opens on New Year's Day, following a stint at a pub somewhere in the cane-growing countryside. The story shows, among other things, just how much discomfort the young are willing to tolerate. Ian sleeps in the cramped quarters of the VW, and when he wakes up he remembers the night before: "watching Helen's eyes bright against her now sun-browned skin, as in the huge pub the Irish canecutters sang mournful ballads in one corner, and the Scots replied in the other, expatriates who had been cutting cane, if they were to be believed, for fifty years; and still remembered their distinct celtic traditions" (70). Among other songs, the canecutters sing the Wild Colonial Boy, though as Helen points out, it's an American version, which leads Ian to think: "Whoever heard of a prairie in Oz"? (70). The reference to Oz, incidentally, indicates its increasing popularity as an insider name for Australia. The contact in this story with working class, blue collar labor is one of the few times in this collection that Wilding's characters are outside the bubble of urban bohemian Sydney—"instant Sydney."

In one remembered scene, from the night before, Ian recalls a one-handed canecutter who was so smitten by Helen's sexual charisma that he proposed to her in the crowded pub. Ian was close to telling Helen how he felt, dancing with her, whispering in her ear how much he loved her, when another Queenslander pulled him away, saying they didn't want that kind of thing in the establishment. Ian envies the directness of the one-handed canecutter, who "was stopped by nothing" (71). Ian recalls the very public declaration of the canecutter, who told Helen of his aspirations, his desire to provide for her, the house they would build, and so on: "And they would live amongst those raw red fields, tracks scored through the thick cane like powdered blood, in that ceaseless sun" (71). The canecutter's urgency and directness bespeak an instinctual energy that the sophisticated, educated intellectual Ian cannot summon. The canecutter might have come from a Lawrence story, in the character's raw intensity and sexual confidence, a kind of maimed Queensland Mellors to Helen's siren from the city.

But awaking in the daylight, inside the VW, Ian feels the heat of Helen's presence and dreads the perception that Andrew "was now thrusting himself into her carelessness" (71). This frustrating dance of desire has been going on for twelve days of the long road trip in the VW. Sleeping arrangements are a particular source of irritation. Somehow Ian always winds up somewhere other than beside Helen, and so instead of sleeping in the tent outside, he has slept in the VW one night, and now does so a second night. Still, inside the car he senses the sexual warmth emanating from the tent. When a fierce rainstorm opens up like "machine gun fire" (72), Ian, in the VW, watches as Pat struggles to get into the car to escape the pummeling storm. As she moves into the vehicle, her breasts are clearly visible, "naked, firm, full" (73), and Ian is certain that she would welcome his physical entreaties, touching her, making them a couple the way, apparently, Helen and Andrew are. But he can't summon desire for Pat, just as he could not in "The Sybarites." He thinks that in any event he has waited too long, ten days in all, to make a move at last. Then Helen comes looking for shelter in the car as well, to escape the storm, the falling coconuts. Ian looks for evidence of her nakedness, but finds none. Still, he is sure that "she could only before have been fucking Andrew, this the first night they had not been slept round by others, the only night alone in the tent" (73).

Helen's presence continues to torment him, and Pat as well. When Andrew enters the car, smirky and edgy, with Helen in the front, and Ian and Pat in the back seat, Ian and Pat watch closely to see if Andrew's hands touch Helen's thighs or breasts. His stomach "sick with agitation at Helen's loss" (73), Ian can't even masturbate, the car is so small, the bodies so proximate. Ian thinks about what he will do when he gets back to the city, but that's five long nights ahead, and in the meantime there is only the burning proximity of Helen: "Five nights of Helen lost to him, her loss so present" (74). The story ends with a jump, a visionary moment: "He wondered if the rains might come down so quickly as to flood the beach into the sea, and drift the VW, which was advertised as watertight, away towards the barrier reef, and beyond" (74). In retrospect, Wilding says of this moment: "The out of body experience was quite something" (Email, October 28, 2009). Despite this comment, no such moment actually appears in the story. Looking back a second time, Wilding has stated, "I thought it was in the story—but it wasn't!" "(MW email "comments and corrections," November 28, 2011).

The next-to-last story in the collection is the only one narrated in the first person.

"And Did Henry Miller Walk in Our Tropical Garden" appeared in two very different publications in the same year: in *Stand*, 11 (1970), 26-30) and the men's magazine *Chance International*, 1 ix (1970), 24-26. The story is the only one from the girlie mags that Wilding included in *Aspects of the Dying Process*. It has also appeared in *Sveske* (Belgrade) and *Ovdje* (Montenegro). In the girlie mag version the title ends with a question mark, but the version in *Aspects* does not.

The story stands out both amongst Wilding's girlie mag stories and in *Aspects* because it is so different from the other works—notably in its narrative strategy and tone. Wilding's narrator is a writer inhabiting a domestic situation with various uncertainties and nervous-making conditions. What is starkly different from the other stories is the vernacular diction, syntax, and overall tone of the narrator—a racy colloquial voice thoroughly at home with modern idioms and grounded in a rich literary tradition. The title alone conveys a kind of jauntiness, and Wilding's commentary on its source and meaning is illuminating:

> The title is of course a version of William Blake's Jerusalem. "And did those feet in ancient times, walk upon England's mountains green." A radical poem—but set to music it was the closing hymn of meetings of the conservative Women's Institutes in England. Ambiguity. So the juxtaposition of the revered Wm Blake with Henry Miller is intended to capture the tonal complexities or collocations I was aiming for. As with the combination of Lawrence and James. (Email "Aspects," November 23, 2009)

The story begins with the first person narrator roused from sleep by the noisy children of "Ross Bilham's wife's God knows whose fathered children" (82). Mrs. Bilham, who also appears in the novel *Living Together*, echoes James' Little Bilham in *The Ambassadors*. It is he, one will recall, who receives the famous advice from the sculptor Gloriani, "Live. Live all you can. It's a mistake not to...." Wilding has commented on the naming: "No special reason, just a tribute to the Master—and the endless quest for usable names for characters. James used to have lists of possible names in his notebooks" (Email "Aspects," November 23, 2009).

The narrator is in bed with his live-in, Judy, and because of the noise and the Indian music that the neighboring woman plays incessantly, he reasserts his desire to move to a quieter location. The narrator quickly complicates the narrative by remembering a drunken evening spent, in part, with Jo, another woman who interests him. The vernacular tone is caught perfectly in his recounting of the aftermath of spending time with Jo: "It wasn't a very cool thing to do, to go without sleep after being sick all weekend, and I ended up with this ache all down my right side for the next two days. Jo just said it was a distended super ego when I told her, and Judy said what did I expect, so I stopped even mentioning it, and it went away by the end of the week" (82).

The colloquial idiom appears in even more evident terms in another passage describing, for lack of a better term, the lifestyle of the narrator: "And I didn't dig the bohemian quarter any more. In fact I'd got to dislike the arty push aspect of it as much as I disliked the brain-damaged bastards who ran up and down the streets all afternoon with plastic machine guns exterminating the Viet-Cong. The whole place was pulsating with sonic or sexual hyperactivity" (83). Here "dig" echoes the Beat origins of this usage, known to Wilding from his admiration for Kerouac's *On the Road* and his enthusiasm for other Beat authors such as Allen Ginsberg and Lawrence Ferlinghetti. The reference to "arty push" is to the Push, the Libertarian movement that roiled and energized the Bohemians and artists and would-be artists of Sydney from the 1940s into the 1970s. The Push was a mind-set, an anti-bourgeois, progressive point of view that was ready to welcome the new poetics, the new fiction heralded by Wilding, Moorhouse, Vikki Viidikas, and all the young writers on the Sydney scene in the 1960s & 70s. Denizens of the Push had, in effect, laid the groundwork for the New, primarily in terms of temperament rather than transformative, lasting creative work. From an American perspective, the Push was like a moveable Greenwich Village.

The title's invocation of Henry Miller enters the story when a girl friend of Judy's comes by one day to minister to the narrator's heavy hangover. She tells him, "Darling, people go on and on about Henry Miller, but man, it's just the way you and I live all the time" (83). The very name Henry Miller signifies liberated, bohemian ways of being. Miller's banned books, especially *Tropic of Cancer*, were, like *Lady Chatterley's Lover*, totemic signs of the break with bourgeois pieties and pruderies.

Henry Miller, D.H. Lawrence, and Jack Kerouac were the holy trinity of the new dispensation of the 1960s. Wilding was influenced by all three, especially David Herbert and Jack.

The Henry Miller reference gets inside the narrator's head and he begins to worry about the existence of some "ex Henry Miller of Judy's" (83). To offset those feelings, he begins to pursue Jo more ardently. In one sexualized conception of her he narrates, "...her suntanned legs were so beaut I'd want to lick the salt of the surf off them, and standing up to get a couple more beers I could look down at her breasts —she didn't wear a bra—and you could almost hear the Hawaiian strings playing and seagulls calling and all that jazz" (83). This takes place, of course, in a pub, the Windsor Castle, which "had only one palm tree, and a concrete floor, and didn't go for pawing in the afternoon" (83). Here the hard-boiled tough guy tone is letter perfect. Wilding recalls that actual pub: "I lived in Windsor Street Paddington at the time, and the pub there was the Windsor Castle, and it had a beer garden called the tropical garden. A very concrete tropic" (Email "Aspects," November 23, 2009).

He invites her to a party, and after drinking a good deal and playing "footy footy" with her, they go outside where "It was raining in a sub-tropical way...". Judy spots them and is "apparently a bit shat-off" (83). Then next, as usual, a terrible hangover ensues, and he has renewed worries about "some ex Henry Miller of Judy's" and he uses this fact to justify his intensifying interest in Jo. So he goes to Jo's flat and they talk and he silently enumerates her library ("Fromm, *Ulysses*, Reich, Ayn Rand, Kierkegaard, Shakespeare, *Breakfast at Tiffs*"—a typical personal collection of that era) [84]. They have a detailed discussion of their "sex lives and...rotten family relationships and ideal relationships we ought to be having" (p. 85), the standard rhetorical background and foreplay of a new relationship but in the end they decide, largely at Jo's guidance, not to sleep with each other but instead to have a "sexy platonic thing" (85). Upon rereading this story recently, Wilding remembers: "I'd forgotten the story and my bad behaviour. Jo was based on the psychology department tutor I knew, a flaming red-head I was fascinated by—Lynne Segal —hence the mention of seagulls in the last paragraph. As her bookshelf shows, she was one of the Sydney Libertarians—that anarchist philosophy, with Freud, Reich & co. thrown in" (Email "Re: Pete Gent," November 19, 2009). In another email he went into a bit more detail about Segal:

> A psychologist, she became quite a high profile feminist in the UK later (University of Middlesex in London) and has published a few books, very bright, very lovely, daughter of psychiatrists, she and her sister seemed to have been left to run wild in a large house in Bellevue Hill in the Eastern suburbs & wild was how they ran." (Email "Re: nostalgia qualified," November 18, 2009)

Two of Lynne Segal's books are *Slow Motion: Changing Masculinities, Changing Men* (1990) and *Straight Sex: The Politics of Pleasure* (1994). Segal, Germaine Greer, Kate Jennings, Vicki Viidikas, Sandra Levy, Elisabeth Wynhausen, and Robyn Davidson are among many Australian feminists of the era who went on to make a name for themselves beyond the anti-war protests, anti-censorship protests, bra-burning protests, anti-male chauvinist pig protests, and all the other protests of that disputative era.

  Back at his noisy house with Judy, the narrator has a child's breakfast, mashed bananas, sugar, and milk, and scans the ads for a new place to move to. "When we were there, in this modern block, looking at the Pacific stretching out Scott Fitzeraldly to America or Antarctica or somewhere or somewhere, stretching out and flecked with bits of foam and wave and seagulls (we'd only got sparrows and mynah birds round the terrace), then it was beaut" (85). Again "beaut" is the signature word of the new idiom of Sydney, of the now. Turning Fitzgerald's name into an adverb serves wonderfully to evoke the last page of *The Great Gatsby* in which Nick Carroway imagines Western U.S. space stretching before him, from Atlantic to Pacific.

The new site with its view of the ocean makes the narrator keenly aware of what he stands to lose if he and Judy break up, but at the same time there is the ongoing problem of Jo, of what to do about Jo. The narrator ruins the day by leaving for Jo's flat, but during his departure he contemplates once again the beauty of their location, in a stirring, painterly description of the view:

> And then, coming down the hill, I saw the harbour, a long glimpse of the vivid blue water beneath the bright sun, yachts and ships and ferries passing across it, and that bright vivid blue reaching out to and beyond the Heads. And I remember why we had taken the flat, because of its view of the ocean, clean and clear and boundless and salt-pure—cleaner, purer than the harbour which had its beauty cluttered with pawing people on ferries, and wriggling grubs and dead fish on fishing boats, and cigarette packets and diesel fumes. The ocean was free from that, possessed an untouched-ness, a great clear blueness, a freedom from intrusion, an aloneness of just the two of us. (86)

He goes to Jo's flat with the intention of ending what is not yet a consummated relationship. He has decided that, as a writer, "I wasn't going to lose that view, all that peace I could write in" (86). So he will end it with Jo. But it doesn't turn out quite the way he has envisioned. He arrives at her place and finds the door unlocked, and when no one answers the bell, he enters and proceeds towards Jo's room where he finds a door half open. Looking in, he sees a man half clad, brushing his hair in front of a mirror. The dominant image is one of sexuality: the man's white buttocks. The narrator-writer steals away, unseen, unperceived. This unexpected voyeuristic moment ends his interest in Jo. As he states, "It formally closed the episode for me, but like the vision of the blue [from the passage above] it had little positive relevance to Judy. She just didn't have a symbolic imagination" (87). The observation about the lack of a symbolic imagination is very funny and reveals Wilding's awareness of the arrogance/pretentiousness of writers as a breed.

Driving back to the flat, he checks to see if "the view of the ocean was as blue as the harbour I'd glimpsed" (87), and finding it so, concludes as follows, with the pun on Segal in the seagulls thrown in for free: "And it was, a deep unpeopled blue, and the white flecked buttocks gave way on my retina to the milky white flecks of seagulls and spray, and I drove home feeling satisfied, and after giving a résumé of it all to Judy, wrote down notes so I could write the buttock image up as soon as we were settled away from the noise we'd been living in, while she packed the stuff for us to move"(87-88). "The milking white flecks of seagulls and spray" betoken another aspect of the dying process (sexual climax). Wilding has commented on the ending: "The episode of visiting and seeing the bare buttocked bloke was true. I left, snuck away silently" (Email "Aspects," November 23 2009).

The narrator-writer's commitment to recording personal experience, immediate experience, is here a reflection of the developing aesthetic of writing about coming into the country, into Australia. In future stories, Wilding would play many turns upon that central early conception of writing, of making it new (the old Modernist ideal enunciated most famously by Pound). Story after story would make it new. This story seems to represent an important stage in the process of becoming a modern Australian. We know nothing of the narrator's earlier life and there is no trace of Englishness.

The title story, the longest in the book, is also the only one previously unpublished, and it brings us back to the Jamesian mode that dominates most of the stories in the collection. It also marks a fitting conclusion to many of the major themes articulated in the artist-writer stories. Typically, the narration is third-person limited, with everything being filtered through the consciousness of a familiar figure, Graham, of "Joe's Absence" and, by other names, Ian and Derek in various of the other stories. In this story, however, Graham is given a last name: Coburn. The setting is urban Sydney, specifically the parties and pubs of the younger members of the avant-garde, who, if we are to believe the previous "Henry Miller" story, would prefer to see themselves as distinct from the Push, that loose confederation of by then mainly older libertarians, artistes, pub crawlers in the name of culture, far-lefties, etc. The Push attracted hangers-on, wannabes, and would-be's of the kind that inhabit the margins of most movements.

The story opens with Graham in a moment of anxiety, much as in "Joe's Absence." He is present at a post-pub party and simultaneously wants to go and wants to stay: "To leave would be to be alone; to remain, would be to have the security of ever believing that excitement was about to arise, the conviction that things might happen he could not miss" (89). And what happens is rather predictable: there's a striking new girl present, and Graham is captivated by her presence. She's not like the usual Australian girls mentioned in "Odour of Eucalpytus": "prettier, browner, easier." Instead, what stands out about this girl is the image of whiteness, the color of innocence: she is slim, with white blonde hair and blue eyes and she's wearing a white shirt. She has a "wide-eyed innocent eager expression" (89). For the attentive reader, this girl is an Australian version of James's Daisy Miller, the innocent American who dies in Rome because of her very innocence, and because of Winterbourne's having given up faith in her innocence and having accepted a cynical, European interpretation of her at times ambiguous behavior. Wilding himself acknowledges the influence of *Daisy Miller* on his own story: "...the Daisy Miller parallel particularly resides in the fact that in James' story the insouciant narrator is clearly responsible for Daisy's death, through his interference in her life. Just as Graham is responsible for the destruction of Jacquie's relationship with Fowler, thro his provoking the uninvited guests at the party" (E-mail "add," November 19, 2009).

Wilding's innocent is not however literally as innocent as Daisy, as she is attached to Fowler, a filmmaker who likes to hear himself talk. The name probably signifies someone who knows how to handle birds or in Fowler's case, "birds." Fowler, Wilding remembers, "was based on someone who was not a film-maker but a folk singer, Garry Shearston (now a clergyman!—saw him singing an Australian folk song on tv a couple of weeks back, now a 60 something chubby old buffer)—had a hit with Cole Porter's I Get a kick out of you, in the cocaine days of the next decade" (Email "Aspects," November 23 2009). Still there is that perpetual air of innocence about Fowler's girl that deeply attracts Graham. He and the girl talk for a while, and among the things about her that he finds intriguing are her jeans, which are carefully faded, and at one point he asks her about "the dyeing process," a punning play on the story's title. The pun, however, is purely accidental, a result of a printing error. Wilding has explained it this way: "Spelling issues messed up my pun on Aspects of the Dying Process. Didn't realize at the time I wrote it that death dying (the little death, orgasm, probably intended) was spelled differently from Thai dyeing" (Email "Aspects," November 23, 2009). Graham's last name, Coburn, in its second syllable—burn— signifies another reference to sexual desire: Coburn "burns" (Email "re: names," November 2, 2009). Then there is an additional meaning, as Wilding explained: "Anyway, the idea of phallic inflammation, whether disease or satyriasis, lay behind calling the character Coburn. Cockburn. But implicit, hidden" (Email "Pete Gent," November 19, 2009).

They talk and they talk some more. He remains enthralled by her "innocence and youth" (91). Amused at something he says, she begins to giggle and tries to suppress her giggling, all the while charming Graham the more: "And laughing, she was pretty. She put her finger tips to her lips as if to conceal her patent giggles. She had all these mannerisms of a child, which he found touching, affecting" (89). Innocent, pretty, child-like—all of these qualities she shares with James' insouciant heroine. Also impulsiveness. She is as impulsive as a child. Graham gets a taste of this when she reaches into his pocket and pulls out a copy of *Sire*, Wilding's fictional name for *Squire*, the girlie mag that he had published a story in back in 1966. From this incident Wilding creates rich comedy:

> But *Sire*. Its name, both hinting at *Esquire* to initiates hard of hearing, and yet evoking rather than the clubman passivity of

> "esquire" the active pioneering life, the cattle station physicality of a stud farm, and carrying too the haunting overtones of a feudal *droit de seigneur*, a courtseying "sire" of consent. And the nudes as nude as any, a little freckled, a little skin-cancered, but fleshly. He wished it had been almost anything else she had found in his pocket. Even *Leather World* might have suggested an exoticism of vice; not simple perviness (92).

This is the kind of analysis of girlie mags that one rarely finds anywhere. And the specifically Australian context of these girls, "a little freckled, a little skin-cancered," is set against the dazzling whiteness of Fowler's girl, the ingénue manqué.

Fowler's girl examines Graham's copy of *Sire* with the close, almost breathless attention of a "child reared away from magazines or books" (92). This lack of exposure to literature, in all its forms, is one of the foreshadowing details in the narrator's eventual turn against her innocence, which can be another word for ignorance, and beyond that, the emptiness of information, the complacency of incurious responses to the world. As she slowly looks at the magazine, the narrative analysis tracks the process: "This way turning every page, absorbing each layout, each title, with every mammary joke, all the grainy nudes. She gave the magazine an examination of the care and intensity usually reserved for rare items in museums and galleries, an examination conducted with a dutifulness rather than spontaneity, but a memorizing dutifulness to provide for the eventual report to be delivered" (92). In short she is like a schoolgirl fulfilling an assignment, and Graham is struck by her seeming detachment from the experience. He thinks, "It might have been that she registered nothing before those bared nipples and shrouded pudenda" (92),

She possesses little self-awareness and her fund of innocence is almost inexhaustible. Upon completing her intense perusal of *Sire*, she asks Graham whether men like such things, and the narrative provides this telling analysis, "As if she had been let out of her convent school for the first time that morning, and stood there, clad in her phenomenal innocence, amongst the crowd of groping hands and shared bottles, the aura of her whiteness creating a restraining, impregnable gulf between her and the crowded room" (92). No one touches her; she is impervious to the random lust of the party, but as we are reminded, "she had been let out that morning from no convent school but the bed of Fowler…" (92). Her innocence, we learn, "was an innocence for aesthetic admiration but surely not of moral intimidation" (92). Thus Wilding shifts the equation from moral to aesthetic, away from James and to a new fashioning of the Master's signature theme (though James himself, in other stories, wrote of terrible women, as he might say, who had lost their virtue and strove on, preying on innocent, or naïve, men).

Their conversation continues. She declares that she couldn't imagine "looking at photographs of grotty men without any clothes on" (93), and she wants to know what Graham does besides write for smutty magazines. He confesses that he is a lecturer, and to his response that his writing for such magazines is something of a "hobby," she responds, "or perversion" (93). She continues in her most animated moment in the story thus far:

> "The only lecturers I've ever met have been such awful bores, really incredible bores. Dirty unshaven men in raincoats with bad breath. They seemed to think if they bought you a crummy meal in a cheap restaurant they always claimed was a special undiscovered place only they knew, and I'm sure nobody else would ever want to admit to knowing it, and dredged half a bottle of warm white wine wrapped in newspaper from their raincoat pocket and then bored you about some ridiculous roman emperor or syphilitic poet you've be dying to leap into bed with them as soon as ever you'd shouted them a taxi." (93)

After this outpouring, they duel a bit, with Graham pointing out that he has a car, and her declaring him to be a "marvelous lecturer" whose students "simply adore" him (93). She asks him for a beer, and when he goes to get her one he is waylaid by another girl, Marianne, who takes him out to the backyard and suggests that they "go off for a fuck somewhere" (93), but Graham is not interested in her; he's only burning for the girl in white. After a time he returns to find the girl alone in the crowded room and he tells her exactly what happened. He also tells her that the other girl's "rampant sexuality" terrifies him (94). Focusing on her, he tells her she reminds him of someone, and she points out that he once tried to pick her up at a party. A bit drunk by now, he conjures up the look-alike: the actress named Anna Karina in the film *Bande à Parte*. (The film's title was *Bande à Part* , "Band of Outsiders.") The girl is very flattered, although she points out that the girl in the film has the wrong color hair. (Karina was a brunette.) The film in question was one of Godard's New Wave successes, in 1964. Graham's flattering comparison of the girl with Anna Karina leads him to think rather highly of himself at that point: "She made him feel chivalrous, very elegantly polished in his compliments, like the hero of a romance. And cinécultured too, which we all have to be these days" (95). At this juncture Fowler comes over to claim the girl and go home, and though she puts up a bit of resistance, the two of them leave and the party is over for Graham.

The next section opens with Graham strolling through King's Cross—a marker of his assimilation into Sydney—and stopping at a crowded little book shop where he likes to browse, where the immersion in contemporary literary magazines and books "gave him the brief feeling of participation in the life and death of literature, consciously creating the illusion and happy to do so" (95). And there, among the books, is Fowler's girl. When he says "You," she says, "Her name is Jacquie," an interesting way of showing that she knows she has been objectified in his mind as Fowler's girl. She's pointing out that she has a name and an identity, and she makes the point further by saying, "You didn't know I could read, did you?" (95). Wilding has explained in detail the choice of the character's name:

> Jacquie is short for Jacqueline. My agent in the UK at the time was called Jacquie Reynolds—so I took the name from her. Being

a UK agent her name probably had those upper crust Lord Snowden associations. It was not unusual in the UK—not sure about Australia, but I don't think it was that rare a name. We published a Jacquie Taylor in Tabloid Story, I recall. Sometimes spelled Jackie. It think it has upper rather than lower class associations—this one in the story was certainly private school moneyed middle class. (Email "Aspects," November 23, 2009).

But it turns out that what she's interested in is *The Penguin Italian Cookbook*, a detail that brings out all of Graham's literary snobbishness: "as if finding someone in a chamber concert listening to a transistor relaying the trots" (96). "Trots" refers to trotting races. The big trotting raceway was at Harold Park in Glebe (Email "Re: query, October 22, 2012).The analysis of his snobbery continues:

> And immediately at that he felt caught out himself in an awful priggishness, holding his copy of *London Magazine* there as a sort of holier than thou thoughts of Chairman Mao before her unhallowed domestic practicality, even if it was a Penguin. And to be put in such a position of assertive superiority made him feel hopelessly conventional, hopelessly academic, before her spontaneity. Had he been carrying *The Penguin Book of Comics* he would have been all right. (p. 96)

In an email Wilding has recalled that exact bookshop: "The bookshop was Clay's bookshop in Macleay Street, Kings Cross, where I used to buy London Magazine, which around this time (when the story is set) I had a couple of stories in, and later reviewed for when I went back to the UK" (Email "Aspects," November 23, 2009). They leave the bookshop together, walking down Macleay Street towards the fountain, with Jacquie chattering to him, and that verb, "chattered," reminds us once again of Daisy Miller, who is always chattering to Winterbourne. In her movements and her essential essence, Jacquie is very close to Daisy Miller indeed:

> She seemed in her lightness, chirrupiness, sunny happiness, her constant chatter and movement, a girl who would always be

> resting hands gently on whoever she was with, always arousing that tactile excitement, touching, stroking, enlivening. Yet she was not true to that impression. She was like a butterfly, always hovering round flowers, twigs, branches, always exciting the stamens with a fluttering hope of contact, but rarely brushing against them. (97)

They continue on to the village centre, which provokes in Graham "his idle morning fantasies of a Village. He wondered whether people who lived in the real village were conscious of its being the village and conscious of playing the appropriate or expected roles, derived from their literature" (97). The village in Graham's mind is Greenwich Village, the storied site and cliché of an American literary tradition based on radical, avant-garde writers stretching from the First World War era through the Beats of the 1950s. Graham has in his hands copies of *London Magazine* and the *Sydney Morning Herald* (and a copy of *Sire* hidden inside the newspaper). Remembers Wilding, "So the mention of the cities in London mag and Sydney morning herald is there to indicate some sort of parallel yet distance from NY" (Email "Aspects," November 23, 2009). Such is the care with which Wilding plants details in this story—and in his fiction generally.

Sitting at a table, he is surprised to learn that Jacquie has a job (she acts in television), and once again misreads her, as Winterbourne is always doing with Daisy. More comedy ensues when she discovers the copy of *Sire* wrapped inside the *Sydney Morning Herald.* She asks him if he carries his "'pieces' around like mascots" (97). The passage is worth quoting: "'To add to your multiple collection,'" she suggested; and giggled. He didn't know whether at the image of his room surrounded with multiple mammaries or multiple copies of his stories, a monstrous grotto of id or ego. Or whether she was just laughing at seeing his name" (97).

Eager to see her again, Graham jumps at the opportunity to attend a party given by David Murray at which Jacquie will be present. David Murray, incidentally, is the boy from ""The Altar of the Family," all grown up (Email, November 23, 2009). Graham finds her at the party and mentions the Italian cookbook but she seems to have forgotten all about it. As she stands with bread and cheese in hand, Graham "found her terribly attractive, like a poster for the Dairy Products Marketing board" (98). That comparison leads to explicit imaginings, "And was filled with the same frustration that makes people rip off the poster across the area of the model's breasts, hoping for revealed nipples and finding only old posters, or that provokes the pencilling in of nipples on to the taut, plumped out blouse, pudenda on to the jeans' crutch" (98).

He finds her "an odd, elusive girl" (98), and, dancing with her, is struck by her self-containment. He can never quite make the contact he wants with her, and David Murray, observing, tells him, "You'll never learn, will you? You're wasting your time on her" (99). He asks her to go with him to another party, in Paddington. As they leave, she tells Fowler she's going to a party and that she will see him later. The narrative skips forward to the drive back to Fowler's place from the party, but Graham, who is "very drunk" (100), cannot remember the exact sequence and cannot remember the second party at all, but he certainly does remember what happens next: he smashes up his car, and Jacquie returns by foot to Fowler's place. Such an incident happened to Wilding, as he recalls in an autobiographical essay, "Cars in My Life": "And then a couple of years later, sneaking off with a girl from a party, I skidded into a culvert in Balmain and the whole front end went out of shape. 'Oh, you silly goose,' I remember her saying. I tried to drive it to a garage the next morning but the police ordered me off the road. They'd seen me around, they said" (77).

The next week there is a reception for a "distinguished writer" and Graham, trying to sort his life out, takes his friend Judy. And there Jacquie is, and again the back and forth flirtation between them starts up. She calls him "professor" and "Dr. Coburn," and he points out that he is neither, that he is a lecturer sans a doctorate. So he becomes "Lecturer Coburn" to Jacquie in a playful mood. They talk about the car, a total ruin, and then she asks him out of the blue: "Do you think I ought to seduce this writer man? Do you think it might cause an international incident?" At the same time, she casts her spell on Graham, who cannot make out whether she is truly "like a child taken to the zoo" (101), full of delight and happiness, or whether she is consciously using the child's persona for her own ends. He cannot fathom "how she could have been unaware of his motives, his aspirations, at that party; how could she treat him with her child's condescension now unless she were unbelievably unaware? Or was all that a façade which she used to deceive Fowler; or perhaps to discourage the unwelcome or intrusive, in whose number she perhaps had placed him" (102). Here Graham is trying to read Jacquie in the same way that Winterbourne tries to read Daisy, and neither is having much success at penetrating the mask of innocence. Wilding employs a traditional image to describe her effect on him: "And so she swung round him, a brighter moth for his candle than the camphored poetesses, at least" (102) At this point Judy comes over and Graham introduces her to Jacquie but the "chill was unbreakable" (102). Jacquie turns the flame of her attention away from him and goes over to join Fowler.

Later, despite his plans to ignore Jacquie after her rebuff, he sees her standing alone, "in utter loss" (102). He asks her if she's still trying to seduce the distinguished guest, and she says she never seduces people, to which he responds, "You let them seduce you" (102) and feels bad about his presumption. She asks him to fetch her a drink and says she has no money, and so he still is drawn to her and imagines spiriting her away, though he has no car and then there's Judy. Observing Jacquie now, with all her defenses down, he makes the most negative assessment yet of her character: "Without her enthusiasm she was nothing. Without her vivacity, she was in suspension. She had not read anything by the distinguished writer nor was interested in discussing him; she seemed not to have read anything; she could remember no films she had seen; and films served only to nail down the image of Fowler into her consciousness with the girl by the bar" (103). Earlier Fowler had been talking to "an elegant socialite blonde" (103). In Graham's further reflections Jacquie is both "a human form preserved in ice" and "a planetary alien" (103). He also imagines that if she had been "like Alice" she "would have drowned the whole assembly without forethought or compunction, perhaps, indeed, without awareness" (103-104). The reference to Alice in Wonderland confirms her childlike nature. Now Graham is done with her, and like Winterbourne after his (mis)reading of Daisy at the Coliseum, where he mistakes her presence as a sign of her lack of innocence, and decides that she is a person for whom he no longer must feel any esteem, Graham sees Jacquie, in a truly Jamesian way, in this manner:

> He saw for the first time that blank emptiness, that beautifully shaped hollowness, that David, that Marianne, that everyone had told him of, he must have presented to everyone else in his pursuit of her, rather than to the engulfing stupidity and petty emptiness she now presented to him. And perhaps her all-consuming selfishness had spread to him; yet how could he be outgoing to her who refused all gestures? He left her there. Slumped on the couch, she no longer seemed even attractive. (104)

With Jacquie out of the picture, momentarily at least, the narrative turns to the comic possibilities of the distinguished writer and his disregard for the organizers of the reception—the Brotherhood of Australian Writers, Wilding's satirical name for the Fellowship of Australian Writers, the organization that sponsored the reading (Email, August 19, 2011). The distinguished writer, incidentally, was Yevgeny Yevutschenko, the ultimate celebrity Russian author of that era. The author of "Babi Yar," his most famous poem, has become a footnote in the literary world today, but back then he was quite popular in America and around the world. Wilding's portrait of the celebrity poet derives satirical humor from Yevutschenko's well-known womanizing. Thus the visiting celebrity gives his attention to "as many of the antipodean sisterhood as his literate hands, his typewriter calloused finger tips, could grasp" (104). And his main interest is in "the prettiest of the younger offerings" (104).

Fowler falls right in line and reclaims Jacquie, and the two of them leave the party with the distinguished writer in tow, "planning his intimate tour of the town" (104). Abandoned, as it were, Graham "toyed with the images of Fowler's ogredom, pimping Jacquie for the rights to a film of one of the writer's trilogies" (p. 105). At the end of this section Graham "was miserable with drinking, with loss, with the waste of an evening in which he had not even said a word to the celebrity, not even acquired an autograph for posterity" (105).

In the next section Jacquie comes to the University where Lecturer Coburn is teaching. At Jacquie's urging the departmental secretary calls Graham away from his tutorial class to meet a "Miss Fowler." Graham is both intrigued and irritated. She wants a drink and with some reluctance, because he has left his students in the midst of a session, he takes her to the nearby staff club where they are able to purchase bottles of beer but not drink them there as the bar is closed. (Today, alas, the staff club is no more. It was closed several years ago. It was a wonderful place for gathering after classes, just a short walk, no longer than a pitching wedge in distance, from the Woolley Building which houses the Department of English.) In his novel *Academia Nuts* Wilding has a character explaining why the staff club was closed: "To stop staff getting together and comparing notes on administrative malpractice and malevolence. It was seen as a site of subversion and potential resistance. A place for people to meet and talk, to sit around and compare notes, to contrast different practices in different departments, to exchange information" (236).

Jacquie fills Graham in on what she has been doing—judging a beauty contest, and Graham "'could have guessed, because Dexter had told him about it and was planning to come up to persuade the winner to pose for *Sire*" (107). As they drink their beers, she teases Graham, "The trouble with you Dr. Coburn is you're just a dirty old perv" (107), and once again he reminds her that he is not a doctor. She goes on to describe her disgust at the participants in the beauty competition, the "daggy girls" and "hundreds of alfish men...all those alfs belching beer" (108). Daggy in Australian slang means uncool, unfashionable, but comfortably so. It

# Varieties of Jamesian Experience

is not as negative as alf, which is used to describe an uncultivated man. When he says that those men were probably engineers, she says she wouldn't have been surprised if they were lecturers. After this exchange occurs the most extensive analysis in the story of Jacquie's Daisy Miller-like persona. Graham still has a hard time reading her, just as Winterbourne does in James's story. Here is the passage:

> At first he had been intrigued by her carrying that aura of innocence and childlikeness in a life that took her through the pub, her acting world, the cohabiting presence of Fowler. He'd found the combination poignantly appealing: but he'd never doubted that her innocence wasn't anything other than a style, he'd never doubted that since she was living with Fowler she would naturally go to bed with someone who attracted her. He had never assumed her style was anything other than an appealing manner. He wondered now, though, whether he had been totally misled, wondered whether she didn't hold that manner with the ferocity of a moral commitment. And yet the episode of the distinguished writer had to be reconciled with this, and yet with this image of innocence, could there have been an episode at all? Perhaps the writer, too, had simply wrecked a car for her and gone his way. (108)

It is only after Daisy Miller's death that Winterbourne comes to realize that he has misinterpreted Daisy's manner and behavior. He was taken in by appearances and by his European cynicism and could not accept the idea of Daisy's innocence. But that is what he learns at the end: that she was truly innocent and that he was wrong to abandon his belief in her innocence. In Wilding's version of that analysis and discovery of the truth, the situation is modernized so that this Daisy Miller—Jacquie—is not a virgin, because she lives with Fowler—but that she is faithful to Fowler and that her ingénue style and childlike charm may be difficult to interpret and may be misleading, but that she is, at bottom, capable of a moral commitment that is very hard to understand because there is so little of that quality to be found among the sybaritic pub and party goers. Wilding is quite explicit in his recollection about the influence of James' precursor story: "I certainly had Daisy, and James's hopeless, culpable narrator in mind, when I wrote that" (Email "Re: nostalgia qualified," November 18, 2009).

Graham is still worried about his having abandoned his students but he is also "committed to a life style of spontaneity" (108) and so remains with Jacquie drinking beer in the empty bar. After they leave, they take a cab and, upon nearing where she lives, they spot Fowler walking. She gets out of the cab and quickly comes back to thank him for "a lovely afternoon" and invite him to a party at her place the next week. She tells him to bring a bird if he likes.

Graham decides to go to the party but not because of her; he believes that he is through being consumed with desire for Jacquie. Thinking about her, Graham confirms a negative view of her manner: "He suspected, indeed, that she was deeply unimaginative, that having Fowler she contemplated no other diversion; unless it were some visiting celebrity, which would not be a diversion but a ladder shooting her up to higher snakes. Advancement to a firmer security might attract her, but a sexual detour offered no appeal. He didn't know; he might have been calumniating her. But that was how he intended to leave it" (110). Ladder and snakes, incidentally, refers to a board and dice game popular at that time (Email "Re: One More (October 22, 2012). At a pub with a girl named Nina, whom he invites to go with him to the party, Nina remarks that she had thought that Graham "was on with Jacquie" (110). When he says no, she replies, "I'd wondered why you alone had been privileged" (110). So in effect Jacquie's persona confuses others besides Graham, who himself finds a bit of consolation in that he, like other challengers, has been unsuccessful. When he arrives at the party, Jacquie is waiting for him but not in any way he wants. She's angry and accuses him of inviting "all these dreadful people" from the pub (110). He denies her accusation and says he didn't invite anybody, but she is still very angry. After she walks away, Graham's friend Dexter comes up. (Dexter appears in many of Wilding's stories.) It turns out that Dexter had dropped Graham's name as entrée to the party. He had heard about it at the pub, and he tells Graham his reasoning: "Well I figured you'd be here after all that *grande passion* stuff with Jacquie, so I figured that would get me in" (111). Graham is nervous about Fowler and in fact Fowler, who is drunk, does confront Graham, charging him with being responsible for "the two hundred bastards who came" (112). They argue about the numbers and though Fowler does not believe Graham's denials, they do not come to blows.

The party is going well regardless of how the pub crowd got there, and Graham relaxes and dances with Nina until he gets bored; he then trains his attentions on Kate and wishes he had his car (they came in Nina's) to go off with Kate. Then Nina begins to dance with Fowler, and Kate directs Graham's attention to Jacquie, who is staring at the couple with "that familiar intensity" (114). Graham then goes up to Jacquie, "a snow child frozen into a pillar of ice" (114). She won't dance or have a cigarette or a drink, and she tells Graham to "Go and talk to the grotty editor of your pervy magazine" (114). Graham apologizes for Dexter, but she tells him to stay away from her.

Graham and Kate dance some more, "his hands feeling the contours of her buttocks, her breasts" (114), and when the record ends, Jacquie confronts Fowler, angry with him for dancing with Nina. Fowler says she, Jacquie, could have danced with anybody she wanted, "even fucking Coburn" (115). So Graham is implicated in their verbal fight. But the crisis is not over. In that "timeless early morning" as the party goes on, Jacquie comes upon Fowler dancing with Kate in a suggestive manner and over-hears Kate say to him, "Why don't we go and have a fuck somewhere?" to which Fowler replies, "I can't right now" (115). Enraged, Jacquie tells him to go ahead, that she doesn't care. Obviously she does and Fowler tries to assuage her by calling her "Jacquie love" which enrages her the more (115). Angered by her attack, Fowler points out that she should have been dancing herself and not watching him all night. When she responds by wondering whether she had cramped his style, he tells her he's not "bloody susceptible to cramping" (116). She calls him sarcastically "Fowler, the big screen lover" (116). Then she tells him to "get out your list of all the women you've got off with and read it out" (116). Fowler asks her if she's sure she wants to hear. Now the earlier whiteness of her beauty has turned "ashen white, drained white with her fury" (116). He asks her ominously if she wants the whole list or just the past twelve months. The passage reads:

> "The last twelve months might be more interesting," she said. And the quaver in her voice showed for the first time her fear. For she hadn't expected it, hadn't expected the list of the women he'd slept with while all the time she'd believed he was faithful to her, and had all the time been faithful to him, she had not, right till the moment he began, expected there to be any substance to his proclaimed roll call. But as soon as he began, she accepted the awful authenticity of it, and never for one moment doubted but that it was true, never allowed the hopeless possibility that he might have been lying and have invented the list; she knew, as soon as he began, that the lying had all been done earlier, all been done in the twelve months whose fabric was now utterly destroyed, against the hurtful falsity of whose dishonest memory she threw herself, hurled the glasses and ashtrays and bottles that were on the floor beside her. (116)

She calls him a bastard and says she hates him and begins to sob. Graham, Kate, and Nina leave unnoticed and get in Nina's car and drive away, Graham between the two girls who are "singing, softly, in unison" (116).

James's *Daisy Miller* ends with the heroine's death from Roman fever; and Wilding's story, a modern version jazzed up with sex, lust, infidelities too numerous to count, ends with the final outrage to Jacquie's innocence. She dies a bit, too, in her sorrow and defeat at the hands of both Fowler and Graham, whose narrative consciousness complicates and implicates him in the destruction of her innocence. Wilding himself has pointed to the usefulness of the James tradition as applied to the age: "At the time, 1960s, narrators were usually endorsed; but I realized from reading Henry James the effect that could be achieved by having a narrator who unconsciously or unawares reveals his unadmirable aspects—as in Daisy Miller" (Email, "Aspects," November 23, 2009). Putting it another way, he added that in both "Aspects" and the Henry Miller story, he employed "narrators who are revealing their own bad behaviour as they narrate it" (Email, November 23, 2009). To a degree often unrecognized by feminist critics, female or male, many of Wilding's stories inoculate themselves from simplistic charges of male chauvinism. Carl Harrison-Ford recognized this feature in Wilding's work early on: "Though constantly aware of sex and occasionally preoccupied with it, the stories contain very little successful wooing or seduction and a number of characters reject direct sexual offers or opt out of initiatives" (178).

The title story is a fitting and powerful close to Wilding's first collection, and *Aspects of the Dying Process* as a whole deserves to be seen as a major contribution to Australian literature. Sydney-sider stories such as "Somewhere New," "The Sybarites," "Joe's Absence," "The Odour of Eucalyptus," "And Did Henry Miller Walk in Our Tropical Garden," and "Aspects of the Dying Process" are among the best short stories to come out of Australia in any era.

CHAPTER 3

# VARIETIES OF KEROUACIAN EXPERIENCE

## THE WEST MIDLAND UNDERGROUND

*The West Midland Underground* (University of Queensland Press, 1975), Wilding's second collection, contains nineteen stories that show the full range of his accomplishments in short fiction. In fact, if one had to choose a single volume to display the diversity of technique, subject matter, and artistry that Wilding brought to the short story genre, *The West Midland Underground* would be exemplary in this regard. The book is dedicated to Sue, Wilding's girlfriend Sue Gregory with whom he lived from "late 73 through mid 75, as far as I can recall the dates. She worked on the ABC science program for a while" (Email "Re: Sue," February 28, 2011).

Eleven stories are set in England, two have indeterminate s/f settings, one is set in Greece, two in America, and four in Australia. The English stories range from the radically experimental "The West Midland Underground," to more conventional autobiographical stories like "Canal Run" and "Jealous of Ali," both of which draw upon Wilding's schooldays at the Royal Grammar School in his native Worcester. "Coming to an End" and "Hector and Freddie" recount various stages of life and experiences after leaving Worcester for Lincoln College, Oxford. Two other English-based stories, "See You Later" and "Tell No More," were both written later, near the end of Wilding's first period in Sydney, 1963-1966. There are enough of these stories in the corpus of Wilding's work, in this volume and in other collections, to constitute a kind of shadow novel of a young man from the provinces.

The volume opens with its dazzlingly experimental title story, "The West Midland Underground," drawing upon the landscape of Wilding's upbringing in Worcester and surrounds. The story begins: "The West Midland Underground goes from to [sic]. Or should I say went? Should I have said went? Should I be saying went? Or even will go. May go. Could go" (1). The paragraph continues to muse upon tenses, ending with: "Perhaps the hitherto impossible tense will bring into being the hitherto impossible West Midland Underground" (1). The sketchy narrative next takes up highly technical considerations of such subjects as verb tenses and syntax in a "Papuan language of average complexity" (1). Then it veers into autobiographical remembrances from Wilding's school days, then into an amazing riff on a plan to broadcast short stories in Sydney cabs, so that the entire city would be filled at all hours of the day and night with riders listening to short stories; this obsessive listenership would devolve into purchasers of short story volumes. Here is a comic exchange generated by such a visionary idea: "Have you got the volume of short stories *Seaforth Crescent, Seaforth to Mort Street, Balmain?*" "This is the last one, sir." "Do I get a 10 per cent discount as a university teacher?" "Not on paperbacks under a total of 23 miles, sir" (7-8). The narrator notes: "The biggest boom in the short story known in history will eventuate" (8). All of this comedy sounds as though it came right out of the schemes and dreams of *The Short Story Embassy*, published that same year. The story returns, surreally, to schooldays and a long meditation on the depredations wrought by modern development upon the old topography of the River Salwarpe and the canals and the River Severn, all haunts of Wilding's childhood. The story's pessimism regarding over-development and pollution is borne out by this description from the 2011 website "Canoe England" (River Salwarpe—river guide): "The last working boat used the canal in 1928, and abandonment in 1939 was followed by much of it being filled in or built over. As can be seen, completion of the cut through to joining with the canalized River Salwarpe has yet to be made." Wilding's story ends with a list of ten advantages to looking for the West Midland Underground. Number 10 is quintessential Wilding: "Hope. Somewhere, over the rainbow, the crock of gold, the gates of Eden, the doors of bliss" (13).

"The Man of Slow Feeling," published in *Man*, 68 (July, 1970), 30-33, 38, is easily the most famous of Wilding's girlie mag stories. It is also his most widely anthologized short story, having been reprinted in four Australian science fiction collections and in four general anthologies of Australian fiction. Rob Gerrand included the story in *The Best Australian Science Fiction Writing: A Fifty Year Collection* (2004) and wrote that Wilding "played a central role as a writer, editor, publisher and critic in the changes that altered the face of Australian fiction in the late 1960s and '70s, helping to foster a literary climate more favourable to Australian SF" (612). Wilding has republished it four times himself, using it as the title story in a Penguin edition of 1985; in *Great Climate* (1990, and in the American edition, *Her Most Bizarre Sexual Experience*, 1991); and in *Somewhere New* (1996). It has also been translated into Serbo-Croatian, Punjabi, and Japanese.

The story is a brilliant subversive response to the girlie mag agenda. "The Man of Slow Feeling" takes place in a modern setting devoid of particularized cultural markers. It could be anywhere in the UK, Europe, or urban Australia. Its true locus is science fiction. Indeed, Wilding has described what he was trying to do in this story in a useful way: It "was one of my attempts to write a sort of Jorge Luis Borges story after reading his Fictions in the mid 60s in Sydney, but it came out more like science fiction. I can't remember why on earth I sent it to Man magazine. Maybe because I thought the lit quarterlies wouldn't like it" (Email, January 22, 2010). The title, incidentally, derives from Henry Mackenzie's sentimental novel of 1771, *The Man of Feeling* (Email "Re: repair work," August 17, 2011).

In "The Man of Slow Feeling," concept and plot are one and the same. A man suffers severe injuries to his nervous system in an automobile wreck. The result is that his sensory apparatus is profoundly affected. He can only feel sensations three hours after an event occurs; whether pleasure or pain, there is a three-hour delay. Thus this story represents the opposite of the "instant-Sydney" aesthetic developed in some of the stories in *Aspects of the Dying Process*. The delayed reaction syndrome is a kind of Orwellian nightmare of being unable to live in the moment, in the immediacy that is the goal of the protagonists in so many of Wilding's stories set in Australia.

Perhaps surprisingly, this is the only one of Wilding's girlie mag stories in which the sexual act is presented. After the protagonist is released from the hospital, he returns with his wife Maria to their house in the country (thus echoing, perhaps, that other man of no rather than slow feeling, Lord Chatterley). The ensuing description of their lovemaking is closer to a reader's expectations of girlie-mag fictional fun than are any of Wilding's other girlie mag stories. But it turns out there is little fun at all in the following passage:

> They made love that first night, but he could not feel her full breasts, her smooth skin, and making love to her was totally without sensation for him. Its only pleasures were voyeuristic and nostalgic. His eyes and ears allowed him to remember past times —like seeing a sexual encounter at the cinema. The thought came to him that the best way to get anything from sex now was to cover the walls and ceilings with mirrors, so that at least he could have a full visual satisfaction to replace his missing senses. (33)

Instead of being titillating, the passage is deeply subversive. Instead of being sexy, it is disturbing. In a sense, then, the desensitized man becomes the voyeuristic consumer of pornography (the cinema) and of girlie mag fantasy (the penthouse pad with mirrors everywhere).

## Varieties of Kerouacian Experience 85

By contrast, the same issue of *Man* contained a story by C. P. Smith, "Night Flight to Amsterdam," that played directly to a stereotypical male reader's prurient interests. It begins, "She was the kind of girl he'd never been to bed with—tall, and with a body that used every last inch for long, heart-stopping curves and hollows" (18); then later, "This one had good breasts. Heavy but well formed. As she leant forward to find the ends of her seat-belt he could see how much of her there was. Junoesque! He wanted her"—and so on (18).

What happens in Wilding's story is the opposite of lust. Vision and hearing are all that remain of the protagonist's five senses, and the trauma of his life becomes evident in an early scene as he tries to adjust to his new reality. Walking in the fields, he plunges his hands into piles of dung placed there for fertilizing the land. Doing so, he feels nothing, smells nothing. Later at table for tea, he experiences a sense of the "foul stickiness" of the dung (33) but is surprised that he is not nauseous. Not yet. But a few hours later, back in bed with Maria, who "made love with him now more eagerly, more readily, more desperately, uselessly, pointlessly than ever before" (33), the earlier expected nausea of the dung overcomes him and he rushes to the bathroom to vomit. Vomiting is not sexy.

Later he begins to realize that he has fleeting dreams of the sensations he once knew, and still later he comes to realize that he has not been robbed of sensation but that the cause-effect between stimulation and sensation has been slowed. Eventually he can measure it exactly: three hours. Three hours after an event he experiences it fully. Thus lovemaking at noon results in an orgasm three hours later when he is in a village shop buying cigarettes. The new knowledge is most disquieting. When he cuts his finger, he "waited tensely for the delayed pain; and even though cutting his finger was the slightest of hurts, it filled three hours of anxiety" (33). The delayed sensations become an agony: "Defecation became nightmarish, could ruin any ill-timed meal, or intercourse. An ill-timed intercourse could ruin any casual urination…" (33).

Struggling to find a way to live in his sensation-delayed world, he starts keeping a written record of everything that he does, in hopes of anticipating the sensations sparked by those actions, but he spends so much time writing that he realizes "he had little time to experience anything" (38). Then he hits upon a new scheme; he dictates into a tape-recorder every sensate detail of his experience, then plays it back three hours later, but the results are unsatisfactory: "And he found that he could not both record his current activities in a constant flow, and hear a constant commentary on his three hours back activities, momentarily prior to his sensations of those past ones" (38). What Wilding seems to be driving at is the burden of consciousness and the burden of recording consciousness whether orally or in writing. The task is all-consuming and destructive of ordinary living. Too much self-consciousness is a curse. The whole story seems to be a rebuttal of Wordsworth's idea of art as emotion recollected in tranquility, and to be a put-down as well of supra-conscious modernism which, à la Joyce, seeks to record every detail of living in an ever-present past/present continuum. The story also would seem to be an inside-out version of Wilding's commitment to a Kerouacian absorption in the present, in the scroll-like recording of experience as close to the moment as possible, an aesthetic that Wilding used to extraordinary effect in his "instant Sydney" program of immediacy and contemporaneous recording of what's happening now. Eventually the man of slow feeling abandons both notebook and tape recorder in an attempt to avoid a kind of over stimulation of anxiety. Again Wilding returns to the recording of sexual experience to register the agony of the protagonist's post-accident life:

> Sex became a nightmare for him, its insensate action and empty voyeurism bringing only the cerebral excitement of gestures of naked women, its consequence a wet dream, the tension of waiting for which (sometimes with an urgent hope, sometimes with resistant wished-against tension) would agonise him—keep him sleepless or, in the mornings, unable to read or move. And the continual anxiety affected his whole sexual activity, made him

ejaculate too soon, or not at all; and he had to wait three hours for his failures to emerge. (38)

This entire passage is quite remarkable in the context of its appearance in a girlie magazine, whose very modus operandi is voyeurism, passivity, tension, sexual dreams, anxiety, and fantasy—all of which are set forth in Wilding's analysis of the slow feeling man who is literally out of touch with himself and confined to the sidelines of sexuality.

Things get worse. He has trouble sleeping; he longs for the sensation-diminished ambience of the hospital, where "in those bare walls of the bare room, he might almost have been in a tomb" (38). Then one day his wife returns home to find him dead, having taken a bath in the Roman way and cut his wrists. She thinks, "Though, she told herself, he would not have felt anything anyway, he had no sensation" (38). But the next sentence, with which the story ends, offers a question worthy of Poe: "But three hours afterwards?" (38).

"The Man of Slow Feeling" is the most intriguing story Wilding published in the girlie mags precisely because it contains plenty of sexual activity and fantasy and yet its sexual verisimilitude is a counter-discourse to the sensations produced by girlie mags: voyeurism, fetishism, auto-erogenous imaginings, desire—all detached, all dehumanized.

The Australian stories in *The West Midlands Underground* include three written to/at/about Vicki Viidikas, the troubled, talented writer and muse whose vibrant, challenging presence appears and reappears throughout Wilding's career: "Writing Again After a While," "Their Minds Keeping on Working," and "Thing for the Tentacle Ladies." Viidikas wrote several poems and stories at/for Wilding. Perhaps the most representative one is "The Incomplete Portrait," which appeared in her book *Wrappings*, published by Wild & Woolley in 1974. The fact that Wilding included her story about him is a testament to his generosity and commitment to literary value. It is the story of VV's that is most like those of Wilding's about her, in that it's also a story about writing, about literature as well as about sex and female/male relationships. It begins, "I am not making love at the time of writing this story..." (124). Then she addresses MW directly: "...you don't want to read about me making love with anyone other than yourself, you don't want to know that I came to you wearing a string of loves, adorned and possessed..." (124). She goes on to explain that writing stories about their relationship is a means of distancing themselves from failure: "...to cosset ourselves in images, cocoons of love made readable—the 'literary' story—when our private acts fail" (124). A bit later she gets down to particulars in her analysis of MW: "I am expected to appear virginal, undiscovered, mysterious, veiled" (124). She continues, "You want me to come to you pure as a lake you may see your own reflection in, blue enough for you to realize the lake has depths, yet safe enough for you to never ride to the bottom of" (124-125). Her job as a woman is to "lie," to "propagate your self-made image even if I don't agree with it, even if it is false" (125).

The scene shifts to a lounge where she is refused access to the public bar. The perfect ironic song is on the jukebox, Tammy Wynette's "Stand By Your Man," and the narrator thinks about her writing in relation to her life: "And I sit knowing I can't keep writing stories of unsuccessful love affairs, of husbands gone back to wives, of lovers in terror of commitment, with the hungry reading these lines as a source for recrimination" (125). In writing such stories, she is writing Wilding's stories, as it were, for many of them are about the desire for and "terror of commitment." Instead she thinks she should construct new myths to define her own persona, tell true stories of the males she has known. She presents these in a list of unnumbered items: "(q) was being unfaithful (as I was probably his mistress.); (m) beat his wife up; (p) has been giving infections to women in that crowd for years. Though (r) wrote a story proving it's the women who always carry infections; that (t) aborted his girlfriend and is secretly homosexual" (125).

But she realizes, of course, the price to be paid for disclosing these unpleasant truths about the males she knows: "It's no good exposing these foibles only to become classified as a man-hater, a castrater, a neurotic terrified child" (125). She declares that women are expected to write "from a peculiar 'other' set of sensibilities" (125). She concludes this commentary in a passage that evokes every manly writer from Hemingway to Norman Mailer: "To be a good male writer might be to have 'guts': to be a good female writer might be to have 'cunt'—yet somehow this predetermines exposures which are not acceptable, and possibly self-righteous" (126).

The next paragraph takes the fight straight to the male lover/writer: "You do not want to read about my sitting in the VD clinic waiting to have my vagina scraped" (126). She points out that he is fine with reading William Burroughs' stories of junkies puncturing their veins but cannot handle the medical agonies that a woman has to endure. He can accept Burroughs' experience because it is "so vividly ugly" but cannot accept her experience: "Yet a woman writing of an instrument stuck up her cunt is being 'self-indulgent' as the doctors make notes" (126). The doctors are both detached and yet writers of a kind, as they make notes. She knows that her lover/writer "will think these stories unnecessary, indicative of a female mind gone sour" (126).

The next paragraph, somewhat cryptic, describes the book jacket of "his serious novel concerning the 'sexual badlands'" (126). Again she uses a list to tick off the content of this novel: the heroine is "beaten up and assaulted by his long-time 'literary' buddy"; the heroine then becomes pregnant, a speed freak, and a kidnapping victim "by a gang of poets"; next the heroine turns to lesbianism because of the way men have treated her; and at the end she's a "used up bag" and is "burnt at the stake at a ritual literary dinner party" (126). It's unclear whether VV has an actual author and book in mind or is offering us a pastiche of a Burroughs-like novel containing elements from writers like Robert Adamson, Frank Moorhouse, and/or Michael Wilding.

Then VV turns to a scathing section on the expectations that a female fiction writer must face. In a very clever line VV writes of the female fiction writer, "...she'll be making phone calls to her sexuality to see how she's all wired up" (126). Because she's a woman, this writer will be "desired (if pretty), admired, abused, mythologised, attacked" (126). She trots out a list of female icons that the writer's femininity will mirror: "Marilyn Monroe, Kali [Hindu goddess associated with eternal energy], Janis Joplin, Medusa, Isadora Duncan, Lilith, and blah blah" (127).

The story ends with "The rejection," a defense of D. H. Lawrence against Kate Millet's charges that he was a fascist and woman-hater. Then she argues that fiction is "always paradoxical" (127). Then she says that this "is not even a story" (127). In any event her non-story ends on an exhilarating note: "The shores of your body are littered with truths. The page should fuck back—I can't think of a more reasonable premise" (127). Here she seems to turn one of Wilding's favorite censorship-smashing words, fuck, against him, but the word "reasonable" is just as targeted since Wilding, in her stories, is always trying to use reason to explain, defend, justify his agenda.

It is impossible to tell which stories were written first, Viidikas against Wilding, or Wilding against Viidikas. But given the intense literary atmosphere of that period, it is almost inevitable that each would write about the other. Wilding himself remembers it this way: "I think the relationship must have been in late 1971. Didn't last that long—a couple of months, maybe. But we kept in touch on and off over the ensuing years" (Email "Re: moving on," February 27, 2011). He adds, "I probably would have shown Vicki the 3 stories in West Midland when I'd written them, but I don't recall any specific reactions (Feb. 27, 2011)."

The first story, "Writing Again After a While," appeared in the creatively titled *The Ear in a Wheatfield*, 3, 1973, p. 40. It is only three pages long but completely brilliant. The "I" narrator begins by saying he has found her address, which indicates a separation of some kind at least, since he is not familiar with her current address. The narrator is in a state of sexual anxiety—not much new about that in a Wilding story —but this time it has to do with a medical condition, a urinary infection for which he is taking antibiotics. He finds that she is living in the "same suburb," which must mean somewhere in Balmain, which VV loved. Wilding's narrator looks about the property only to find that she's not there, and later he returns to learn that she no longer lives there but has moved in with someone named Angela (still in Balmain, though). About Angela, Wilding has commented: "I don't know who Angela was —can't remember—not sure if I had anyone particular in mind" (Email "Re: Robert Z," February 28, 2011). Sometime later the narrator runs into Robert Z. and asks him where VV is because he wants to see her "about those stories" (p.167). Robert Z. is the poet Robert Adamson, a familiar figure in Wilding's stories. Wilding explains the name: "Z because it's the opposite of A, and because he used the name Zimmer from Bob Dylan aka Zimmerman for his Zimmer's Essay, his prison memoir we published with Wild & Woolley" (February 28, 2011). Robert Z. tells him where Angela's house is, but he can't find it, and so he goes to the pub, only to return later, and this time he does find her at a waterfront house on the harbor. He is not seeing her for sex, that is over and done with, he is seeing her for writerly purposes, for "new idioms" (p. 168). Everything is source material, every experience, whether a success or a failure (and often failure is best, as in all the plaintive lover stories). He expatiates upon why he needs to see her:

> Her idioms are different from those I've been amongst. I'm not seeing her to fuck her. She doesn't use fuck or screw in her vocabulary. The only expletive she uses is flipping. I stopped saying flipping fifteen years ago. I learned to say fuck and screw and idiom and expletive. I say she expresses surprise at my visit. "What a flipping surprise visit this is," maybe she says. (168)

This commentary is extremely interesting. It is, once again, a process story about writing, authorship in the absence of sex.

Together they sit on a wall of the old house near the water. She's wearing a bikini and the narrator is fully clothed. Their bohemian world is marked by contrast with nearby "bikini'd, mascara'd, hair-done sunbathers" who "do seem of a different world" (168). Later, while VV is getting ready to go out to meet a man, the narrator is reading a new story of hers about a woman who is going out to "screw somebody." The narrator worries that he's reading a predictive story, and when she returns he concludes, "She did screw somebody" (168). They talk and get stoned and he leaves with a folder of her stories.

Sometime later he returns to "tell her how fantastic" her stories are (169). Then he shows her his latest work, and she quotes a sentence derisively: "'Despite her protestations,'" she says, it's insane, what an incredible thing to say; 'insisted on accompanying her, despite her protestations that it was not worth his while.'" He thinks, "I seem to be getting stoned a lot" (169). Is this the reason for the elaborate diction, or is the elaborate diction a carry-over from his earlier Jamesian manner? All we know is that he seems to take her criticism to heart: "I don't write 'despite her protestations' or 'insisted on accompanying her' or 'not worth his while' any more" (169). In fact, he stops writing altogether for a while.

The story ends with her announcing that she's living in a "very dirty house" and that she's going to see a doctor about an infection. He tells her to move and "On Saturday we drive down to pick up her double bed" (169). We don't know where she is moving, but the implication seems to be that she is moving in with the narrator, for a time anyway but probably not for long. So the story begins with one infection and ends with another. These were the days of the infection stories.

The second story about Viidikas, "Their Minds Keeping on Working," was published originally in *Stand*, 18 iii (1974), 58-59. It picks up where "Writing Again After a While" ends, with the narrator commenting on VV's criticism of his diction, "Making love (and even in this beginning I'm using my old insane vocabulary as you call it, but that's what it has to be here not screwing, you know that), I say, 'I thought this was supposed to be a literary relationship'" (171). Then he recounts her astrological interpretation of his problems, how Capricorns have "to put everything into words, their minds keeping on working" (171). His intellectuality versus her spontaneity is a motif running through the story. But the real problem, he maintains, is not the words but "those protective questioning ironies" (171).

Another problem is his commitment to books, to "those dead men's brains stacked in rows across my wall" (171). Wilding has explained the exact source of this image: "When my boxes of books arrived from England on my return to Sydney in 1969, one of the removalists commented, dead men's brains. So that's where that phrase comes from, books as dead men's brains" (Email "Re: another vv story—powered books," March 7, 2011). The narrative continues, the books "just crumble down into sudden soft heaps on the carpet like skulls in old catacombs" (171). The narrator concedes that VV is doing the opposite from him, that she's writing him poems that are "Celebrations" (171). And these poems go against prevailing literary decorum: "Things you're not supposed to write poems about; because people like me have preferred ironies and negativities and all those elegant safe self doubts. Your poems to me have feathers and shells and stones, gifts of perfumed drugs and shamans' magic" (171). He concludes his description of her poems by contrasting them with his stories: "My stories to you have urinary infections and tentacles. I have a long way to go to where I am already" (171). Here the reference to infection points to the prior story "Writing Again After a While," and the reference to tentacles points to the third story in the VV series, "Thing for the Tentacle Ladies."

The next topic in this literary relationship is VV's request for him to "look at [her] stories and fix up the tenses when I should be asking you to fix up my head" (172). Towards that end, they "lie naked against each other and the story between. The first falling apart is at aggravate" (172) —a very funny line, by the way. Clearly, in some story VV has misused the word "aggravate" because the narrator quotes the entire entry on the correct and incorrect usage of this word from his copy of Fowler's *Modern English Usage*, 1926 (Prize for Eng. Literature, Middle School, Dec. 1956— a self-referential reminder of Wilding's precocious academic accomplishments). "There you are, see, uneducated feminine child," the narrator says humorously upon ending his recitation of the official Fowler position on proper usage (172). VV's response is an Australian one: "Things are changing. That's how people say it. Out here, where people say things, that's what they say" (p. 172). Just before that the narrator imagines her thinking of him and his manner, "pedantry, insane, trapped in the academy, pressed like an old flower in the Oxford dictionary" (172). Stylistically, they are at an impasse. She won't "emend," and he refuses "to continue the story" (172). He re-embraces his "old polysyllables" and has to find new ones in a thesaurus to combat her straightforward vernacular (173). Impasse leads to shouting "for two hours, our limbs not always intertwining" (173). The narrator employs martial imagery to dramatize the outcome: "We move on heavily to our doom. Unwilling trucks towards the minefield, khaki invaders of your mysterious desert" (173).

He turns to another literary source for inspiration, *New Directions 22*, with comic results: "I have read it since and am not directed; it is you who are doing the saving" (173). The new books he bought have not helped him, and so he returns to the present literary problem, VV's stories that he can't read without pain: "That has been hurt enough. I do not want to lie in bed next to you reading stories of someone you've been screwing. Correcting the tenses" (173). The next paragraph merges his voice with VV's concerning tenses and sex and ends with VV's voice: "I am so disgusted with this freak complaining about me screwing you in my story" (173). The issue is inescapable: "I do not want, about to make love to you, to read about you slowly undressing some eighteen year old pusher. A thirty-eight year old pusher would not be better" (174). He continues to mix memory and desire: "Well not wanting to read about other screws right here now in this double bed of yours we have picked up from your husband. I know that's a bad line but some ironies I cannot easily forgo. And I know they get me using words like forgo" (174). Years later, in *Wild Amazement* he gave Valda this dialogue in one of their set-to's: "'If you want some squeaky clean virgin fresh off the shelf, why don't you go out and buy one?' Valda would say. 'She'll wash your socks for you. She'll sew your leather patches on. Go on, piss off, don't hang around here asking me all those stupid questions, go out and buy yourself one'" (51).

He can't finish reading her story, and VV responds with her own literary credo: "That's what writing is isn't it writing's telling people things you better not read anything else I write if you don't want to know things you'd better not read anything at all ever again…" (174). After telling him to "crawl back into the woodwork" (174), she continues, "The flipping irony of it I can't stand the flipping ironies I try and say how things are put it in the first person and be honest and what do I get for that flipping abuse and madness I just can't stand it it's just not worth—" (174). There it is again, "flipping," Viidikas's vernacular caught perfectly. Christina Stead recognized Viidikas' importance, as revealed in a letter to Wilding: "As for V.V., her portraits of men instant and sharp, could only have been done by a girl who took those chances (and had talent). She has tremendous talent" (*Wild & Woolley* 75).

The literary/sexual dialogue continues and can never be resolved. VV tells him, "The irony of it is it isn't true, it didn't even happen, he's based on some guy I knew but I never did get off with" (175). Things look better the next night until they don't: "I lie next to you on this next night. We are very close. You tell me things to tell me how close we have become: When we first meet you are still having a scene with someone else—" (175). The verb "lie" might be more consoling if it meant that she was lying about the facts of her life, but she is a truth sayer (when she isn't "lying" in fiction), and the old bugaboo of jealousy on the narrator's part resurfaces, as in these stories it always does.

The story ends thus: "This is no page I can refuse to turn. This tense is unalterable. These are not the words of a literary relationship.

My powdered books offer no refuge" (175). The last sentence, which sounds like a quotation or allusion, is not, however. Wilding thinks in retrospect that the line is meant to echo or fulfill the earlier image of decaying books: "& I think the idea of their crumbling into powder, dust—that must explain the last line of the story" (Email "Re: another vv story—powdered books," March 7, 2011). The story's last paragraph feels like the end of a relationship, both sexual and literary. Rereading the stories recently, Wilding has commented, "But these two stories—I hadn't looked at them for years, they belong to quite another era. The surreal touches make it hard to remember what reality underlies them. So for once I am puzzled and find it hard to explain things!" (March 7, 2011). In his memoir *Wild Amazement*, however, Wilding revisited his relationship with Valda and concluded:

> Things just were and then they ended. And that's how it was with Valda and me. Undoubtedly there were recriminations, resentments. But I have no recollection of things working up to a climax. I have no recollection of the slow, or rapid, unravellings of plot... It is tempting to write that it was just one of those things, and to succumb to the temptation in no way undercuts the painfulness of it all. Those things were often very painful. (56)

The "surreal touches" reach their apotheosis in the last story in the MW/VV sequence, "Thing for the Tentacle Ladies," published in *New Poetry 22* i: *The Ear in a Wheatfield*, 8, 1974, 23 (joint issue). The briefest of the stories, it is just two and a quarter pages, and the most opaque.

No characters are identified, but it is clear from the diction that the tentacle lady in the story is VV and the narrator is a surreal version of MW. The first section seems to take place in an aquarium, and the female —figured as an octopus—has the male utterly in her power. Such identifications can be seen at the end of the first section:

> "If you want it that flipping much why don't you just cut it off?" she said. "Here take this oyster knife."

She put it in one of the tentacles. And the translucent green of their aquarium reddened with a spreading dusty cloud of blood. Like drifting powder. (178)

"Flipping," of course, is one of VV's signature words and appears in all three stories, and the elaborate diction of the narrative voice in the second paragraph is in the Wilding manner.

The story is dominated by an overmastering image/metaphor/symbol —the idea of woman as a biological creature that seeks to capture, hold, and immobilize the male. It reads like a Freudian nightmare brought to life. Her power over him is so great that he severs his arm in order to possess the tentacle holding it.

The next section takes place at a beach where the further empowered tentacle lady nurses the maimed male. The male remembers an earlier time when he had been "dragged ... out of the giant clam," a reference to another female relationship imaged in determinist biological terms. Queried about the possible identities underpinning this imagery, Wilding replied, "I have no idea who the friend or the clam were, nor the specific incidents this might refer to. Not even sure if it was specific or generic. Deeply repressed, I guess. I don't even know what provoked the story" (Email "Re: last mw vv story," March 7, 2011).

In the encounter/relationship with the clam, the narrator lost his toenails. Women as tentacles and clams that diminish the male form: again, how very Freudian. The closing sentences of this section describe the rescuer and the rescued: "And he and his rescuer walked along the beach and trod on the cunjevoys till they spurted. His rescuer carried a knife too: he liked to prize oysters off the rocks and cut the eyes out of seagulls" (178). "Cunjevoy" is an Aboriginal word for "sea squirts," defined as sedentary, filter-feeding, cylindrical or globular animals, usually found attached to rocks, shells, pilings or boat bottoms.

Regarding the source of this passage, Wilding has recalled some possible origins of the story:

> But one time I helped Vicki move house. She had been staying with her ex-husband and his partner down the coast south of Sydney, Coalcliff or somewhere, amazing region, like all those B movies shot on Pacific Coast Highway north of LA up to San Francisco—winding road along a precipitous drop to the ocean. We put her mattress on the roof of my Mini and drove up to Sydney with it. She complained that the mouse that lived in it must have fallen out. I remember walking on the beach with Vicki on that occasion down the coast and her jumping on cunjevoys revealed at low tide on the rock shelves. They would spurt out water when jumped on. So I think that was the setting" (Email "Re: last mw vv story," March 7, 2011).

The opening of the next section shows just how complicated the narrative line is: "'Here,' she said,' he said, "'stand in this bowl of alligators while I write you'" (178). Placing the tentacle lady in a bowl of alligators is in keeping with the other surrealistic water/sea creature imagery in the story. "While I write you" is one of the best formulations of this entire strain of writing stories for/at/about someone that Wilding uses in his stories of personal address as well as his stories about VV and Frank Moorhouse, and they in turn in the stories they addressed in various ways to Wilding himself.

The next section begins, "Oh, you get let off do you?" she said, "you can't be a very good writer then, the writer never gets let off" (178). Wilding has recently confirmed the identification with VV evident in this passage: "And that's certainly her utterance about the writer not getting let off" (Email "Re: last mw vv story," March 7, 2011). The narrative continues, "Toe-nail less and one armed, he did not feel let off. They sat high on the cliff and watched the waves beating beneath them. He loved her very much then" (178). He accepts the vision of himself as reduced to a dependent biological creature: "If he cut enough off, he would always stay there. A headless limbless trunk on the basalt rocks. There would be no pain. He would like to feel the tentacles of the tentacle ladies wrapping round him but unable to move he would not feel any possibilities. Or see them" (178).

The story ends in a lovely flurry of allusion and imagery, beginning with: "Old Aeschylus died when a seabird thought his white head was a chalk rock and dropped a shell fish on it" (179). The most common apocryphal version is that an eagle dropped a turtle on the dramatist's head. The vision of death leads to another allusion, "Those are pearls that..."(179), a line that may refer to the original, in Shakespeare's *The Tempest*, or to its Modernist incarnation in Eliot's *The Waste Land*. Following that, the story comes to its visionary close: "Oh my ever renewing tentacle ladies, which of you comes to take another limb, over which of the seven seas will I be scattered next? Across the grey landless surfaces beneath the low clouds, what solitary bird will be my dying cry?" One might conclude that this is Wilding's most Prufrockian story, with no mermaids on the horizon, only more tentacled ladies.

A word about the title: "Thing" seems to echo the phrase "to have a thing for somebody," but it also refers to the fact that the male figure in the story becomes a "thing" to the tentacle ladies, a physical part and nothing more. Finally the story itself is a thing, and as Wilding makes clear in *Wild Amazement*, "thing" was a Vicki Viidikas word, the word she used for story: "The stories were of course less stories than things, they had that indeterminacy of things, they floated there with an undoubted specificity but unanchored in consequence or cause, never located that minutely in time or space as a realist treatment might have required" (51).

Decades later, Wilding generously recognized the importance of Vicki Viidikas' writing, including those pieces aimed directly at him:

> Thirty-five years after they were written, her searing attacks on male self-involvement and overall unsatisfactoriness still make me flinch. No doubt they should, since a couple were written at

me. Not written for me, or to me, but confrontationally at me. Writing was part of an ongoing dialogue with the world for Vicki and other writers of the 1970s. Pre-dating blogs and the web, it was a direct and instant medium of exchange, inviting rapid reaction. We used to respond to each other's stories and poems with stories and poems in reply. It was not a matter of manufacturing a product and marketing it. Of course, some were doing that and have been most successful. But that was a world for which Vicki had nothing but scorn. (*Wild & Woolley: A Publishing Memoir* 15).

In conversation with me, Nicholas Birns, editor of *Antipodes,* remarked that Vicky Viidikas was "the girl in the band" (AAALS Convention, Fort Worth, February 19, 2011.) That seems about right, but VV, as Wilding has always claimed, was quite simply one of the most talented writers of that generation. Together and independently, Wilding and Viidikas in their work and in their lives were testaments to the continuing power of writing fiction.

In "Bye Bye Jack. See You Soon" Wilding turned to one of the most important influences on his writing, Jack Kerouac, and produced one of his greatest stories. Broadcast on ABC Radio in 1974, it appeared in *Stand*, 16, ii (1975), 64-70. An excerpt was published in *Contemporary Literary Criticism*, vol. 5, edited by Carolyn Riley and Phyllis Carmel Mendelson, Gale Research Co., 1976, and Brian Kiernan included the story in *The Most Beautiful Lies* (1977). It also was published in *Noc Na Orgiji* in 1982 and translated into Punjabi in 2001.

In a recent essay collected in *Car Lovers* (2008), Wilding recalled the early impact that Kerouac had on his thinking: "I remember being in Oxford when I was offered the job in Sydney, and announcing I was going to go out to Australia and buy a Mustang and drive across the continent. Those were the days when the influence of Jack Kerouac first overtook me" (75). He goes on to mention that Robert Adamson bought a Mustang for the same reason: "The Beats were very influential in those decades" (76). Wilding has also made an interesting connection between Borges and Kerouac, one that he had not thought about until much later:

> At the time Borges read as if he was writing very carefully constructed, almost arid, encyclopaedic entry type stories. After reading a life of him a couple of years ago, I discovered he dashed off these stories for a weekly paper—they were very much spontaneous, improvised. The sort of thing I was trying to do, influenced by Kerouac especially. (Email "Re: James crossed with Lawrence," November 8, 2009)

Wilding continued to draw upon Kerouac in stories written later. "In the Penal Colony," for example, collected in *Reading the Signs* (1984), has an epigraph from *On the Road*: "Somewhere along the line I knew there'd be girls, visions, everything; somewhere along the line the pearl would be handed to me." In this story Wilding describes a wild, alcohol and drug-induced reading tour in Tasmania with some familiar faces (Robert Adamson) and some new ones (Dorothy Hewett) added to the mix. In "Midnight Readings" Wilding introduces his story of surveillance (collected in *This is for You*, 1994) with a passage from Kerouac's *Vanity of Dulouz* about surveillance. Early and late, Kerouac has been an abiding presence in Wilding's life and fiction.

"Bye Bye Jack. See You Soon" is the fullest and richest embodiment of Kerouac's importance. The story begins with the news of the American writer's death a fortnight after the fact, a reminder of the tyranny of distance. The narrator immediately concludes that it's "like the end of an era" and thinks Kerouac's death should be somehow commemorated (p. 181). So he sets about organizing a wake. Only his uni students don't even know who Kerouac is; they ask him, "What's kerouac?" as though the name signified an object instead of a person. That question leads the narrator into a reverie about the role Kerouac played in his life back in England. First he mentions that he doesn't even have a copy of *On the Road* in Australia and then reports: "I had shipped all my Henry James. Kerouac stayed behind in the cold damp shelves in the bedroom that had been mine in my parents' house" (p. 182). But he remembers Kerouac's influence on his life then: "The poetry of hamburgers, apple pie and ice cream, waitresses, bus stations, of trying to hitch rides and getting soaked when the night came down and there weren't any rides" (p. 182). He also invokes *The Dharma Bums* and remembers masturbating in a canoe on the river Severn. Other memories are pure Kerouac:

> We used to drive around in an old upright Ford Anglia, talking to the waitresses in coffee bars and hoping for girls in country pubs. And that was no more like Dean's Hudson, though probably of the same year, than the Severn was like the Mississippi:--my beloved Mississippi River, dry in the summer haze, low water, with its big rank smell that smells like the raw body of America itself because it washes it up. (182)

The prose after the dash is a direct quotation from Chapter 3 of *On the Road*.

The next section also begins "What's kerouac?" and answers the question thus: "Kerouac is a registered code name, like Kodak or Coca-cola. It is a magic incantation. It represents the out, the other, the away" (182). Then the narrator plunges into a beautiful Kerouac-like riff consisting of one sentence twenty-five lines long. It begins: "Like this weekend: I am in this unit in Elizabeth Bay and a bit of research later could've checked out the phenomenal amount such units cost, with this as Kerouac would say chick, and it has three locks and a chain and a spy-hole and a grill on the door, so I can imagine it's like I'm in an apartment in Manhattan, except that it looks on to not the Hudson but Sydney Harbour, in all its wide beauty..." (183). The sentence goes on to recall the girl's talking about her school days and the narrator's liking her in spite of that bit of upper class nostalgia; in the meantime as she plays Tchaikovsky and Buddy Holly, the latter reminds him of girls back in England who played Buddy Holly and of his masturbatory fantasies. The whole riff ends beautifully: "and I'm reading *On the Road* there, having brought it out this time, while she is out there making food so we can eat by 4:30 p.m. and lying in bed I don't have to put my tweed jacket back on, but can lie there holding my kerouac, that's what it is, a talisman" (183). Here the tweed jacket, as in Vicki Viidikas's stories about Wilding, signifies his Englishness.

When she asks him what he's reading, the narrator provides without further explanation the content of the front and back cover of "Pan Giant On The Road Jack Kerouac Explosive epic of the Beat Generation…Unmatched descriptive excitement…A stunning achievement" (184-185). Rarely has collage been used to better effect. Then he begins to tell her "the story of the Jack Kerouac Wake" (184).

He mentions Kerouac's football days and rebukes himself for putting down his girlfriend for her remembrances of sports at school (Wilding hated sports at school). Then he launches into a commentary on the Sydney Uni faculty:

> My colleagues, of course, knew what Kerouac was. They laughed. I said, Let's put Kerouac on a modern fiction course. Wow how, how they laughed, the wittiest thing I'd said all morning, they really enjoyed laughing at that. They dug life that morning with a huge beatitude, Satori at Sydney U. (184)

The concept of *Satori*, incidentally, was the subject of an elaborate joke in the girlie mag *Chance International* (9, No. 1, 1970), the issue in which Wilding's story "And Did Henry Miller Walk in Our Tropical Garden?" appeared. In a full page joke titled "Don't Knock Zen" Larry Lawrence told the story of Foo-lo and his wife. He's in his "fat middle years" and she's a beautiful woman. He believes that he will achieve "SATORI: the term used in Zen to describe a state of consciousness beyond discrimination and differentiation." To do so he practices "long periods of contemplation and meditation." Meanwhile his wife gives birth in the following years to three children. Upon the birth of the third, Foo-lo is certain that satori is near at hand. And it is. When he asks his wife, "What can you know of such things, Mother of three?" she replies, "Then you may reach your SATORI, Father of none" (p. 43). Like the word *beaut* the word was percolating through the culture.

Then the narrator returns to the question of why he is criticizing his girlfriend—"that's the sort of thing I learned from Henry James," he adds (184), and in the new, freer Kerouacian mode he notes that putdowns have a way of rebounding on one, sort of like bad karma one might add, and mentions a post card sent him signed Dean Moriarity (Kerouac's muse and companion in *On the Road*). The narrator, however, thinks instead of another Moriarity, the master villain who appears in many of Sherlock Holmes' stories, and by way of suggestion, of Holmes in association with the Moorhouse persona, Joseph Wendel Holmes, though the text does not say this (185).

But the connection is unmistakable in the next paragraph, as evident in its beginning, "Reading an MS of Joe's one morning, coming into the living room where he'd set up his typewriter in that house in Drummoyne..." (185). Looking at the manuscript page (as in the much earlier "Joe's Absence"), the narrator sees a long list of music titles including Bach, Strauss, Elgar (a Wilding favorite and like him, a native of Worcester), and other classical composers, a Buddy Holly item, and so on until he realizes:

> What's all this? I called out as he did his exercises in his track suit in the fernery, what's all this culture? not his scene at all. And then as he strode in, which is the only word, strode, in his track suit, I said, What the fuck are you doing, these are all my records you're copying down here? That's right, he said, since the story's about you, and took it out of the carriage right there as I stood there. That couldn't have been too long before the wake. (185).

The narrator is almost as irritated about Joe's working out as he is about Joe's appropriation of the music, the culture, to be used in a story about the narrator.

The next paragraph continues the debate about writing, about the entire aesthetic of immediate/instant experience:

> I phoned him up. I said, I'm writing the story of the Jack Kerouac Wake. Like this minute. I wonder if it's like my story, he said. I said, I've been changing a lot of things; not of the story but of myself I meant, but who knows, who knows what our words reveal of us; yes, and now I'm writing instant experience. That's a good phrase, I'll use that he said. No longer emotion recollected in tranquility I added as he wrote it down. What do you mean, he said, instant experience, that happened ten years ago. Four, I said. (186)

The dialectical exchange is the best single passage in all of Wilding's work on the aesthetic of instant experience. There is a similar moment early in *On the Road* that captures the spontaneous excitement of writing instant experience. Dean Moriarity is spurring Sal Paradise/Kerouac on:

> He watched over my shoulder as I wrote stories, yelling 'Yes! That's right! Wow! Man!' and 'Phew!' and wiped his face with his handkerchief. 'Man, wow, there's so many things to do, so many things to write! How to even *begin* to get it all down and without modified restraints and all hung-up on like literary inhibitions and grammatical fears... (4).

The passage ends with another nod to the Americans: "On the shithouse walls of California they write Ginsberg revises. You're writing a story a day now, are you? he said, like the poets" (186).

Wilding then goes into an account of the actual wake itself, of its failure. The room at the university was too large and boringly historical, and worst of all, only five, or maybe seven, people showed up for the wake. At this point the narrator points out that the "five of us" kept "our eyes averted," which reminds the narrator, as nearly everything in the story does, of a passage from *On the Road*, "'I wanted to jump down from a mast and land right in her, but I kept my promise to Remi. I averted my eyes from her'—averted in memoriam J.K." (186).

Worst of all, no one thought to bring anything of Kerouac's to read or anything to read at all, not even the narrator, who, sick with a cold, is depressed at the whole outcome. The only one named among the five who came is Big D, based on Don Anderson, the University of Sydney lecturer and literary critic who was friends with everybody in the Wilding circle it seems, particularly Moorhouse (Email "bye bye jack," June 20, 2011). While they wait for somebody to read something, the narrator comically imagines what might have happened if there had been a large crowd: "And what if no one in the whole wide audience had've had a thing to read, what would we've done then? Had them reading driving licences? Check stubs, Famous Australians stamp booklets? Were the famous Australians stamp booklets current when Jack Kerouac died?" (187-88). This riff segues into the quotation of two stanzas from a poem by Adam Lindsay Gordon, a Wilding favorite, a 19th century English émigré to Australia who had attended the same grammar school as Wilding in Worcester a century earlier. In *Wild Amazement* (2005) Wilding credits his own decision to leave England for Australia as in part related to Gordon's own similar journey. Wilding's discomfort in England was "inextricably linked with class, class perceptions, class roles, class possibilities. I might have learned from that. Or I might have suppressed it. Or I might have suppressed it and learned subconsciously. The slow incubation of an English disease. No wonder I followed Adam Lindsay Gordon to Australia" (19). The wake lasted all of twenty minutes before the five stragglers went their separate ways. The sequence ends with another direct quotation from *On the Road*, a scene in New York in which Kerouac can't locate Hassel or Dean or anybody and so retreats to his home.

But the narrator of the story then goes to a pub, the "dear old great old memorious badly sceneful Forth and Clyde" where of course Joe turns up in short order. Joe arrives in character: "...what a ridiculous name, why do you call me Joe, Joe for chrissake, why pick a name like that? Joe said. I don't think it's any worse than Carlo Marx [Allen Ginsberg] and eventually I'll get a surname for it that'll redeem the Joe, just that I can't think of one" (189). In real time, the Wake would have occurred in 1969, the year of Kerouac's death. When asked where he was regarding the Kerouac Wake, Joe says that he was there, and the narrator has to concede to himself that it's possible that others turned up at the Wake too late to find anybody there. The poet Robert Z. (Robert Adamson) was there, for example, as the narrator learned later.

Joe is up to his usual tricks, having visited four pubs and having invited everybody at those four pubs to a party being held at the narrator's house. The narrator is quite upset about this turn of events and asks Joe why he didn't invite them to his place, and Joe says that he no longer has a place because the narrator had thrown him out. To Joe, having a party after the wake (which was an abysmal failure) is like having a baby or not; "there's no in between" (190). Hearing this, the narrator reacts, "I particularly disliked his folksy quasi-psychological determinism, his reactionary sentimentally corny pessimism. I tried to say that, something I'd been wanting to say for a long time" (190).

The narrator decides to have the party anyway and drives around Balmain collecting people to attend the party. Big N, rolling a joint, is the poet Nigel Roberts who, according to Wilding, "was a sort of fixture around Balmain" (*Wild & Woolley* 52). "Nigel was an early resident, and lives there still; 'a pusher and a poet and a problem to his friends,' he used to intone from the Kris Kristofferson song" (52). Wilding describes him and the antics surrounding typical readings at that time: "He had also been active in the Balmain readings, at which the literary folk, pub crowd, and not so beautiful people of the peninsula would gather on the waterfront and get drunk and stoned and hear each other deliver their latest compositions. Sometimes hurling emptied beer cans at readers they did not appreciate" (52). An untitled poem by Roberts appeared in the anti-Vietnam war anthology *We Took Their Orders and Are Dead.* It's interesting today in part because of its nod to Wilding and his influence and life-style during those heady days of the early Seventies:

> the marie Antoinette / slice
>
> of cake / was awarded
>
> to the poet who said
>
> 'let's go back to wilding's place
>
> & smoke / some good
>
> Vietnamese shit.' (152)

The poet alluded to could have been just about anybody in the frenetic confederation of anti-war protesters and Push veterans that made up the moveable-party zeitgeist of that time.

At the house in Balmain the post-wake party keeps building in crescendos of drunkenness and excitement. The Dean of Arts is there and "Paddy the blond anathema." The Dean of Arts is based on Leslie Rogers, McCaughey professor of Early English Language and Literature at the University of Sydney. Wilding recalls that "he used to go round the department ripping down the notices of anti-war demonstrations I had posted on the walls" (Email "Re: more on bye bye jack," June 20, 2011). According to Wilding, Paddy is based on Paddy Dawson, "a provocative activist around the student left at the time. White, almost albino, hair. So rather than blond beauty I called him a blond anathema" (June 20, 2011).

As with all spontaneous parties, there are unknowns: "some lady swimming amongst the sharks and them all sitting down there on the waterfront looking across at the old prison island now Cockatoo dockyard that convicts got taken by sharks swimming away from" (191). Joe the joker turns up again, announcing that "those pages of your film script on the table and jesus where were they all laid out ready for collating, we used them as beer mats" (192). Angry, the narrator tells Joe that is "a fucking nough" and Joe says he will go, which he does. Big D. is worried about him, however, because he's so drunk, and the narrator says "Maybe he swam" (192). Once the party ends, the narrator concludes, "It was a good party. The best parties are always the unplanned ones. I must phone up Joe and ask him if that's true of babies" (192-193).

Some time later the narrator receives a postcard from Dubbo then another from Bourke, or perhaps Wagga Wagga—all country towns from the provinces—and all with the message **DEAN MORIARTY FORGIVES** (193). Wilding remembers,

> Moorhouse sent me those postcards, as I recall. Signed Moriarty after Dean Moriarty (Neal Cassady) in *On the Road*. But my immediate association when they arrived was Sherlock Holmes's Professor Moriarty, the arch criminal, who plunges to death with Holmes at the Reichenback falls, though Holmes miraculously survives in later stories. (Email "Re: more on bye bye jack," June 20, 2011).

Indeed he does. The story in which Sherlock Holmes returns after a three-year hiatus and during which time everybody, including Watson, believed him to be dead is "The Adventure of the Empty House." Arthur Conan Doyle had killed off Holmes in 1893 but brought him back from the dead in 1903. Instead of falling to his death at the Reichenbach Falls in Switzerland, Holmes, using his knowledge of "baritsu, or the Japanese system of wrestling," had managed to escape Moriarty's clutches and survive whereas the arch criminal fell to his death in the foaming waters of the Falls. (Doyle 9).

Of course the narrator knows that Joe is the author of the postcards: "As he was always saying in that folksy reactionary etc way, A man's got to do what a man's got to do" (193). The narrator returns to a description of Sherlock Holmes's suicide before returning to the present and the narrator's anger at Joe: "Forgives *me*—he does the forgiving. I was outraged. I screamed with outrage" (193).

The next paragraph is a tour de force, Wilding channeling Kerouac in a passage that derives, in a general way, from Moorhouse's story "Across the plains, over the mountains, and down to the sea," the same story, incidentally, alluded to in "Joe's Absence." The passage reads:

> While he took his American lady and her car out into the Western plains, out into the big red barren centre of the land, all detail, all individuality, all definition falling away, to the great flat desert and the bare cloudless dome of the sky, the flat red line of the ever receding horizon and the blue dome of the infinite sky and the yellow sun scribbling lines across it day after endless day. (193)

Wilding has explained: "This is my own writing, but it refers to a story by Moorhouse—he has a story called 'Over the Mountains and across the river into the plains,' or some such title, which deals with driving some poor American girl he was no doubt exploiting at the time to the beach. . .I may have recycled some of his lines, though it reads too well so maybe it's my own work rather than his..." (Email "Re: more on bye bye jack," June 20, 2011).

> The story ends with a magnificent lengthy quotation from chapter 4 of *On the Road* in which Kerouac recalls a strange dream that he discussed with Carlo Marx [Ginsberg] about an Arabian figure who haunted Kerouac and who, they concluded, was death. The passage ends: "I told it to Dean and he instantly recognized it as the mere simple longing for pure death; and because we're all of us never in life again, he, rightly, would have nothing to do with it, and I agreed with him then" (*On the Road* 115; "Bye Bye Jack" 194).

Kerouac meant many things to Wilding, among them being a freeing up of style and narrative energy, but it meant something else as well, a point that Wilding makes emphatically in a passage from a late story, "Red Rock," collected in *This Is For You* (1994): "And this morning I started to read Jack Kerouac and like every time I read Kerouac I put down the book, whichever book, and want to write, always his note is the note of memory and search and wanting to write it as close to as it was as you can dare, as at this stage you can try" (66). In conversations with me, Wilding stated several times that reading Kerouac always had the effect of making him want to write.

Back in the early 70s Brian Kiernan commented on the ongoing oral history of the Kerouac Wake material:

> Another example of adjustment to reality is "The Jack Kerouac Wake", a story not yet published that turns up at Sydney readings in different versions. One version is by Michael Wilding (whose own collection, which includes stories of Sydney push life, has just been published by Queensland University Press), others are by Moorhouse. Each claims to present the "true" account of a chaotic night. Each is close to the truth—but what is truth?" ("Notes on Frank Moorhouse" 9)

Later, in his anthology, *The Most Beautiful Lies* (1977), Kiernan pointed out the importance of this work, noting that it is "an example of a story first 'published' at poetry readings, where the audience could enjoy recognizing real-life models for the characters, most of them being present in fact..." (206). Kiernan simultaneously discounts the realistic base of the story, adding, "However, enjoyment does not depend on being able to read it as a *conte à clef* but on appreciation of the contrast between its elegiac unfolding and the frenetic randomness of literary 'Push' life it structurally mirrors" (206). I would suggest that the story invites the reader to have it both ways. We can read *The Sun Also Rises* without knowing the real-life counterparts of Hemingway's characters, but once we know them the novel gains that much more historical interest and authenticity.

Wilding himself has addressed the importance of readings in the development of new writing: "We weren't getting a lot published though we were writing a lot. We did a series of readings in Balmain. People had low rent houses on the waterfront and we'd put on a reading in a boatshed or a garden" (Syson 283).

For Wilding, the readings encouraged a post-Jamesian style. He spoke of this development in an interview with Ian Syson:

> The other thing, reading to an audience encouraged the development of a more colloquial style that directly engaged readers. Not everything I've written works well when read aloud, some of it is very much for the printed page. And as I was developing this through having to do a lot of lecturing, I decided that since I was having to give lectures, then I would put the work into developing new ideas in them so that they could be published. This in part involved adopting a style that would work both as a lecture and in print. So out of the lectures emerged a more accessible style. Otherwise I might have gone the other way into Henry James or Joyce or something like that. (283)

The Kerouac manner of course fit in beautifully with the emphasis on an aural style aimed at readers as listeners. Recently, however, in *Wild & Woolley: A Publishing Memoir* Wilding has distanced himself from oral performance art: "But theatre, readings, performance, radio, I always found too transitory, too ephemeral to be ultimately satisfying." (9). It was all right to write it but not always meaningful to read it before an audience. Or not meaningful enough.

But Wilding's story was not the end of the telling of the Kerouac Wake event or non-event. Moorhouse had his say too, in "The Jack Kerouac Wake—The True Story," a work that was also read at poetry readings. It is one of a half dozen stories targeted at Wilding that are collected in *Tales of Mystery and Romance* (1977).

Heretofore the closest that Wilding has come to offering an account of the breaking of that friendship appeared in *Wildest Dreams*. The occasion was a trip that Wilding was going to make with "Bobbie" (Pat Woolley) to visit California, her home state. Moorhouse was also planning a trip, with "Rachel" (Sandra Levy), to visit the U.S., and he proposed meeting up with Wilding and Woolley in America. Hearing about it, Valda advised Wilding not to tell Moorhouse anything about his itinerary. Instead Wilding wrote Moorhouse a letter detailing his reasons for preferring not to spend time together in the states. He wanted to be free of Balmain associations. In *Wild & Woolley: A Publishing Memoir*, published in late 2011, Wilding restates the account of his grievances and the content of the letter, but adds a paragraph about the aftermath:

> And that was the end of a beautiful friendship. When I phoned him on my return Frank was decidedly chill. He declined invitations to meet for lunch, for drinks, for old times' sake. And he declined the offer to republish his underground collection [a small out-of-print collection of three risqué stories]. (113-114)

Rivalry, competition, and hurt feelings seem to be at the heart of the rift that, once articulated, would only grow wider with the passage of the years. The powerful autobiographical content of "Bye Bye Jack. See You Soon" defined the end of a ten-year period of friendship 1964-1974 (although for two of those, '68 and '69, Wilding was in the UK).

## Chapter 4

# Writers Living Together

## The Short Story Embassy: A Novel

*The Short Story Embassy: A Novel* was Wilding's second book of fiction to be published in 1975. It was also his first book with Wild & Woolley, the press that he and the American Pat Woolley had launched two years earlier, at the end of 1973. Wilding chose to go with his own press, he has explained, because the new work was "a novel quite unlike anything else I had done before, and quite unlike anything else in print in Australia—short, self-referential, post-modern before the term was current. I doubted that UQP would appreciate it" (*Wild & Woolley* 24-25). Wilding also has commented at greater length on the importance of this novel in his career:

> By the mid-1970s I had committed myself to exploring a more open-ended, spontaneous form, to moving on from the aesthetic of Henry James into the spontaneity of Jack Kerouac, Leonard Cohen, Richard Brautigan. *The Short Story Embassy* was the breakthrough. Yet, as Carl Harrison-Ford gleefully pointed out, the spirit of Henry James was still there; what was the title *The Short Story Embassy* but another formulation of James' House of Fiction? ("Writing Humour" 174)

This was the era when American fabulists like John Barth, Donald Barthelme, Richard Brautigan, and William Gass were turning fiction inside out, exposing its presumptive fallacies of offering a realistic, naturalistic description and analysis of experience, exploding formal properties, using disruptive techniques such as collage and headlines and other at times almost stunt-like techniques to, in a postmodern sense, make it new. There was even a French novel that did away with page numbers. It came in a box and the reader was invited to shuffle the pages like a deck of cards and read it in whatever random disorder one wished.

Wilding's book stacks up very well against American titles such as Brautigan's *Trout Fishing in America*, Barthelme's stories and his "novel," *The Dead Father*, and the stories of Barth and the lesser fabulists. Thinking back on his influences, Wilding has written, "From the late 60s I began to read and to be influenced by Richard Brautigan, Donald Barthelme. Admired but not sure whether or not I was influenced by William Burroughs, Paul Bowles, Ed Sanders, from the 70s onward" (Email "Re: Bukowski," November 28, 2009). Before the Americans, there was the Argentinian Borges, and Wilding sometimes wrote fables in the Borges manner.

*The Short Story Embassy* is Wilding's most ingenious and intriguing postmodernist performance. A highly original work of fiction, it received excellent reviews in Australia ("an interesting book, one that you will want to read again," *Sydney Morning Herald*), England ("considerable entertainment," *Times Literary Supplement*), and America ("The best of the talent emerging from Down Under," *San Francisco Review of Books*) [excerpted quotations from ad page in *The Phallic Forest*]. Christina Stead told Wilding in a letter that she enjoyed the novel and read it three times (*Wild & Woolley*, p. 75). For readers familiar with Australian literary culture, the novel offered a set of recognizable figures, as the principal characters are all *roman à clef* versions of persons in Wilding's circle. Wilding himself has mused perceptively on the inclination to search for real-life models in fiction. In "Characters" in *Newswrite* (2002) he stated:

"One of the functions of literature is that of assisting the understanding of life; and you are likely to understand more if the characters you read about are based on actuality" (3).

Of the four characters in this house of fiction, three are authors: Laszlo (Wilding), Wendel (Frank Moorhouse), and Valda (Vicki Viidikas). Laszlo is an unusual name for a Wilding surrogate; usually it is Graham or another English-sounding name (Ian, Derek). The name, Wilding remembers, was "taken from Laszlo Toth, an Australian who smashed Michelangelo's Pieta or something in protest about something. World wide outcry. I think I took his name because the issue of art vs humanity always interested me, as from an English puritan background, I tended to feel humanity should have priority" (Email, June 17, 2010). Born in Hungary in 1940, Laszlo Toth was an Australian geologist who did indeed attack Michelangelo's Pieta statue, on May 21, 1972. Shouting that he was Jesus Christ risen from the dead Toth struck the statue with fifteen blows, using a geologist's hammer. The Virgin's arm was knocked off at the elbow, a part of her nose was broken off, and one of her eyelids was chipped. Toth was judged to be insane and spent three years in an Italian hospital before being deported to Australia in 1975, where he still resides.

Wendel is part of the alternate naming system Wilding devised for writing about Moorhouse. Wilding derived the name from the American jurist Oliver Wendell Holmes, who had been in correspondence with Marcus Clarke, the subject of considerable scholarship by Wilding. Thus, according to Wilding, "Holmes = homes = [moor] house—so I called FM Wendel from that" (Email, June 17, 2010). Valda is based on Vicki Viidikas, and *The Short Story Embassy* is in fact dedicated to "Vicki." Wilding remembers that she never said anything about the book's dedication. He adds, "She was ropable that the copy I mailed to her had a section missing. She thought I'd censored the copy, cutting out something bad about her. It was just a binding error" (Email, June 17, 2010).

The fourth character, named Tichborne, is a critic—and therefore in the view of the writers in the novel not a real writer. The name Tichborne has complex associations. First of all, it echoes the famous Tichborne claimant case in 19$^{th}$ century England involving an imposter named Arthur Orton who maintained that he was the missing heir Sir Roger Tichborne. Orton, born in London, was living in Australia when he presented himself as the missing Tichborne heir. The story of the Tichborne claimant has been the subject of many retellings, from Borges to Patrick White to a Simpsons TV episode. The most relevant in Wilding's case was Marcus Clarke's use of it in *For the Term of His Natural Life* (MW email, June 17, 2010).

Wilding also had in mind Chidiock Tichborne, the Renaissance plotter and poet, about whom Clarke had also written a novel, *Chidiock Tichbourne*. But the actual person on whom the character Tichborne is based is Brian Kiernan, a friend of Wilding and Moorhouse, an important critic and historian of Australian literature who taught in the English Department at the University of Sydney from the early 70s until his retirement in 1998. Like the character in the novel, Kiernan had come to Sydney from Melbourne. Australian literary scholar Laurie Hergenhan has written of those days: "The first clear picture of Brian I recall is of meeting him at Sydney University Staff Club, since abolished. The time would have been around the later 1960s. I was waiting with Michael Wilding, who told me that Brian was visiting from Melbourne and would meet him shortly. Then Brian entered, looking eager and alert" ("Brian Kiernan, Critic and Editor: Some Reminiscences" 12). As Wilding remembers it, "BK coming from Melbourne was on the receiving end of Frank's rather cruel wit. BK was eager to be accepted, which of course gave FM ample opportunity for torture. I am afraid I rather went along with this. And since BK was a critic not a fiction writer he got a rough deal" (Email, June 17, 2010). Addressing the other aspect of the name, Wilding observes, "The possibility that he was an impostor in a world of writers added to the note of paranoia in the book, sexual paranoia and political" (June 17, 2010). Tichborne narrates several chapters and plays an important, though often unwitting role, in the life of the three writers living at the Embassy.

The novel is intensely literary; indeed, virtually every page hums with discourse about writing, writers, critics, strategies, competition, envy, paranoia—all the tools of the trade. The site of the Short Story Embassy is a large two-storey house seemingly located in one of the Sydney inner suburbs. Though the book is thin in geographical and sociological detail, there are references to the Harbour and to the Cross (King's Cross). In fact, Wilding has confirmed that the house "was in Balmain, where I was living at the time, and where Frank & I had shared a house for a while when I came back from UK 1969" (Email, June 17, 2010). That ended when "his girlfriend threw us out (it was her house, she was living in the Cross), and I got a place in neighbouring Drummoyne, with Margaret Clancy, and Frank came to stay, and Margaret left. . ." (Email, June 17, 2010).

Unquestionably, Balmain was *the* literary place to be in the late 1960s and '70s. Elisabeth Wynhausen in her memoir *Manly Girls* (1989) recalls the dismay expressed by her mother upon her decision to move to Balmain: "'Balmain' she had snapped, in the last act of the drama played out on the day I said I was leaving home, 'who ever heard of Balmain?'" (117). But to Wynhausen herself, Balmain was "almost European, with those winding little streets..." (116). According to Wilding, the mother was doubtless remembering the Balmain of old, originally a "dangerous working class dockside suburb" (Email, October 12, 2010). After the docks moved to Botany Bay in the 1960s, Balmain began its ascension to "le ghetto de Balmain" (October 12, 2010).

For many writers, artists, and Push layabouts Balmain was a romantic haven, an island of Bohemia. To Moorhouse, it was John Steinbeck's "Cannery Row" reinvented in a Sydney suburb: "As we said, the book [i.e., *Cannery Row*] is about lazy days in the sun, not having a job, boozing and whoring. The adolescent dream of avoiding conventional life" (*Days of Wine and Rage* 121). Pradeep Trikha, author of a book-length study of Moorhouse's fiction, writes of Moorhouse's experience in Sydney and surrounds: "It is here he read American writers like Hemmingway, Stienbeck, Kerouac, Ginesberg, Burroughs and others [sic]. He settled himself in the suburbs of Sydney, in Balmain, where fresh blood replenished his intellectual zeal and made him a freelance writer (14)." Trikha adds, "Another positive factor which constantly contributed to his creative writing was healthy, honest and useful reactions of his Balmain friends like Stephen Knight, Michael Wilding and Don Anderson" 14).

According to Wynhausen, "Reporters wrote about the place as if the dust from the Balmain collieries had no sooner settled than we found ourselves in the middle of Bloomsbury, figuring out whose turn it was to play Virginia Woolf" (150). Vicki Viidikas, on the other hand, loved its déclassé down-market feel: "so it was neighbourhood to me, though a piranha tank with unnecessary teeth" …("Vicki Viidikas Born 1945" 419). Later it would become gentrified and by the 1980s most of the artists and writers and would-be artists and writers and hangers-on and nymphs had departed.

During the late 60s/early 70s Wilding and Moorhouse were key figures in the literary life of the Push. According to Wynhausen, Moorhouse was "the standard-bearer of a division of 'the Push' identified with Balmain" (131). The Push was a loose coalition: "The Libertarians were famous for believing in Free Love, and by the 'fifties, wayward students were following them around. With little else in Sydney in the way of bohemian subculture, 'the Push' had come to include academics, artists, and writers, as well as dissenters of every stripe…" (Wynhausen 130). Wilding appears in Wynhausen's narrative as an Englishman and as the writer Michael Wilding. She remembers once that she and "an Englishman" were in bed when they were repeatedly interrupted by someone bursting into the bedroom. She recalls that the Englishman had also acted strangely as well: "He had once arrived unannounced, by shinnying up the drainpipe and coming into the bedroom from the first floor balcony, perhaps the only sign he gave of being anxious to see me" (133). The Wilding identification is confirmed by another Push member who asks her, "Remember when Wilding got into your room by climbing up the drainpipe?" (135). She concludes, "Though the Englishman continued to call in from time to time to badger me with questions about my alleged infidelities, the affair was over" (137). Today Wilding recalls that time: "I'm the mad Englishman obsessed by Wynhausen's past affairs, in *Manly Girls*. Retrospective sexual jealousy was one of the themes of SSE. I was aware of my problems. Didn't seem to help deal with them" (Email, August 30, 2010).

The Wilding-Moorhouse branch of the Push hung out at the Forth & Clyde in Balmain. According to Wynhausen, "The Forth & Clyde hotel in Balmain was the focus of our social life… Several scenes merged at the Forth & Clyde, the local for the contingent from 'the Push' as well as some of the campus radicals" (134). To Wilding, the "world of the Libertarians," the Push, was improbably a "site of the exotic" (*Wild Amazement* 57). Years later he offered an ironic analysis of the animating principles of the Push: "Sexual exchange was what it was about and jealousy was, though not unknown, frowned upon. And in theory, of course, sexual exchange was not what it was all about, it was about other things too. Anarchism. It was about Anarchism." (*Wild Amazement* 58).

Wilding summarizes the politics of the Push thus: "…there were no taboos, do what you want was the whole name of the law, as long as what you wanted was not Socialism or Communism or religion" (58). For a committed Leftist like Wilding, the Push was never wholly authentic.

The idea of a short story embassy came from the example of political activists of that era. There was an Aboriginal Tent Embassy established outside Parliament House in Canberra in 1972, and closer to home, in Balmain, gay activists had set up a Camp Embassy (Email, June 17, 2010). Having a Short Story Embassy seemed eminently logical if one wanted to write about writers and their ambitions. The book covers a three year time period—1969-72—the height of political and cultural activism in the run-up to the transformative election of Gough Whitlam and the Labor Party.

The three fictional characters live at the house/embassy; it is their center of operation. Here they write, steal from each other's writing, and plot their schemes for disseminating their stories and taking on the formidable outside world of publishers, agents, and various control systems put in place to stymie and suppress the great work being done at the Embassy. There are numerous references to the Literary Police (enforcers of the Literary Establishment) and in one very funny sequence Wendel will not permit the mention of a prominent journal published in Melbourne (where Tichborne-Kiernan comes from). That journal is the *Meanjin Quarterly*, edited by Clem Christensen. Wilding recalls his own antipathy to *Meanjin*: "The Meanjin editor was always hostile to Frank's work and mine. This wasn't helped by Frank getting me to review an issue of Meanjin for his journal Australian Highway. Christensen was annoyed by this" (Email, June 17, 2010). Wilding's remembrance of that time captures the clash between the new writing and the "wide brown land" hegemony held by conservative quarterlies of the period. By the mid 1980s, however, with new editors at *Meanjin* the resistance to the New Writing had given way to acceptance of work by both Wilding and Moorhouse.

The House's literary aura is represented by a panoply of allusions to famous short story authors. A full rundown includes the Earlier Brautigan potting shed, the Henry James carpet (echoing the "Figure in the Carpet"), the O. Henry guest suite, the G. K. Chesterton refectory, the Borges library, the Edgar Allan Poe graveyard, the Pat Hobby construction room (which refers to Fitzgerald's Pat Hobby magazine stories), the Maugham verandah, the Borges chicken run, and the Katherine Mansfield sanatorium. The novel's title has a jokey quality as well: *The Short Story Embassy: A Novel*—a novel made up of short stories, essentially.

And it even has a plot. In the first chapter, "Tichborne describes his arrival," the critic from Melbourne narrates his entry into the impressive house/embassy. The scene, it turns out, derives from Henry James' opening page of *The Turn of the Screw*. Wilding himself has pointed out this influence and the general importance of James in his novelistic imagination. In his 1977 essay "A Survey" Wilding addressed the continuing relevance of James: "When Robert Duncan called James the first of the moderns I felt much relieved; I could bring out dear old HJ from the closet again. I could admit that *The Short Story Embassy* which commentators linked with Brautigan (and fair enough), took its first paragraph direct from *The Turn of the Screw*" (p. 119). As in James' short novel, Tichborne is a stranger entering an "old house" (James) amidst an aura of both excitement and anxiety. How will he be received? Will he be received? The rest of the story will have gothic overtones, though a comedy of anxiety predominates. Tichborne is drawn to a large table upon which lie "copies of short story magazines from throughout the world" (7). He is attracted to one in particular, "that small local product in which I had reviewed Wendel's collection" (8). The collection is probably Moorhouse's *Futility and Other Animals*, published in 1969. Wilding reviewed it in *Southerly*. Tichborne then relates a familiar feeling in the Short Story Embassy—pride of authorship and fear of criticism: "I wanted to leaf through it to see if there were any annotations or signs of reaction to the review; but the possible embarrassment of being found standing there reading it prevented me" (8). In the second chapter, "Wendel and Lazslo crouch at the window watching Tichborne's arrival," the two writers speculate about Tichborne's appearance and motives. It becomes clear that Wendel does not like Tichborne's review of his book.

Wendel's suspicions and hostility towards Tichborne come out in this passage typical of the book's manner and themes:

> 'He'll probably expect us to get him a fuck now, he probably expects we've got a woman laid on for him ready, he's probably even got a particular one in mind, he probably wants to fuck someone from the book like Wesley.'
>
> 'Can we arrange that? Who was Wesley?'

> 'Oh Laszlo, you know we cannot be caught out like that. You know the basis of fictional creation, that we cannot make these simple identifications.' (9)

The question of the fictional Wesley's real-life basis comes up repeatedly in the novel, but remains unanswered. Wesley appears in Wilding's "The Nembutal Story," written to rebut Moorhouse's "The Oracular Story," which featured a character named Wesley. Wilding is playfully commenting on a reader/critic's desire to identify the source of a character.

The back-and-forth between Lazslo and Wendel in this chapter is also indicative of much to come in the novel. In the following exchange we witness essential differences between Laszlo (Wilding) and Wendel (Moorhouse). Laszlo speaks first:

> 'You're an offensive, sexist, chauvinist, alfish bastard sometimes.'
>
> 'Ageist. You forgot ageist. Add that in.'
>
> 'Mockery of the concepts doesn't destroy the validity of the analysis.'
>
> 'Is that from your calendar of epigrams you're writing? It's rather good. Can I copy it down? I'll put it under the notes on dictionaries, here we are.' (10)

The word "alfish" needs a bit of explanation. According to Wilding, "The libertarians called males who were not hip, cool, liberated, libertarian, or one of us, &c 'Alfs'. A condescending term of dismissal by the initiates. A sort of petit bourgeois name to have. Alf. It's probably obsolete by now" (Email, August 27, 2010).

Here we see the same rivalry and competition between the two writers that Wilding first wrote about in "Joe's Absence," and which he —and Moorhouse—would write about many times in those years and afterward. There are also marked political differences evident in this passage. In Wilding's view his friend and housemate was a reactionary masquerading as a libertarian. Certainly they were very different politically. Wilding was far left, and Moorhouse was, to use his own favorite terms, an "anarchist" in search of "volupté."

That rivalry and the interest in who Wesley is (from Wendel's story) seeps into another early chapter, "Valda and Laszlo discuss a fictional character." Valda wonders who Wesley is, and Laszlo, who doesn't know, is preoccupied at the moment with Wendel's analysis that found a heavy preponderance of animal metaphors in Laszlo's fiction, moving Laszlo to shift to vegetable rather than animal metaphors. The two male authors are obsessive about each other's work, while Valda plays the role of visionary hippie chick. In a previous chapter she has enchanted Tichborne and annoyed Wendel with an account of how she once turned into the cat's milk. The conversation goes back to Wesley's identity, and Laszlo makes much the same argument about fiction and its real-life sources that Wendel had made earlier, saying that "we don't write like that… we don't just take characters and incidents and change the names and places and use them like that. It's much more complicated than that" (18-19). Then Laszlo suggests that Wesley may be a female name. Valda says the name is "hermaphroditic" and Laszlo replies, "Bisexual would be better" (19). The puzzle of Wesley's identity (and gender) continues unsolved through the rest of the novel.

If Wesley, a fictional character, can arouse so much interest and anxiety, imagine what the characters in the novel can arouse when it comes to each other's sexual anxiety regarding each other's various liasons and affairs and live-ins and one-night stands, etc. Valda is the central figure in this ongoing sexual who-done-it or did-you or didn't-you sleep with Valda and who has Valda slept with previously. Three young men in a house with a young woman—writers living together and writing about each other covertly, directly, obliquely, obsessively, etc. —such is the hyper-tense world of the Short Story Embassy. An early indication of the preoccupation with Valda appears in "Laszlo sits at his typewriter and recalls first being on with Valda." Laszlo is very worried that Valda has "got off" with Wendel. Certainly he cannot ask Wendel because, given the nature of their relationship, he can't tell whether Wendel would answer truthfully. For example, Laszlo writes, "Some people have a vocabulary of shared words that between them have a private meaning. Wendel and I had a shared vocabulary of private words that between us had no meaning; truth was one of them" (21-22). Valda, however, intuits Laszlo's anxieties, and Valda answers those this way: "'I'd like to write him [Wendel] a story about a prostitute and take it round to him to read. Of course he'd have to think it was me. What else could he do? Then he wouldn't know where he was. He's one of those people who likes to give the impression he's got off with me'" (22). Then she tells Laszlo that of course she has never got off with Wendel. Laszlo's last statement in the story is, "So you weren't on with him" (23). In Wilding's stories about sex and fiction one can never be sure what the absolute truth is.

Tichborne, meantime, is becoming an increasing problem. He has set about chopping down trees in order to build up the supply of wood for the fireplace. The noise of his ax is bothersome, especially to Wendel, who is already hostile because of the review of his book. Wilding, too, was irritated about a review of his own book, *Aspects of the Dying Process*, that Tichborne (Kiernan) had written. According to Wilding, Kiernan "banged on about the UQP paperback prose series being a workshop for new writing. I rather felt my writing was complete and didn't need workshopping, which I felt a rather condescending concept. And have a sheltered workshop created in the novel. I was rather peeved" (Email, June 17, 2010). In the novel Wilding presents this criticism of Kiernan in such a way that only the most inside reader would make the connection. It is Wendel to whom Wilding gives the critique that he himself personally felt—and which doubtless Moorhouse did as well. Wendel tells Tichborne that he is to begin building a "sheltered workshop" (45). When asked what that is, Wendel explains, "It's an important project to emotionally cripple and retard writers. It promises to fulfill a valuable role for new and experimental writers of fiction, a role that the underground poetry press and the theatre workshops have already performed for younger poets and playwrights" (45).

In fact, Wendel's statement follows very closely what Kiernan had written in an article in the *Australian*, so much so that the last portion is a direct quote: "It promises to fulfill a valuable role that the underground poetry press and the theatre workshops have already performed for younger poets and playwrights" (quoted in "Adventurous Spirits," 86). After Wendel adds that "the writer of fiction faces obstacles different from those of the poet and dramatist," Laszlo chimes in, "'You can increase those,' Laszlo told Tichborne" (45). The practice of workshopping still irritates Wilding, as it does many established authors in Australia and the U.K. Wilding recently seized upon a statement he ran across in a Kingsley Amis novel, *Jake's Thing* (1978): "'If there's one word,' said Jake, 'that sums up everything that's gone wrong since the War, it's Workshop" (149; Email, July 24, 2010).

In the important short chapter, "Laszlo's statement of poetics," placed near the middle of the novel, Laszlo lays out a formal and thematic distinction between short story and novel: "The difference between the novel and the short story is between re-creation and prediction. The novel structures what has happened to us; with the short story we sketch out our future actions" (51). Laszlo also draws an important philosophical distinction between himself and Wendel. Laszlo identifies himself with the Jains, proponents of Jainism, an ancient Indian religion that stipulates a path of non-violence towards every living being. Wendel, on the other hand, in Laszlo's formulation, is a believer in "cosmic toryism," which connects him with imperialism, nationalism, conservatism (51). Laszlo is fearful of Wendel's paranoia and aggression, though Laszlo himself is certainly no stranger to paranoia. Laszlo is worried that Wendel's stories will create an antithetical reality of aggression. At the end of this chapter Laszlo concludes, "I would rather that Wendel wrote my novel and I wrote the short stories. I have a happier vision" (52).

In the next chapter one can see Wendel's aggression very easily. When Tichborne asks Valda about a poem of hers that he has read, Wendel says, 'You writing poems again? Slut.' Wendel, and Laszlo too for that matter, are both very opposed to poets. The poem in question, "Poem to All the Ladies," is in fact a poem titled "Punishment and Cures," published in Viidikas' 1973 collection, *Condition Red*. The poem is a harrowing account of two rapes.

Reacting to Tichborne's praise of the poem, Valda observes that it was important for her to write it, that it served as a kind of therapy, a way of going forward instead of going mad. Later Laszlo digs up that poem and others of Valda/Vicki's early poems and reads them. After he reads "Poem to All the Ladies/Punishment and Cures" this is his reaction: "Spectre, spirit, shade, goblin, wraith, spook, boggart, banshee, he watched " (56). Later in conversation with Valda, he asks her what she did "after the—" and she says, "What could I do? Nothing. Didn't do nothing. Just went mad for a while" (58).

In one of the loveliest sections of the novel, "Statement of poetics by Valda," Wilding vividly captures Vicki Viidikas' voice and manner. In a sense this piece of ventriloquism is an act of writing against himself, for Valda/Vicki depicts certain attributes and habits that are quintessential Wilding. Says Valda, "Laszlo spent all those years with books and libraries but it doesn't seem to have done him any good" (59). Laszlo depends upon the wisdom of the ages. Literature shields him from life. According to Valda, "He cannot take the life as it surrounds him" (59). "The girl in the room he never notices," she adds a bit later (59). Valda sums up the differences between them at the end of her "Statement": "I offer him new futures, new idols. I drape the room in feathers, tinsel, gold paint. But he stacks the old books against every wall. He aims, though does not know it, to block the door with them. Statements of poetics are for what has happened. Feathers are to carry us forward into the sun" (60). It is interesting to note that in Laszlo's "Statement of poetics" he defined the novel in very similar terms as Valda defines her Statement of poetics: as a record of what has happened. Laszlo sees the short story form as future-oriented; Valda sees life as future-oriented. Thus Wilding grants her the most visionary power of any character in the novel. Valda's previous sexual episodes torment Laszlo, and she runs circles around his paranoia and envy, telling him at one point, "There are a lot of things I never said before" (62). Everything in this section sounds like a restaging of images and ideas evident in the stories about Viidikas in *The West Midland Underground* and moreover, in Vicki's stories about Wilding.

To the two male writers, Tichborne is becoming an even greater irritation. Wendel meets conspiratorially with Laszlo to discuss what to do about Tichborne. Laszlo is upset at the destruction of plants and insects during the building of the sheltered workshop, but Wendel's views and proposals are even more disturbing to Laszlo. The differences between the two can be seen in their view of nature: "Wendel rested a foot on a fallen log. He started to carve at the bark with his Bowie knife. Laszlo watched the sap bleed out, heard the thin high scream of pain" (65). Wendel's action and Laszlo's reaction here are in line with this earlier exchange from the same section. Laszlo: "I note your concern with words is greater than your concern with nature." Wendel: "Nature can look after itself; words can't" (64).

Wendel's proposal is to "condition him [Tichborne] so that he can operate for us. We have to feed him ideas so that he can go and persuade the media and publishers and the publicity channels into what we need" (65). To do that, Wendel reveals a plan, and the technology, to use "subliminal persuasion" (66). The attic of the Short Story Embassy, it turns out, is full of recording equipment. Wendel wants to playback subliminal messages while Tichborne is sleeping in order, for example, to convey instructions such as "Tichborne, today you go to the Penguin organization and propose a volume of new urban short stories," or, in a parody of Nazism, "Teachbone, todie you vill go to zee Pengvin orga-nizazione und propvose eine folum von neuen urban schtorien..." (66). Though concerned for Tichborne, Laszlo is more worried about how the recording equipment came to be in the attic. He fears surveillance by the authorities.

Wendel offers other possibilities for controlling Tichborne. He suggests using the equipment to record Tichborne's dreams, and Laszlo, always on the look-out for material to write about, likes that idea, and Wendel agrees that it would be good material for a writer like Laszlo. Wendel also proposes using Valda to influence Tichborne, an idea that does not appeal to Laszlo so much. Wendel stirs the pot by showing Laszlo what Tichborne has been reading: poetry, especially Valda's poetry. Once again, for Laszlo, the personal and the political have been joined in paranoia. The chapter ends with Wendel's telling how he sent Tichborne and Valda into the city to shop for books. He sent them on bicycles with punctures to insure slow leaks and a long trip.

But of course they return, and laden with books. One of them is that literary quarterly from Melbourne that Wendel has forbidden the mention of. He is furious and won't permit its name (*Meanjin*) to be uttered. Valda points out that Tichborne has a literary article in the issue on the "state of new writing" (71). Incensed, Wendel responds: "'What do you know about the State of New Writing?' Wendel asked. 'This is its Embassy and we are its Ambassadors. Any pronouncement comes through our press officers'" (71). Brian Kiernan did indeed later write such an article, "Recent Developments in Australian Writing with Partic-ular Reference to Short Fiction," *Caliban* (Toulouse), XIV (1977), 123-134. That same year, 1977, Kiernan edited a useful collection of the new writing, *The Most Beautiful Lies––A Collection of Stories by Five Major Contemporary Fiction Writers: Bail, Carey, Lurie, Moorhouse and Wilding.*

A one-page section presents a fantasy of the Laszlo-Wendel commit-ment to prose fiction and rejection of poetry. Valda has to pay for her violation of the rules of the Short Story Embassy, so in this brief paragraph she is "marched naked from the Embassy" (73). They lash her with whips, "beating her for reading poetry, for bringing poetry books into the Embassy, for secretly composing poems in her head" (73). Although Tichborne tries to stop them, the ritualistic fantasy proceeds: they set her poetry books on fire, they use burning pages to torture her further. The scene is both bizarre and, in a strange way, comic in a manner.

Following this fantasy scene, the novel grows more self-referential by the page. An unnamed chapter begins, "I am of course Laszlo," though most readers would have reached this conclusion on their own. In any event, Laszlo discloses his identity in an effort to head off Wendel's appropriation of Laszlo's subject matter. On a "fiction finding mission" (itself an hilarious conceit) at a pub, Wendel announces: "The first of the Embassy stories is on its way today. It has you in it and Valda and some of your characters and some of my characters and Titbone [one of his names for Tichborne] and Titbone's professor and the literary police" (75). Laszlo feels instantly threatened. He sees that Wendel, writing short stories rapidly and putting them through his usual seven-revision process, intends to beat Laszlo's slower-proceeding novel into print, described by Laszlo as a "long story in the form of a novel" (the book we are reading).

This little piece of literary paranoia ends with further paranoia, as Laszlo speculates that Wendel may in fact be fabricating the advent of his, Wendel's, Embassy stories, and further, Laszlo is worried about what sort of research Wendel might be undertaking with regard to Valda (literary paranoia is never far from sexual paranoia in this novel), and finally, he worries that the devious Wendel is merely creating real-life situations as subject matter for his future stories. In the world of this novel, whatever one can think of is a distinct possibility either for fact or paranoia.

In another chapter Lazslo's paranoia reaches new heights. Wendel's day begins with exercise, an activity that Wilding hated going back to his school days in Worcester. Even worse, Wendel ascends to the tower of the Embassy where he writes, an act that causes much anxiety on Lazslo's part. Lazslo believes that "Wendel could be writing this whole narrative and presenting it under my name. Wendel would like us to think we are all creatures of his imagination" (83). Lazslo takes it one step further: "If he chooses to write as me, who will ever be persuaded that it is not me?" (83). But it's not just Wendel about whom Lazslo is worried; it's Tichborne (or Titbone or Titbun, Wendelisms for Tichborne) (84). Lazslo thinks that Tichborne is becoming "increasingly furtive" and conveying a sense of "nudging camaraderie, as if to claim a shared heritage" (84). Even worse, and funnier, is Lazslo's fear of Tichborne's Wendel-like subterfuges: "If I do not trust Wendel not to use my name and persona in his writings, how much less do I trust Tichborne not to steal my manuscripts and translate them into Italian and publish them as his own work. I have begun to keep everything locked" (84).

Three closely related stories explore Laszlo's and Valda's relationship. In all three Laszlo is tormented by Valda's past, by the men she has known, by whether she has worked as a "harlot" (her word) for a time (85). The first story in this sequence flashes forward to some time in the future when they have broken up and have moved separately and apart from the Short Story Embassy. They lie on a beach, something they never did while at the Embassy, and Valda talks about her desire to be a prostitute because it would both give her time to write and an opportunity to gratify her need for sex. Such talk greatly troubles Laszlo, who is sick at his stomach over such information, if information it is, because he can't tell from Valda's words whether she actually was a prostitute at one point and he can't tell from her stories either, especially the one that deals with a guy who was stoned all the time and who ran five girls on the street at a time. Was this true or just a story? Did he "run" Valda as well? At the beach he reads her new stories but they only create a sense of lost opportunity. One is about groupies, and Laszlo laments that they never had groupies at the Embassy. Valda's explanation why is perfect: "You've got to change your image; short story writers just don't have the image" (87).

The second story in this sequence deals again with Laszlo's preoccupation and paranoia regarding Valda's sexual experiences when she was a girl and before she met Laszlo. Addressing her in his mind, he asks, "Valda, why do your stories always contain uncertainties, Valda why do you never pin them down into specificness, but leave those things I do not know, those things I cannot ask?" (89). He wants to know, but cannot bring himself to ask, how old she was when she lost her virginity and how many boys or men she had sex with in her teenage years, and he concludes a paragraph of speculation about this subject with a self-question, "...when is this ever going to stop?" (89).

The third story in the sequence focuses on Valda and Laszlo in the Embassy where Valda is writing a story about a girl "screwing pushers." She shows it to Laszlo but he says she shouldn't show it to "people" (91). This irritates her, and Laszlo goes on to say that he had rather wait till the story is completed and then he can read it "and get over it" (91). Which also irritates her. His reason is familiar and predictable: he can't handle her past experiences with other men. Since he always assumes that any female protagonist in her stories is in fact Valda, this irritates her as well. Finally, she reads him the riot act on his jealousy and paranoia: "'Your head is incredible,' she said. 'You're so busy thinking of things you never live; think think think think think. And what do you know at the end of it? Nothing. You never even try" (92-93).

According to critic Jennifer Maiden, Wilding's various fictional portraits of Vicki Viidikas captured her personality so accurately that "Vicki was over-defined early as the wayward, kind-hearted, promiscuous druggie in Michael Wilding's prose." (quoted by Kerry Leves, "Foreword" 16). Kerry Leves, who knew Viidikas, makes the same point even more forcefully, pointing out that "Wilding's 'Valda'--an uncannily accurate mimesis of Vicki's vocal cadences, of the way she spoke—didn't seem to bother the model. When I tried to quiz her about 'Valda', Vicki shrugged—writing was (is) an open field" ("Foreword" 16).

Valda, champion of spontaneous feelings and sexual honesty, is rather stunned at Laszlo's comeback to her withering analysis of his shortcomings. For Laszlo proposes that Tichborne may in fact be an actor that Wendel has hired. Indeed, he might even be Wendel. These comic paranoid levels are beyond what Valda has contemplated.

In the last thirty pages of the novel, things get wilder and wilder. There is a brief, three paragraph segment detailing the arrival of a dog, Sluggo, and Wendel's excited expropriation of the dog as accessory to his big-game hunting persona. Wendel parades around the grounds of the Embassy with the dog, a hooded falcon on his wrist, and a hat with trout flies adorning it. He carries a rifle and a whip.

The next chapter is brilliant. It is narrated in first person by Tichborne (or Laszlo impersonating Tichborne, because by now in the narrative, everything, narratively, is up for grabs). Enthralled by Valda's beauty and talent, Tichborne sees her as potentially becoming "one of the great writers of our time" (95). Her subject is one reason: the "raw material of our time; attempting suicide, having abortions, being raped, walking the streets, catching venereal disease, participating in multiple sexual situations, lesbianism, fucking dogs" (95).

Infatuated with Valda, Tichborne tries to puzzle out her relationships with Laszlo and Wendel. He also asks a very naïve question; he asks whether any of them has written about the Embassy "and what goes on in it" (96). Valda laughs and the three writers suddenly leave the room after which Tichborne can hear the "clatter of typewriters in the rooms above" (96). Tichborne is pleased because he sees himself as playing a role in "the germination of literature" (p. 96) and compares himself to Thomas Ellwood. Ellwood (1639-1713) was a prominent Quaker and a friend of John Milton and William Penn. His best known book is *The History of the Life of Thomas Ellwood*. Wilding includes Ellwood here because of the Milton connection. The context is the question that Ellwood asked Milton after he, Ellwood, had just finished reading *Paradise Lost*. He asked Milton whether he was going to write a poem about "Paradise found," and, prompted by this question, Milton later produced *Paradise Regained* (Email, August 27, 2010). The allusion and the quotation from Ellwood illustrate brilliantly Wilding's incorporation of Renaissance literature into his own modern works set in Sydney.

The chapter ends with an eruption of violence. Valda and Tichborne are in the chicken-run and Valda is feeding the chickens when suddenly a chicken explodes right in front of them, shot by Wendel from the window of his room in the Embassy. The next paragraph is an interpolation from Wilding's story "From His Apperceptions of the Terribleness of Things." That story ends thus: "'Hemingway once said the greatest practice in concentration a writer could have was big game hunting,' Joe said, aiming again. 'This is my practice'" (*The Phallic Forest* 106.). In *The Short Story Embassy* the sentence reads: "'Hemingway once said the greatest practice in concentration a writer could have was big game hunting,' Joe said, aiming again,' he called." (97). The insertion of Joe's name into the text dispels any doubts one might have about the identification of Wendel with Moorhouse and provides a playful bit of intertextuality.

The next chapter further intensifies Wendel's role in the novel. Tichborne discovers him engaged in engraving epigraphs on tombstones. Laszlo collects them, and Wendel engraves them. Wendel runs through a long list of how epitaphs have been used in the past, to cover virtually every category and sentiment. He concludes: "But no Epitaphs for Reviewers and Critics. Perhaps they never died. Perhaps they were buried in unconsecrated ground. Along with Publishers. There aren't any Epitaphs for Publishers listed either" (100). Wendel also has a stack of wood nearby, and at night Tichborne is kept awake by the sound of Wendel's carpentry. It seems clear to the reader if not to Tichborne that Wendel is fashioning a coffin. The constant sawing of the wood for the coffin recalls the famous scene in Faulkner's *As I Lay Dying* (Email, October 12, 2010). Another Faulkner allusion to the same novel appears in *Living Together*: "Maybe he's ploughing a field to buy a horse" (51).

In the next chapter Wendel interviews Valda regarding her sexual history. He types everything she says, source material for a story he's writing. He wants to know how many men she has slept with. At one point Valda tells him he asks the same questions as Lazslo and then tells him the kinds of detail that Laszlo wants to know, numbers, places, physical details of her sexual life. Lazslo himself emerges from behind the arras (just as in *Hamlet*) and wants to know why he's asking her these questions, and Wendel says for a story he's writing: "About Valda?"... "About you" (102).

"Laszlo's work in progress" is the title of the next chapter, a dialogue between him and Valda. As usual, most of the conversation is about sex and their relationship. Laszlo thinks he is falling in love with her: "She answered everything, mother, moll, madonna" (105). There are questions that he can't ask her, ones that he has been worrying about the whole novel: had she been a prostitute? was she camp? did she love him? The chapter ends with her talking about how hard it is to live in the city. She mentions prostitution; she mentions begging.

In the next chapter Valda discovers one of Laszlo's manuscripts in progress, a story about a prostitute that she believes is based on her experience or, that is, on Laszlo's understanding of her experience. They argue about who knows the most about prostitution, and Laszlo offers his aesthetic of the short story: "Look, you know stories aren't based on events. They're predictive. If I write about a moll in a story today, I meet one next week" (106). Valda counters with her own aesthetic: "When I write stories they're about what's already happened. What I decide doesn't have anything to do with it" (107).

Following the fluid, shifting point of view technique, a chapter narrated by Tichborne exhibits the critic observing large sheets of strawboard being brought into the Embassy and wonders if a play is going to be put on. Lazslo tells him that he and Wendel are "assembling a chart of literary affiliations, groups, power bases. We have isolated the CIA group, the translated into ten languages Communist group, the

# Writers Living Together

Literary Police, the Daily Poets, the Dramatists, the quarterly **** from Melbourne, and so on" (109-110). Explaining further, Laszlo says the goal is to disclose "the recurrence of names, the exercise of power, the distribution of patronage, and Mr. Big" (110). Both Wilding and Moorhouse are on record as having constructed such a schematic to show the power relations among the literary establishment of Australia in the 1960s and '70s.

In a hilarious half-page follow-up chapter Tichborne sees that more sheets of strawboard have been delivered. He takes them to Wendel's room, where he hopes to see "the chart of literary affiliations" (111), but Wendel says the boards belong to Laszlo, who is "assembling a chart of Valda's lovers" (111).

Another short chapter develops Wendel's ideas about Laszlo's chart of Valda's erotic experiences. Again Tichborne is the narrator and it is he who draws Wendel out on the supposed chart. Wendel explains that its purpose is to "track the course and carriers of the disease" (112). Flustered, Tichborne ticks off a list of possible diseases, all being varieties of sexually transmitted disease. Wendel goes on to expatiate on possible cures and protections against the diseases. Wendel here is perversely exfoliating upon concerns about hygiene and disease that Laszlo himself has raised with Valda. This is Tichborne's last appearance in the text; he disappears in the first sentence of the next chapter.

While Laszlo and Valda are in the dark about Tichborne, Wendel argues preposterously that Tichborne has been kidnapped and is being held in the Philippines. He even has a kidnap ransom note to prove it. It's clear that Wendel has gotten the idea from the fact that embassy officials are subject to being kidnapped in the outside world.

And since embassies issue communiqués, so too does Wendel begin to send out communiqués. There is also a skeletal finger bone that Wendel claims is Tichborne's. Laszlo is skeptical, but they bury the finger bone in the Edgar Allan Poe cemetery anyway. And Lazslo is quick to construct his own fantasy, that Tichborne has been called back to his base in Melbourne. The fear that Tichborne is a double agent involved in surveillance and spying remains a viable paranoia. The next one-page chapter ends thus: "This is a recorded message: Valda tells me I must escape from Wendel's paranoias. This is a recorded message: Wendel tells me I must escape from Valda's paranoias"(120).

The penultimate chapter consists of a one-sentence introduction to "TICHBORNE'S ELEGY, WRITTEN IN THE TOWER BEFORE HIS EXECUTION" (121). Then follows the famous poem penned by Chidiock Tichbourne on September 20, 1586, on the eve of his execution for having plotted against Queen Elizabeth in a conspiracy to murder her and place Mary, Queen of Scots, on the throne. At the end of the quotation, the narrator (Laszlo) observes, "Even this was not his own work." The last chapter is titled "From Laszlo's papers." It is paranoia to the max. Laszlo "is terrified to write any more" (123). He is very worried about VD. He mentions his prior definition of the short story as being predictive of the future but is worried now that his preoccupation with Valda's possible prostitution has led him to meet a prostitute. He fears that what he has been writing is becoming true. He concludes that "My novel has come to its sudden and curtailed end; has become a short story; its events are predictions" (123). He wonders if it was T (his new shorthand for Tichborne) who introduced VD from Melbourne. He worries about a fire consuming their writings. Wendel has finished the last chapter of his Embassy novella, but a fire had destroyed some earlier chapters.

The novel (now a collection of predictive short stories) concludes with Wendel's vision of himself and Laszlo living in exile in Mexico, older and wearing beards and evading the Literary Police. The last sentences, from Laszlo, imagine them on the beaches of Acalpulco: "From Thirroul to Oaxaca we will carry our fireproof boxes. A new Embassy will arise from the ashes of the old" (124). The place names allude to D.H. Lawrence, who stayed in Thirroul on the NSW south coast where he wrote *Kangaroo*, before going to Mexico (MW email "comments and corrections," November 28, 2011).

*The Short Story Embassy* may well be Wilding's most underrated work of fiction. The portraits of the three writers and the critic are dead on. Elisabeth Wynhausen describes a typical evening at the Forth and Clyde that captures the kind of tensions between Wilding and Moorhouse that lace the novel's narrative:

> Frank Moorhouse, who could be at his most engaging at a party, had decided there and then that he was being persecuted by Michael Wilding, another writer. The two of them were always making wild claims to keep the atmosphere sufficiently charged. Not knowing much about it, I assumed that it inspired them to dramatize their rivalry. They liked to write stories which played off each other's neuroses and it gave them more than enough scope. "He's been trying to find out what I'm working on." (136)

Vicki Viidikas died on November 27, 1998 at age fifty, of a heart attack. In Wilding's obituary for her, he wrote of her presence in relation to Balmain: "Balmain in the late 1960s and early 70s was home to a horde of writers and publications. Viidikas was a striking, effervescent figure around the pubs, the parties and the waterfront readings of those years" ("Trenchant Writer Blitzed Bohemia"). He added, "In that time-honoured tradition of the avant-garde artist, she preferred bohemia to bourgeois existence, and she preferred the demi-monde to bohemia." Calling her a "fiction writer of genius," he summed up her career in these terms: "In recent years she became a myth, lost to view of the literary world that she had inspired, stimulated, informed and reviled. It is a tragedy and a scandal that so comparatively small a part of her work appeared in print." But he predicted that more of her writing would be published and that it would eventually receive the cult status that it deserves.

There are recent signs that this may happen. In 2010 a collection of her work, *New and Rediscovered*, was published. Wilding's review of the book offers his most current assessment of her importance. First, he praises her subject matter: "She eagerly seized the opportunity to record what had rarely been explicit before, a world of gays, lesbians, prostitutes, rapists and their victims, drug-dealers and their junky clients." Continuing, he observes, "These are sketches from the life, not narratives manufactured for commercial gain or propagandist agenda. Vicki presented no agenda: other than the agenda of the clear-eyed writer, the Isherwood 'I am a camera'" ("Vivid Sketches" 1-2).

He concludes that the volume "has assembled the materials for our own cult. Vicki would have been wryly amused. But with that puckered smile of satisfaction. It was worth it, after all, despite the cost. But it was at a cost and she paid the price."

As for the Tichborne figure, Brian Kiernan remains close friends with both Wilding and Moorhouse. In an email Wilding recalled Kiernan's reaction to reading *The Short Story Embassy* when it appeared: "'I felt myself becoming more deeply involved the further I read.' But it was left at that enigmatic note, and we said no more" (Email "Re: update,: July 31, 2010). In the 2004 festschrift *Running Wild: Essays, Fictions and Memoirs* Kiernan embraced the Tichborne connection in a critical essay titled "Tichborne Redivivus: Re-Viewing Michael Wilding's Fiction."

While postmodernism is sometimes subject to devaluation because of its provisionality, its formal eccentricities, its sheer random experimentalism, *The Short Story Embassy: A Novel* is at once a highly entertaining and deeply serious corrective to such an easy dismissal. It offers a profound inquiry into the nature of fiction, writing, and perhaps best of all, writers living together.

CHAPTER 5

# POST-MODERNISM IN HIGH GEAR

## SCENIC DRIVE

Published by Wild & Woolley in 1976, *Scenic Drive* continued the narrative experimentation evidenced in *The Short Story Embassy* and *The West Midland Underground* of the previous year. The censorship battles had been won, and writers in the mid-70s were free to explore previously forbidden topics. None did so with more daring and verve than Wilding. Radically postmodern in form, *Scenic Drive* consisted of twenty-two stories, nineteen of which appeared in magazines in 1975 and 1976. (The other three were later published in magazines as well.)

Even the cover art of *Scenic Drive* sought to kick against the pricks. The front cover depicts three photographs: a section of an elegant building reminiscent of the "embassy" photo cover of *The Short Story Embassy*; a man, possibly a mime or clown, with mouth wide open; and a frontal nude shot of a female's pudendum. The back cover continues the nude motif with three small photos of female nudity overlaying eight Kodak photos of a casual Wilding sitting in an office and displaying various modes of facial expressions ranging from thoughtful to whimsical. The "pix" of Wilding are by John Delacour and the cover "art" by SSSSSharp! The last named is Martin Sharp (1942-), a major painter, illustrator, and cartoonist. Wilding wanted him to do the design because he had illustrated the story "The Vampire's Assistant at the 157 Steps" when it appeared in the *Sydney Morning Herald* (Email "Re: Axel," May 10, 2011). Sharp's long career includes covers, illustrations, and cartoons for the magazine *Oz*; album covers for groups like Cream; co-authorship of a famous Cream song, "Tales of Brave Ulysses"; posters for rock icons like Bob Dylan, Donavan, and Jimi Hendrix; and a film about Tiny Tim. All the visual elements of the cover's front and back contribute to the meaning of the title, Wilding's "scenic drive" through contemporary culture.

Wilding intended originally to dedicate the book to Pat Woolley, friend and co-publisher of Wild & Woolley, but Pat declined "on the ground she was the publisher" (Email "Scenic Drive," March 20, 2011). He then dedicated it to Colin Talbot, a good friend of his in that era. Talbot was one of the people who started Outback Press in Melbourne at the same time as Wild & Woolley in Sydney. Talbot published a couple of novels, wrote new journalism essays, and eventually, from Wilding's perspective, "vanished." Wilding considered him "a very talented writer" (Email "Scenic Drive," March 20, 2011). It was not until 2012 that they made contact again.

Multiple strands of intention mark the plan and execution of *Scenic Drive*.

One strand, as Wilding has recently explained, was "part of my exploration of the literary life. Inez Baranay [a novelist friend] remembers my recommending she read *Lost Illusions* back then. And I recall her visiting the house of the 157 steps. So I had been reading Balzac. So I was clearly exploring the interrelationship of literature, commercial publishing, the market place, sex & so on" (Email "SD further," March 21, 2011).

Regarding the literary scene, he also "wanted to explore the continuity between the high end glossy women's magazines coming out then, and the sleazy end inhabited by Dexter of the girlie magazines, the performance art and avant-garde sexual themes of art and movies at one acceptable end, and the vampire vamp porn at the other, & ask, what if any are the differences? What are our values, art, hypocrisy &c" (Email "SD further," March 21, 2011). Such explorations led him in turn to question which markets were available for these stories, and he points out that "the publication history of the episodes in SD enact the theme —everything from the reputable newspapers—Sydney Morning Herald and National Times and Nation Review to the commercial magazine about sex, Forum, through the respectable lit quarterlies like Southerly and Stand, to the avant-garde mags like Krausmann's Aspect, and the ephemeral Dodo" (Email "SD further," March 21, 2011).

Although "my magazine lady" is a recurring figure in the novel, none of the women's magazines printed any of the stories. Wilding, however, had had some previous success in being noticed by those magazines. *Vogue Australia* ran an excerpt from *The Short Story Embassy* in 1975, and *Cleo* carried Elisabeth Wynhausen's interview, "Wild Man of Letters," also in 1975. That same year he was selected as a *Cosmopolitan* Bachelor of the Month. And the year before, Jan Meek, in *Vogue Australia*, had reviewed his novel *Living Together*. "Wilding's pen is sharp as a rapier." As for the women's magazines, those were the good days, but by 1976 things were changing. Says Wilding, "Those days are now historical. Women's magazines don't mess with writers any more—we're no longer on the agenda" (Email, "SD further," March 21, 2011). Especially, one must add, male writers.

The magazine ladies conveyed a particular sexual charge, in Wilding's view: "So the magazine ladies were part of the milieu I was inhabiting, exploring, thinking about and fantasizing about—the journalistic young ladies emanated a pervasive sexuality. Or I thought they did" (Email "SD further," March 21, 2011).

To Wilding, there was a particularly Australian element as well, in the wide range of possible publishing venues compared to Great Britain. Recently, he summed up the aura of freedom that animated that period:

"This was all interesting, too, in that the UK tradition I came from had a hierarchy of values, deemed to be exclusive. So to publish fiction across the board from lit quarterlies through women's mags through girlie mags through avant-garde and alternative papers was something new, something taboo breaking &c &c" (Email "SD further," March 21, 2011).

The fluidity of the literary marketplace found a corollary for Wilding in his interest in an immediately responsive prose. He has explained his intentions regarding his aims in writing Scenic Drive:

> ...while on the socio-political side I was exploring the sociology of the literary publishing magazine worlds, on the aesthetic side I was also practicing spontaneous writing. I had no overall plan for SD. Just sat down and wrote each morning, as with SSE. Later I shaped, edited and reordered the material. But it wasn't written sequentially. Though I put it into a sort of chronological order so it could read like a novel or a narrative. So I would write bits of dialogue, bits of narrative, sometimes full episodes, sometimes fragments I would glue together later into blocks that looked like episodes. But in fact it doesn't matter which order the stories are read in. Out of this spontaneity came fantasies, alternative versions, speculative versions about what might have happened, what could have happened, what might happen. So the narratives shift from reportage, actuality, into speculation and fantasy, and back again. (Email "SD further," March 21, 2011)

For a reader coming to Scenic Drive in the natural progression of Wilding's work, following it chronologically, the novel seems both familiar and yet in some ways a bit different, at least in the degree of explicit sexual content. Indeed, a contemporary review of Scenic Drive dismissed the book as "crude masturbatory male chauvinism" (McLaren 64). Wilding would say that the book is "an exploration of sexuality, of course, male sexuality at that" (Email "SD further," March 21, 2001). Like it or not, male sexuality includes masturbatory fantasy. In condemning Wilding for this presumptive breach of correct feeling, there is a double standard at work. In the same period Anne Sexton, the American confessional poet, wrote "The Ballad of the Lonely Masturbator" and received no condemnation at all. Masturbatory fantasy does not automatically mean "male chauvinism." One is biology, the other is ideology. Years later, in the chapter "Libertarianism" in the fictional memoir *Wildest Dreams*, Wilding has Joe wittily say, "In the past when they cleared out writers' desks they found sheafs of unpublished pornography. We publish our pornography. It is realism that is our dirty little secret, ... that is what we try to hide" (61).

The novel opens with a bang. In "My Magazine Lady" an attractive young woman brings photographs for the writer/narrator to comment on: "colour transparencies of naked people in groups of three or five. They were always odd numbers, three or five" (p.7). The photos are suggestive, to say the least. One depicts a naked man sitting on a chair, with a bowl of "small brown objects" (walnuts or feces) beneath him. A second man stands beside him, and together they observe a nude woman lying on her back who seems to be "proffering them"—the small brown objects (8). "Coprophilia" is one of the interpretive remarks that the writer or reader might bring forward. The magazine lady remains neutral throughout, listening, observing, and recording his comments in shorthand.

The narrative moves seamlessly between the mode of interview/commentary and sexual fantasy on the part of the narrator. At one point he imagines himself fondling her with her full consent. He comments on the fantasy, "Defilement, oh defilement. That nervous well-bred voice, that demure manner, that fragile, vulnerable posture, the nice girl who thinks she should be ambitious, who becomes a journalist and spends her life showing quasi-pornographic slides to people whose responses she records" (11). Numerous sexual fantasies and interactions follow as the story moves towards its close. The magazine lady asks him if he can help her secure a quiet room at the university where she can write; her own workplace at the magazine is too noisy. He thinks, "I cannot imagine finding a room in a university for a journalist typing up people's fantasies about pornographic pictures.... All week I sit in my room in the university typing up my fantasies about a journalist showing people pornographic pictures" (13). The rich comedy of Wilding's self-reflexive posture here is characteristic of much of *Scenic Drive*. He continues, "At the end of each thousand words, my quota, I stop writing. At the end of the week I walk across to the post office to post a story to *Sire*. I do not feel I can get that through the official mail" (13-14). Obviously, in the light of Wilding's actual, mostly English-set stories that he published in the girlie mags, he is fictionalizing by implication the erotic content of the story that he sends to *Sire* in this story. In sum, the girlie mags had faded away, to be replaced by women's magazines. The old male chauvinist images of masturbatory desire were displaced by fashionable female pornography, by perversion, by feminist sexuality in all its polymorphous manifestations. Then the males disappeared from the magazines, except as objects of delusion, oppression, and fantasy.

Wilding recalls the actual circumstances of "My Magazine Lady": "The magazine lady—this was a true episode. Can't remember her name. She came with this bizarre project for one of the new glossy women's mags. Looking back on it, she seems more like someone doing psychological tests for the security services. Her alleged article never appeared. Anyway, it gave me an idea for the string of stories, which were like interpretations of objects or photos put before me by her" (Email "Scenic Drive," March 20, 2011). Further, Wilding explains that the motive for the novel came not from surrealism, as one might expect, or from cinema, as one also might suspect, but rather from a "self-referential" conception, a "subtext, or residual text" (Email "Re: Scenic Drive 2," March 21, 2011). He elaborates, "So the idea at one point was all the ensuing stories would be stories created for the Magazine Lady, from those dodgy photos she showed me. Just as with Wildest Dreams the idea was all the stories could be examples of Creative Writing, triggered by the story Creative Writing, which ended up concluding the book. None of these grand narrative ideas was ever quite fulfilled. But they served as jumping off points" (Email "Re: Scenic Drive 2," March 21, 2011).

Only Ken Gelder and Paul Salzman in *The New Diversity: Australian Fiction 1970-88* seem to understand and appreciate the novel's method and objectives: "Indeed, these stories contain their *own* attempts at self analysis, offering...a plurality of questions and positions in a willingness to show how 'open' they *are* (to interpretation). In these stories, analysis becomes psychoanalysis: every (sexual) relationship is not only represented but analysed by Wilding's narrator" (167). Nix the annoying parentheticals, and what they say is essentially correct. Close analysis of every story amplifies and enriches the unfolding experimental narrative.

The second chapter, "Dexter Has Been Sending Me His Books," reintroduces a familiar figure in Wilding's stories. Dexter was based on Ron Smith, an American from New York who edited the girlie mag *Squire* which published Wilding's story "They Might Have Been Brother and Sister" in 1966. Smith and John Baxter collaborated on science fiction stories under the pen name of Martin Loren. Wilding called him Dexter, he has said, "because I found him Sinister, playing on the Latin" (Email "Scenic Drive," March 20, 2011). According to Wilding, Smith "survived in publishing and sex industry fringe—moved to Melbourne, don't know what happened to him" (Email "Scenic Drive," March 20, 2011). In *Scenic Drive* Wilding focuses on another of Smith's activities in that period, writing soft porn narratives with vampire motifs.

The books that Dexter sends the narrator have titles like *2 plus 1=Orgy* and *Headmaster's Wife* (15). (Wilding doesn't remember whether Dexter's titles were real or made up.) Having taken the books to his room, the narrator is chagrined to see that every visitor wants to leaf through them instead of talk "about art and life and sex" (15). Embarrassed, the narrator pulls out copies of magazines to cover them up, but "copies of *Sire* spill out across the carpet. My entire world has become a manifestation of Dexter's handiwork" (15). Dexter has some much harder-core publications that he prefers, such as *Call Girl*, which displays pubic hair, unlike *Sire* which did not. The rest of the story involves us in Dexter's hyper-fantasy mode in which he is starring in his own pornography, in publications like the photo book *Launching Party*, featuring him as a "novelist surrounded by the beautiful of the art world" (18). The book reveals him "covered with books and naked ladies, and a fair smearing of chocolate" (18).

The next entry in fantasyland takes us back to the world of *The Short Story Embassy*. In "The Death of Fiction Cemetery" writers go to the cemetery who are "in deep grief for the recent loss of a story, the barrenness of their current life now" (20). Girls also visit the cemetery, some by means of the "death of fiction freeway" (20), and the girls make the forlorn writers happy by performing acts of fellatio because "The girls know this makes the writers feel fulfilled and significant, givers of status and makers of dreams" (21). Wilding recalls that Kate Jennings "denounced this story in a letter to *Nation Review*" for being male chauvinist, since the 'writer' in the story is a male. And we'd been such friends!" (MW email "further," November 29, 2011).

Not surprisingly, the old rivalry between Wilding and Moorhouse resurfaces in the next chapter, "The Great Past Age of the Girlie Magazines." Looking back retrospectively, Wilding has stated, "The competiveness and mistrust of the Moorhouse relationship is one theme. This was written after our big rift. So I could see things more sharply. Perhaps" (Email "SD further," March 21, 2011). The story begins with a riff very much like the telephone exchange that takes place in "Bye Bye Jack. See You Soon": "I told him I was writing about Dexter. On the phone I would tell him these things. He did not even have to ask them" (22). Instead of Joe, the Moorhouse figure is named J. W. Holmes (Joseph Wendel Holmes) throughout *Scenic Drive*. The reason, apparently, is to present Joe as a kind of businessman of letters—a respectable sounding name instead of the friendly, former friend, Joe, of several stories or Wendel of *The Short Story Embassy*. Hearing the name Dexter, J. W. Holmes urges the narrator to wait a bit, a month perhaps, because he's not yet ready to write about that character. The narrator then defines a version of instant writing similar to that of "Bye Bye Jack. See You Soon":

> For a while we had been writing things not together but in unison. One theory was that with simultaneous composition you both tuned more readily into the psychic vibrations writing about characters always created; we are drawing on the same dynamo, absorbing the same generated electricity from the air; without the need for cables. But energy is not illimitable. I began to suspect somebody had to lose. (22)

The scene shifts from the telephone conversation to a visit by the narrator to J. W. Holmes' domicile. The floor is covered with "back copies of *Sire*, opened at their centre spreads" (23). J. W. Holmes urges the narrator to be careful because these are his file copies. On display are nude photos of the girls who appeared in the magazine. (Everywhere in his stories Wilding uses *Sire* to stand for all of the girlie mags.) J. W. Holmes queries the narrator whether he remembers the various girls. Each has trouble remembering or identifying them. J. W. Holmes then launches into a commentary on the publishing situation at that time: "We were just pimps. We were so desperate to see our stories in print. The literary quarterlies rejected us at every mail" (24). He goes on to illustrate how each of the two friends was a pimp. According to J.W. Holmes, the narrator used his position at the university to offer girls "a big break" (24). And J. W. Holmes does not exempt himself from the charge of pimping: "In despair and self-disgust I would go down to the pub where girls would come up to me and offer me their life stories to write. I did not want stories to write; I had a lifetime of stories already written; I wanted a publisher to accept them" (25). In this story and some others, Wilding gives the Moorhouse figure some of the best and funniest lines. One of the best comic riffs, if one is not reading the story from a politically correct anti-male chauvinist position, appears in J. W. Holmes' reaction to the sheets lying on the floor:

> Those girls you lured out of your lectures are spread over every sex magazine and postcard collection in the world. Eskimos pull themselves off over them in the long winter nights and then

> scrape the semen from the pages and use it for blubber. CIA men trade postcards of them to get diplomats to defect: 'Look at the West. Tits as big as the setting sun. Every night.' They're pedalled round Vatican City where vacationing nuns get this itch of delight thinking what their favourite pupils might have grown up into—little thinking that it is their favourite pupils they pore over by candlelight. (25)

J. W. Holmes would talk to the girls and eventually he would get round to telling them about "this friend who is always looking for models" (26). That friend, of course, is Dexter, and it is Dexter who sleeps with the girls, not Moorhouse or Wilding (at least according to this story). For J.W. Holmes, it's an endless cycle of frustration. The girls tell him their stories, and for him to get Dexter to publish his stories, he has to send Dexter more girls. Or had, to be more accurate; the time of the girlie mags is over, a part of history. J. W. Holmes summarizes his response to that era thus: "What a squalid, seedy, dirty lot of girls. Why do we never see the beautiful women? Why do we lack elegance and volupté? Why are our lives doomed to be spent amongst the squalid and distasteful?" (28). *Volupté* is Moorhouse's signature word and appears throughout his fiction and in conversational remarks into this century. The story ends on a strange yet also familiar note, as J. W. Holmes tells the narrator that recently, he, Holmes, was in a room in the nearby Travelodge motel looking into this very room—this motif of self-surveillance will resurface in a later story in *Scenic Drive*.

The next chapter has a jokey title, "J. W. Holmes' Morning Sickness." Early one morning J. W. Holmes comes to the narrator's domicile to tell him about his experience the evening before. He had sex with a prostitute "who was the exact image of your student friend" (29), who he then identifies as the "literary barmaid." The literary barmaid figures in several Wilding stories, most prominently in "The Girl Behind the Bar is Reading Jack Kerouac," which appears later in *Scenic Drive*, and "Yet Once More," collected in *Reading the Signs* (1984). J. W. Holmes' story leads the narrator to reflect upon the differences between himself and

Holmes: "J. W. Holmes offends me by the transparency of his subconscious motivations. I like ambiguity, I like subtlety, I like a range of levels and interpretations. But the uncertainty Holmes creates is the simple uncertainty of not telling the truth" (30).

Next the narrator speculates that J. W. Holmes' goal is to convince the narrator to have sex with the prostitute/literary barmaid: "Then we would be sharing the same woman, whoever she might turn out to be. This is something that has been appealing to him ever since he read the life of Jack Kerouac and found Kerouac shared his women with Neal Cassady. Or vice versa" (30). The narrator sums up J. W. Holmes' view of women: "I know Holmes thinks that all barmaids are prostitutes; just as he believes all women journalists, all women models, all women writers are. But he knows I do not accept most of his world picture" (30). The story continues open-ended, unresolved. Holmes tells the narrator that he suggested that the girl write a story about prostitutes and their clients, a ploy that the narrator believes, if true, is intended to "get his name into the magazine for more PR" (30). Finally, at the end, J. W. Holmes says that the reason he came by so early in the morning was in the hope of finding the literary barmaid at the narrator's residence so that he would know that the girl the night before had been a double or her sister. Told that she did not spend the night there, Holmes replies, "Then it could have been her after all. What do you make of that?" (31). At some point in their relationship, everything became a game, it seems, between the two writers.

"Her Most Bizarre Sexual Experience" is one page long. Wilding reprinted the story in his 1991 collection, published in England as *Grand Climate* and in America as *Her Most Bizarre Sexual Experience*. The narrator, taking his lead from a magazine he's looking at "in which eight men and women describe their most bizarre sexual experience" (32), asks the host of the party he's attending what her most bizarre sexual experience was. She recalls that when she was a schoolgirl she was invited to a house by a woman who did all sorts of erotic things: "I only watched.

It was only voyeurism" (32). Then she mentions a second incident that happened at a cocktail party—two women making out while the party swirled around them. Again her experience was voyeuristic. But the irony of the title is borne out in what happens in the second paragraph of this six paragraph story: while she is responding to the narrator's question, her husband is in the kitchen with his girlfriend, and the paragraph ends with this bit of bizarre sexual experience: "She has asked her husband and his girlfriend to stay there the night so she won't be left alone." The story ends on a suggestive note: "'You're looking very well,' she said, 'very together'" (32).

"A Night at the Orgy" is another comic tale based on a reversal of one's expectations, especially those of feminist critics. It is, Wilding has stated, "fiction," "though [it] draws on my interrogation of an individual who shall remain nameless, about her experiences at such an event, and her evasions (four or five)" (Email "further on JWH," April 28, 2011). The narrator, as is often the case in this novel, plays off of J. W. Holmes: "Ever since J. W. Holmes couldn't get a grant to go to Vietnam to write an action novel I have been thinking of nearer fields of action to go to" (33). The narrator's field of action is an orgy—peace not war—and he decides to attend an orgy and realizes that he needs a partner, that one can't attend orgies alone. When he talks to the magazine lady about his intentions, she volunteers to go with him to gather material for a story. The story then jumps to the early morning when the narrator and the magazine lady decide to leave. Part of the joke is that the narrator did not take part in the orgy, but the magazine lady did—repeatedly. Instead the narrator spent his time at the orgy talking to people, after which he would go outside into the garden and write down what they had said. This is a very briefly delayed version of instant writing and offers another insight into Wilding's sociological curiosity regarding the behavior and motivation of his characters drawn from the life around him.

## Post-Modernism in High Gear 153

As they drive away from the party, the magazine lady is eager to recount her experiences of having had sex with four or five people at the orgy. The one she mentions the most is another writer who was gathering data on Vietnam Rose, a term from the late 1960s. Vietnam Rose refers to an urban legend, a deadly STD that was thought to be spread by Vietnamese prostitutes and was believed to constitute a severe threat to soldiers in Vietnam. It was also called the Black Pox. Neither term has any medical standing. (The Straight Dope: Fighting Ignorance Since 1973—It's Taking Longer Than We Thought). The writer asked her to mention his name to the narrator (though the story does not divulge who the writer is). But the reader, remembering the reference to J.W. Holmes and Vietnam in the story's opening, would be warranted in guessing that the writer who took part in the orgy is in fact JWH. Wilding confirms this assumption in his account of the story's origins: "But JWH's researches here draw on an event related in "Mateship" in *Wildest Dreams*, p. 58, where Joe aka Moorhouse or Whoremouse, after the event narrated, started to create anxieties in my mind about Vietnam Rose" (Email "further on JWH," April 28, 2011).

After reporting this, the magazine lady remarks in a put-down of writers: "You're all much better talking about sex than doing it" (36). She mentions two other figures who participated in the orgy: the ubiquitous Dexter and "some bikie," a figure who achieved fame from a "pack rape case" and who wrote a memoir about it that he sold to a newspaper, and who plans to relate his experiences at the orgy to a ghost writer. Everything is grist for everybody's writing mill. At the end of the drive to her place, she invites the narrator to have sex with her, but he declines. Attacks on this novel as a male masturbatory fantasy do not account for the female gender of sex and desire in stories such as this one.

The recurring character Dexter gets a story of his own in "The Vampire's Assistant at the 157 Steps." In the story Dexter calls the narrator and asks him to find a girl to pose for *Vampire Vamp*. His requirements are that she "has to be beautiful and look like a vampire" (37), and she also has to have "a certain sort of teeth" (37). The narrator immediately thinks of "Valda," but, he says, "I didn't want her tits and cunt exposed to any more men. There were some books I would prefer to close. Not reissued in runs of 10,000 copies" (37). Dexter's next request is a place to stay while he completes *Vampire Vamp*. The narrator invites him to his house, and the troubles multiply. There aren't enough bed clothes to go around, and when the narrator gives half of his to Dexter, then the narrator is cold. He remembers that things were no better in Valda's house. He was always cold there, and her bed "sloped to one side," though she denied anything being wrong with her bed (38). Faith, another girl friend of that period, offered nothing better in the way of sleeping conditions either. She slept with her windows open because of asthma, and it was freezing at her place. Faith, incidentally, was based on Elizabeth Fulton, an editor for Angus and Robertson publishers. She also appears, though not by name, in the story "Bye Bye Jack. See You Soon." (Email "SD further," March 21, 2011).

But such discomforts are nothing compared to the nocturnal disruptions of having Dexter underfoot. Dexter, as would be expected of a vampire's assistant, is up all hours of the night, and his entrances and exits are fraught with peril. Wilding describes the house in some detail: "The timber frame house is at the bottom of 157 steps, surrounded by eucalypts. Another 157 steps further is the water of the bay. The cliff face is nearly vertical" (p. 39). According to Wilding, "the house was in Seaforth, upper reaches of Middle Harbour, just by the Spit Bridge" (MW email "Scenic Drive," March 20, 2011). A bit later he provides an even fuller description of the site, tracing its sociological origins from a suburb that offered "a place for weekenders" to a bypassed and decaying area where the house is located, a prefabricated fibro: "Like a Mayan temple overgrown in the jungle, it is a monument to a creed; it is a statue to loss of faith" (43). The narrator is fearful of all sorts of disasters, death from fire set by Dexter's carelessness, death from electric cables strung up the side of the cliff, death from the cliff itself, from falling off the 157 steps to the Harbour waters. With Dexter there is always a new problem, the latest being an old commode that he has found and that he wants to use in his newest vampire project, *Garbo Girl*. The story ends with the narrator in a state of anxiety: "I wish he would go soon. I am afraid the neighbours will burn the house down if they work out he is living here. We are such natural suspects, such natural victims. The next morning I find that someone has shitted at the top of the steps, and the commode has gone altogether" (45).

Brian Kiernan thought enough of this story to include it in his anthology, *The Most Beautiful Lies* (1977). He states that it represents "something very characteristic of his [Wilding's] fiction as a whole" (207). Kiernan identifies those typical features as "its bemused narrator and its entertainment of his fantasies and fears" (207). Certainly living with Dexter is no fun except in comic retrospect. Finally, writes Kiernan, "Also characteristic is the openness of the story, which conveys the essential openness of Wilding's fiction to new experience and to new forms in which to express it" (207). All of these points are true, and true also is the wry comic sense that pervades many of Wilding's stories. The other point to make is how nervous and often chaste the male narrator is, how often in the stories of *Scenic Drive* sex is anything but the triumphant progress of one conquest after another, as Wilding's misguided Feminist and Post-Feminist critics (male and female) would have it. Often there is no conquest at all, and often in this book it is the women who are the aggressors.

"Reading Axel's Art Book" is another scenic trip into the world of writing, photography, and film. Axel is based on Aleks Danko, a conceptual artist friend of Pat Woolley's. It was he who repainted a used Honda van for Wilding and Pat Woolley's publishing firm in bright red with graffiti on the sides and a Milton quotation for literary effect. According to Wilding, it garnered them mention in the *Sydney Morning Herald* and possibly even sold a few books (*Wild & Woolley* 97).

What might appear to be satirical exaggeration in the novel is actually very close to the facts of conceptual art during that period. In his recent history of Wild & Woolley, Wilding begins by recounting a quintessential scene from the performance art world:

> I met Pat Woolley at a performance event in Bay Street, Broadway, one of those performances where the performers took off their upper garments and exchanged them with each other, so there were bare breasts along with the changing and singing, which in 1973 was considered the height of the avant-garde. Robyn Ravlich and Aleks Danko presented a piece called "The Path of Poetry" and Tim Burns filled up the stairway with Styrofoam. People had to crawl over it to get to downstairs. (1)

Another example of Danko's performance art is "Day to Day," an event that was staged at the Central Street Gallery, 1 Central Street, Sydney, in 1974. In this one Danko was gagged, blindfolded, and tied to a chair while holding a stopwatch. Recently his work has focused on his mother's embroidered cushions.

"Reading Axel's Art Book" is of course more about the narrator than about Axel. As usual, the narrator is busy doing extra-literary things instead of writing. He has recently gone on a radio show to talk about "the new novel" (46). On the show they talked about the old novel as well, and Wilding lists fifteen writers who were brought up for discussion, from George Eliot and Dickens to Robbe-Grillet and Richard Brautigan and Morris West (the latter of whom lived in Sydney and whom Wilding knew). The narrator tells J.W.H. that "living the literary life is much pleasanter than actually writing" (46). On the day of the story he has to read Axel's latest book and he hopes that it is pornographic like the previous one was, and the next day he has to appear "as a voyeur in an art class in a film" (46). Wilding seems to be poking fun at all the mixed media aspects of experimental writing in the 60s and 70s. He remembers how a pornographic experience led to excited sexual coupling and then recalls the larger context of the event: "It was an art show. We read our stories. Our innermost sexual anxieties, our most hurtful intimacies. Ra-ra. How the applause rang out. More wine. More dope. Most intimate revelations. Ra-ra. Robert Z. reads a poem about the female person of my story" (47). Robert Z. is Robert Adamson, poet and long-time friend of Wilding. The "female person of my story" is Valda (Vicki Viidikas). Her presence haunts much of Wilding's fiction in the mid-1970s.

Sexual anxieties, hurtful intimacies, deeply personal revelations—these phrases offer an excellent summary of Wilding's concerns in this collection and in many of his stories. Such themes and disclosures are hardly the stuff of male bravado and sexual trophy-hunting. Feminists need to reread—or read—Wilding's fiction before they thoughtlessly attack him for being a male chauvinist. He is far more with-rue-my-heart-is-laden than gather-ye-rose-buds-while-ye-may. There are more sexual failures in Wilding's fiction than there are conquests.

The story veers off from pornographic imagery (tits, cunts) to another meditation on writing and the cemetery where "All fiction lies buried there" (48). For Axel's current book is not pornographic at all. Instead it is an experimental text combining the techniques of instant writing with photography: "It is a book of which he writes a page every day; plus a picture" (48). On bad days "he writes how he can think of nothing to write" (48). In a way he is something of a mirror image, a doppelganger of the narrator: "I half expect him to say he has no time to write or take photographs because today he has to read a novel" (48). The story ends with both writers lost in the death of fiction cemetery: "We feel, but do not know what we feel; whether we run against nothing and the pain is the constant pain of life or death; or whether we are pressed against granite fog and tombs and are pained from that" (48-49).

"Bikie's Moll" brings J. W. Holmes and the narrator into contact with a bikie and his girl friend at a pub that both writers and bikies frequent. The writers are excited at being so close to a subculture that has been making the news. The narrator, as usual, is looking for story material:

> I know the bikie has just been acquitted on a pack rape charge [gang rape in American parlance]. I would like to talk to him

> about it. The pack rape, not the acquittal. I would like to win his confidence so that he would admit me to their brotherhood and to rites that I could write about, the inside story of onions, gang-bangs, pack rapes, drinking menstrual blood from petrol cans, taking part in battles with rival gangs and capturing their slave women and doing our will with them on deserted beaches, on sunny heathlands, in the steamy valleys of tropical rainforests. (51)

When the bikie's moll asks them what they do, they're excited to say they are writers. The narrator identifies his friend as "J.W. Holmes the pornographer" followed by Holmes' demurrer: "Writing stories for *Sire* is not true pornography" (51). The girl announces that she has always wanted to meet a pornographer and then goes on to state that what she really wants to do is to get into live "sex shows" (52). J.W. Holmes says he knows a great deal about "Mr. Sin," a figure who is behind such sex businesses. The story trails off with the bikie girl being entranced by J.W. Holmes' presumptive familiarity with a sexual underground that he actually knows nothing about.

The next story, "She Wanted to Write So She Did What Was Wrong," opens with a familiar figure, Dexter, coming into a pub to meet the narrator. The barmaid is the reason he and Dexter are meeting in this particular pub. "I have been thinking about her for some time now," the narrator observes (54). She will appear in several subsequent Wilding stories. Dexter has brought along his latest pictures, and they reveal the magazine lady engaged in sex with a rock and roll singer and then with another woman. Once again in these stories the women are engaged in pornography and group sex while the "male chauvinists" are onlookers. Meantime, the literary barmaid suggests that Dexter's next book should be about "young women writers" (56). Dexter, however, is skeptical that there are "any attractive young women writers" (56), whereupon the barmaid announces that she is a woman writer and, bending over to get something from behind the bar, exposes her breasts for Dexter's delectation. He gives her his business card and she gives him a sheaf of manuscripts titled SHE WANTED TO WRITE SO SHE DID WHAT WAS WRONG (56). The story ends with the narrator repeating his interest in the attractive barmaid.

"You Will Come Back to Us" takes us away from the exclusive focus on Australia, back to Wilding's England, back to his younger days there. The story opens with a woman assuming that the narrator is an atheist. He is unwilling to say yes and flashes back to a memory of being in a pub next to a graveyard. In the pub a vicar told him, "you will come back to us" (57). Then the scene shifts to the death of fiction cemetery where "gravestones mark the end of narratives" (57). The narrator resumes his dialogue with the woman at the pub who wants to know where the church was, and he tells her that she just wants "to look at slides of the Church of the Martydom of Short Story Writer and the dungeon of the literary police" (58). Then he begins to question her about her own childhood in England, and bit by bit she tells of her posh schoolgirl background and of the working class boys who she let "feel [her] up along the riverbank" (58). She apparently enjoys recalling those Sunday mornings of adolescent lust and forbidden fondling: "I was as clay in their hands" (59). The story has a very strange and haunting ending. The narrator recalls that "This was the river the Danes came up, harrying the citizens, who took refuge on an island in a marsh" (59). He goes on to recall the legend: "They came for the danegeld, and the citizens caught one of the taxgatherers and flayed him alive, and nailed his skin on the Cathedral door" (59). Noting that this event occurred in 1049, the narrative shifts to a passage from Old English: "Her let harthacnut hergian call Wihracest'scire, for his twegra hus thingon the the strange gyld budon. Tha sloh the fole hi binnan port. Innan tham mynstre" (59). In a translation of this passage from the *Anglo-Saxon Chronicle* by medievalist scholar Mary Blockley, the text reads: "In this year Harthacnut allowing the harrying of all Worschestershire for the sake of the affair of his two house carls [personal elite household corps] who collected the severe tax. The [English] people slew them [the two Danes] inside the door, within the church." Wilding has stated, "I remember a showcase in Worcester

Catherdral with some of the skin, like parchment. No doubt it's no longer on display (Email "Some Further Minor Corrections," July 31, 2012). By using this incident of political revolt from the 11$^{th}$ century in his native Worcester, Wilding seems to be drawing a parallel about class structure and power still evident in the U.K. when he was growing up.

The quiet classicism of this story contrasts sharply with "J.W.H.'s Zoo Story," one of the most surrealistic pieces in the collection. It begins, "J.W. Holmes beats out an assignation on his typewriter. He is taking my magazine lady to the zoo for her to write a feature story" (60). The verb in the first sentence suggests a masturbatory fantasy. In any event the incidents in the story are fantastical. At the aviary Soviet spies are transacting business with high ranking public officials while CIA agents and secret service men observe birds, "Beautiful Mata Haries... their mascara'd eyes fluttering, their breasts slipping out of their fur coats" (60). At the kangaroo enclosure J.W.H. tells the magazine lady that "Henry Miller said the kangaroo had a double penis, one for weekdays and one for the weekends" (61). At the same time a group of college professors from Boston arrive to see the kangaroos:

> 'On page eleven of the local Panther edition of *Tropic of Cancer* there is this interesting reference,' their convenor addresses them. He has a loud hailer [portable loudspeaker] and an identity badge. He is identified as coming from subsection WL 901 of the MLA annual convention, American literature at large charter travel group. (61)

The story is one of Wilding writing Holmes/Moorhouse in a particular kind of way. In the next sequence J.W.H. is taking down the experience as fast as he can, but with a certain ambivalence. At the camel enclosure, for example, the magazine lady says she has "never been screwed by an Australian camel," which causes J.W.H. to ponder "whether the emphasis is on Australian or camel. It remains an ambiguity that will always distress him" (p. 61). Now models, nude models appear, along with a photographer who asks J.W.H. if he would like "to stand in for Rudolph

Valentino would you, dearie?" (61). To this offer by the gay photographer, "He finds himself blushing and his prick growing hard" (61). The ambiguity of which excites him more, the photographer or the models, remains. At the tortoise pen more comic banter ensues as J.W.H. tells her of something that Thomas Browne wrote about the copulation of tortoises and adds that one of the tortoises is 200 years old and was Captain Cook's pet. The next sentence states jokily: "Carved on top of its shell is 'Cook this side up" (62). At the vampire bat case, not surprisingly perhaps, they see Dexter and a vampire bat engaged in amorous foreplay, with the bat sucking at Dexter's throat through the glass.

The story ends with the usual competition, resentment, and one-up-man-ship that characterizes the Holmes/narrator relationship throughout *Scenic Drive*. The narrator charges: "I refuse to accept any more. Holmes has stolen information that I have over the years acquired in the academy he so despises. He has also stolen my magazine lady. He has adapted events and phrases from my own stories" (62). One obvious example of such borrowing is the reference to Sir Thomas Browne. The narrator makes this obvious in this further elaboration: "I could do much better with her alone in my room. Sir Thomas Browne, Henry Miller and myself accessible on the shelves, my Durer engraving of a rhinoceros on the wall, my carved Indian elephant on my desk, and the stuffed swordfish hanging from the ceiling" (62-63). The next sentence ties this story together with the previous one: "One day she will come back to me there," recalling what the vicar had said (63). As for the magazine lady, Holmes claimed to be as shocked as the narrator is. He had thought, he says, that the magazine lady was his alone. The story concludes with Holmes observing: "I found it all a fascinating display of your disturbed inner life. If I had known there was any truth in your talk of her, we could all have gone to the zoo together" (63). This story is probably, narratively, the most complex one in the collection. At times it is impossible to tell who is narrating and whether we are in a Holmes story or a narrator's story, or both.

"This Evening I Take Part in a Film" offers a complex commentary on filming, fantasizing, and writing. The narrator has been invited to be in a women's film: "I cannot think why around the concept of a women's film hovers hopefully the idea of a pornographic film. It is quite unjustified, I know. As well as being unreconstructed sexism" (64). The narrator's reference to sexism shows that Wilding is well aware of the new context for thinking about sex. There is always that dangerous possibility that sex = sexism, the new paradigm of the women's movement. The role they want him to play is a voyeur, "A perv in an art class, as we put it" (64). The model in the film is someone he has wanted to have sex with for a long time, so that the offer is a definite fantasy plus. The plan calls for the model to be an "object" while twenty male onlookers look at her. "What the film is to ask" is what the fantasies of the objectified model are (64). Naturally enough, the narrator's first thoughts are that she is fantasizing about having sex with each of the different men, and then he concentrates on the possibility of his having a relationship with her. All of this is prelude to the evening; these are all preliminary fantasies and thoughts of fantasies. But the narrator becomes anxious at being cast as a voyeur and recalls that he himself has already made a film about a voyeur, an exhibitionist, and that the film "treated him well" (65). Obviously this is a reference to Wilding's own film "The Phallic Forest" which had produced public outrage in Melbourne when it played there. He imagines various forms of perversity and thinks comically of Dexter: "Dexter, for instance, he would have an erection at the first sight of bondage" (66). Then he has a darker vision: what if her fantasies are physically aggressive, what if they involve mutilation of the male sexual anatomy. His worst fear is of mutilation, even death: "Then they would produce the knives. This is all in the cause of art; we are filming in the Fine Arts Workshop where the usual inhabitants are heavily into the cause of art, everything modern, everything conceptual, like Axel's book" (66). Then, in turn, he thinks of the worst-case scenario, a Dutch conceptualist who sliced his penis into pieces and died as a result of blood loss. (Incidentally, searching the

Internet for information on this topic can result in extreme anxiety and horror.)

A headline in bold print introduces the next section, **Now for the instant writing bit.** In this self-reflexive riff, Wilding comments at length on the problem of instantaneous writing:

> The difficulty of writing this is of someone reading what you're writing. That suddenly emerges as the major inhibition. The need to write in the closed room. In the closed room I can sit naked at the typewriter. Yet here she sits naked before the desks, the easel desks. What does that tell us? The room full of naked men sketching the clothed model: someone has already suggested that to me, the old cartoon. If I don't paragraph no one will be able to pick out the major points. It will be like a medieval manuscript, all run along line after line, poetry or prose all written solid to economise on the parchment. The point, anyway: this doesn't look like being the great pornographic experience I predicted this morning. But if it were how could I be writing this at the same time? Already I have looked for five minutes at this paper, following my pen. (66)

The writer's difficulty is further dramatized in his speculation about how to use the time to the best purpose: "To write down the ideas that well up. May well up. Or to look at the novel. The model. How interesting: a genuine Freudian slip. The model asks do we want a different pose. Axel says he doesn't care, he's making up fantasies here" (67). The narrator/writer continues to ponder the ontology of instant writing:

> I wonder what of what is happening I write down; what I select. Out of that infinity of other things going on. If we could find a total film of the events. And correlate the things I miss, exclude. A total inventory of events listed. And a tick against the ones I include. The minority. The difference between events and writing speed is large. Possibly not infinite. But very large. (68)

Thus the impossibility of matching instant by instant what is happening with what one is writing in the (doomed) process of instant writing. Still the results can be exhilarating as evidenced throughout this novel and in many of Wilding's stories. Further on there is a post-commentary on the instant writing phenomenon: "That was the instant writing bit, unrevised, unprocessed, unfulfilled. More happens than can be written, and less happens that I would write. Back to the naked mornings at the typewriter now. Fantasy recollected in tranquility" (p. 68). Here Wilding, as in "Bye Bye Jack. See You Soon," recasts Wordsworth's famous definition of poetry. Immediately we are plunged back into the ongoing fantasy and it reaches its climax, literally, when the model and the narrator "screw there while they load more film in the camera. We have to have a very quiet orgasm, so as not to draw too much attentions to ourselves" (69). The model returns to her station—a couch—and engages in sexual self-play, leading the narrator to comment, "Sometimes, I feel, the directors of this film are not concentrating on the most interesting material. I watch her to see what sort of orgasm she will have on the couch there" (69).

The story ends with the narrator and the model spending some time together watching television and talking and the model tells him "about the stories she is writing" (69). Which is funny: everybody, it seems, is a writer or about to be a writer. He drives her to her home and thinks about making sexual advances but then considers it absurd because he has been looking at her breasts for at least five hours. In another funny bit, after she goes into her house, he drives "the twenty yards up the street back home" and the story ends (69). It ends on page 69. Whether this is an accident or not is part of an ongoing low-grade mystery.

"Business Lunch" begins with J. W. Holmes calling the narrator to express anger at a "situation of embarrassment" caused by the narrator. This comic story is divided into four headline sections. **What happened** tells how the magazine lady invited JWH to lunch to discuss the promotion of a new book of his and JWH in turn invited the narrator to join them: "So I went along and had lunch and then dipped out. I found her insufferable and why should I help him promote his new book anyway?" (70). When he left, he said he would leave them together and JWH interpreted this as code for an opportunity for him to have sex with the magazine lady. **What happened next** recounts what happened next. The magazine lady invited JWH to have a drink at her place, and once there, he kissed her only to be rejected when she asked him, "Affection" and he said "Just sex" (71). She tells him to leave and he does, first trying to exit through a storage cupboard. **Happy ending** finds him finally out of the building, but in the basement parking garage where, here's the happy part, she's waiting for him. "I love that coarse honesty," she says, placing his hand on her breast. They talk about whether to have sex on the concrete floor or on a car. He points to a Falcon panel van but she considers it "too vulgar" and selects instead a Mercedes convertible. **So what's he so unhappy about?** concludes the story in three sentences: "I send him the happy ending to cheer him up. I like thinking of happy things for him. Maybe she'll promote him in *Modern Auto*" (72).

One of the most transportable stories in *Scenic Drive,* that is, one that is less dependent on the specific context of the novel, is the comic sexual fantasy titled "The Girl Behind the Bar is Reading Jack Kerouac," which is also the first sentence of the story. The literary barmaid has appeared earlier in *Scenic Drive,* but here she is the center of the story. The narrator considers the Kerouac book "an omen" and tries to strike up a conversation. He asks her what time she gets off, but she says that she never gets off, "She is a writer. A writer's work is never done," playing off the familiar line "A woman's work is never done" (73). She tells the narrator that she needs "someone to look over her stories" and give her "advice on the markets" (73). So they go to her place and lie on the bed and talk while he looks over her stories. The first one is "about a girl working in a bar and being picked up by a man" (73). The second story is more complicated. The barmaid meets a Scandinavian and they have sex and then one day when he comes back into the bar with another girl, he tells her that the barmaid is a writer and the barmaid is ecstatic at being so defined. The narrator tells her he likes the irony and eroticism of that story and says that's hard to do and she says "it's not really hard" and undresses and they have sex. The next story is a very clever bit about a girl who went to a seminar on writing and had sex with each of the panelists: "The story related their different screwing patterns to their different writing styles" (74). The narrator wants to take a coffee break or something, but the girl is insatiable and forces him to read another story; this one is about a girl who is so busy writing that she doesn't have time for sex but pleasures herself with bananas, etc. because she has a strong sex drive. Then she picks up a banana and begins to enact the story. This excites the narrator, and in fact the next story the narrator reads is about a "jaded writer" who can only become aroused by watching a woman pleasure herself like the one in the story that he just read. He and the barmaid have sex again, and she showers and dresses and prepares to go to work at the bar and upon leaving him there, gives him a story to read: "It was about how this man kept coming into the pub where this girl worked and kept talking about writing and eyeing off her tits so one day she took him back to her place and showed him her stories and they re-enacted the fucks in them all afternoon till she had to go back to work" (75). The story goes on to recount her departure and then details the erotic pleasure the man enjoys just thinking about her being eyed by the other men in the bar, which leads to the narrator-in-the-story masturbating and drifting off to sleep.

The last paragraph of the story depicts the girl returning and asking, "Have a good time?" and taking off her clothes (75). In a story just two and three quarters pages long, Wilding combines fantasy and narrative complexity with an enviable economy of method, and a great deal of comedy.

"Visiting My Publisher" is the second shortest story in the collection, one paragraph, 3/4s of a page. Whimsical might be the best word to describe it. The narrator visits his publisher at the university press (probably University of Queensland Press in Brisbane). The comedy begins immediately, as the publisher also operates "a fashionable hair-dressing salon" and in this capacity he cuts the writer's hair while wheeling him around the campus where a young writer is waiting to meet the narrator-writer. The story ends with an encounter with a professor from the English university where the writer once taught (probably the University of Birmingham) and a professor from the department where the writer now teaches (University of Sydney). Both professors pass them by "without a smile" (76). The story ends, "The publisher's distribution manager remarks on this chilliness of attitude, though says obviously the English dislike us the most" (76). Here Wilding seems to confirm his identity as an Australian writer.

Of this piece's origins, Wilding has stated, "This was a dream, which I wrote down on waking. Don't often remember my dreams, so rarely get to write them down, thank heavens. But Burroughs and I think Kerouac were into doing this, so I tried doing it too. The publisher was Frank Thompson at UQP, an American and someone who greatly supported my early work" (MW email "comments and corrections," November 28, 2011).

"Our Lady of the Magazines" is a bravura rendition of themes and techniques on display throughout *Scenic Drive*. It opens with the narrator/writer at his desk in a house with a harbor view (water glimpses in Australian argot); he is absorbed in the cover of the magazine that she writes for, a cover of a "naked woman sitting up with her hand on a man's head" (77). He believes that the woman on the cover is the magazine lady and he spends a good deal of time analyzing the details of the photograph to prove his point. The animus against the magazine lady becomes apparent when he says that when he had seen her before, she "seemed almost dowdy" (77). He decides that it is not her small breasts or her hair color but her hand, "lined" and "worn," that gives her away (77). But since only one hand is in the photo, he begins to fantasize about the other hand, whether it is involved in erotic play with herself or with the man in the photo. He comes out of his reverie to the sounds of dogs barking and cruising ships in the harbor, "But for that moment we had been together, my morning quota [of words] has been fulfilled" (78).

In the next section J.W. Holmes phones to tell the narrator that the magazine lady is doing business with Dexter. He elaborates that Dexter and the magazine lady have outfitted themselves in ecclesiastical costumes for Dexter's latest book, *Choirgirl in the Belfry*. He suggests that the narrator would make a good addition to the book: "Then you could have stood in the pulpit and fulminated against the fornication going on beneath you. I think you'd have found that very exciting" (79). The next section reprises a motif running through the collection: the preoccupation of the new women's magazines—supposedly liberated—with celebrity, sexuality, and male fantasy. Looking at a new issue of the magazine lady's magazine, the narrator reads and views a piece that interviewed eight prominent figures in arts and business regarding the way women respond to them. "Joseph Wendel Holmes (Saggitarious) replies that he has never identified with sex heroes like Rudolf Valentino and Clark Gable and women don't respond to him as though he was one" (79-80). The narrator is shocked, he says, at what JWH is not telling him and shocked too at the duplicity of the magazine lady. He imagines a scene in which JWH is staring out of the window of his dwelling while looking at the Travelodge motel (a totemic aspect of modernity associated in other stories with JWH's mode of voyeurism) and talking to the magazine lady. He tells her, "I have been treated as a sex object in numerous encounters with women who don't care how distinguished a writer I am but just want me for sex. I dig that" (80). This quotation is priceless. JWH appropriates one of the talismanic phrases of the women's movement—sex object—and turns it to his advantage; he reveals his vanity as to his presumed status as a writer; and perhaps funniest of all, he borrows Beat idiom, specifically from Jack Kerouac or Kenneth Rexroth (who appears as a major character in Moorhouse's "The American Poet's Visit"). The narrator's comment seals this analysis: "Even his jargon is inauthentic" (80). A few lines later the narrator states, "—and I transcribe his words from the hurtful page beside me, though I can only speculate on the circumstances surrounding his uttering them, 'I mix mainly with women who have achieved things in their own right and who react to my intellect in a comfortable way'" (80). What is the hurtful page? At this late date Wilding cannot recall, though he believes that "if anything it's from an interview rather than a story" (Email "Re: one more SD question," September 13, 2011). Then the narrator imagines in the conditional "would," would the magazine lady have offered herself for cunnilingus? In the imagined act JWH whispers that women sometimes write up such experiences as those they have had with him, but the narrator has the last word: "But I do not know that she thought I would write it up" (81).

The next paragraph continues the ongoing rivalry between the narrator and JWH, certainly a constant concern in virtually every story involving the two characters/authors. The narrator is worried that JWH is gaining advantages with the magazine lady, specifically: "For every horoscope of mine I let them cast, Holmes is asked to reveal his most bizarre sexual experience [thus echoing the title of "Her Most Bizarre Sexual Experience"]. For every list of the ten women in the world I would most like to meet, J.W.H. is asked the ten most appropriate sexual situations in which to eat the following menus" (81). The funniest bit, though, is this exchange: "Sometimes I feel the things they ask of him are more exciting than those they offer me. They phone me for my new year resolutions. 'Do I get to take my clothes off?' I ask. 'We're using the same photograph,' she says" (81). Clearly one writer is advancing thanks to the magazine lady, and the other, the narrator, is not.

The story ends with a mock religious invocation of the power of the magazine lady to influence one's literary future in the marketplace of promotion: "Oh our lady of the magazines, reveal yourself to us, tell us your plan, walk on the still blue waters of the harbour before us, make it all come clear" (82).

"J.W. Holmes Has Installed a Second Phone" is a zany story about J.W.H., Dexter, and the narrator-writer based upon a premise of J.W.H.'s:

"He has read somewhere that in this century you write between phone calls. The tension of awaiting the calls stimulates his writing" (83). Acquiring a second phone, J.W.H has taken to calling everybody who is a writer, and it seems that everybody is, in order to disrupt their writing. And Dexter, always up to something, has installed a telephone answering machine under a woman's name so that he receives thousands of sex calls and plans to make a book of them. When the narrator tries to call J.W. Holmes, both lines are busy. The girl on the telephone switch tells him she can't put him through or cut in on his line because "he's a writer, he mustn't be disturbed" (85). Then the story goes into full fantasy mode, as Dexter, whom the girl knows, cuts into the line and through the use of his new videophone, instructs the telephone girl and the narrator to have virtual sex while Dexter participates pornographically. The story ends with J.W. Holmes knocking on the door, saying he's been unable to reach the narrator all morning and the narrator wishes "he would go away so I could get back to my typewriter" (86).

"Gallery" is another riff on conceptualist art. It begins: "One room of the gallery has nothing but a bed and a girl in it. The walls are flat, white and cold; the floor is concrete. In the middle is this double bed, with a girl lying spread out on it...She has a necklace round her throat, but otherwise she is naked. The necklace enhances her nakedness" (87). The girl is silent: "If she said anything it would no longer be a work of art" (87). The narrator then describes various classic positions that the girl adopts and imagines having sex with her on the basis of reproductions of nudes in paintings from the past, but the story soon devolves into the kinds of pointless debates that go on all the time among those who like a little conceptualist art with their pornography. Topics include model vs. prostitute, replication vs. imitation of reality, etc.: "We argue about art. We argue about the denigration of masturbation" (88). The story ends in a bravura comic move with the gallery owner deciding to expand the exhibition to include the whole gallery:

## Post-Modernism in High Gear    171

> Each room will have a different image from classic and contemporary works of art. Single girls, single boys, double girls, double boys, black and white and red and yellow girls and boys, Modigliani and Rubensesque boys and girls, the three graces, Guernica for the necrophiliacs, bowls of grapes and hanging hares for those who get it off on still life. (89)

In "Four Episodes in the Office of J.W. Holmes" the first episode describes a conversation taking place between J.W.H. and the narrator. They are looking at the city skyline from the room where J.W.H. writes, and J.W.H. describes something that happened the week before. He was in the nearby Travelodge motel looking at his own room observing his typewriter and so on. The narrator picks up the narrative: "Then you saw someone come in through the door, sit down and start writing" (90). Here Wilding is recreating the Travelodge incident of the earlier story "The Great Past Age of the Girlie Magazines." The narrator concludes that he does not believe J.W.H.

**Two** describes J.W. Holmes in a room at the Travelodge motel "writing stories about bikie girls in black leather" (91). Clearly this bit derives from "Bikie's Moll," in which J.W.H., it will be recalled, spent an evening at the pub gathering information about biker culture from the bikie's moll. But the narrator of the present story (who is of course the narrator of "Bikie's Moll" as well) takes exception to J.W.H.'s command of detail: "They drive their motorcycles down unknown bush trails. Doesn't he know you ride motorcycles, you only drive cars?" (91). The narrator also criticizes other details in the J.W.H. story, implying that the story of sex on a motorcycle with the bikie moll is inauthentic. Elements of this story have occurred before, in Moorhouse's "The Oracular Story" and in Wilding's "The Nembutal Story." A cluster of brand name references, Castrol XL motor oil, KY jelly, KB lager, PK chewing gum, and IXL tinned fruit uncannily illustrates the kind of reliance on commercial names to authenticate fiction that would characterize the works of such American writers of the 80s as Bret Easton Ellis and Bobbie Ann Mason. Wilding ends this segment with a zinger: "And ultimately he can abort her in the name of ZPG"—Zero Population Growth (92).

In **Three** the narrator and a girl climb through a window into J.W. Holmes' living quarters. J.W.H. appears in the doorway and, when questioned as to why he hadn't let them in, replies that he wanted to see if they could get in by the window. He immediately leaves. In the morning he fixes breakfast in bed for the narrator and the girl. The narrator explains to the girl J.W.H.'s possible motives: "He could be making breakfast to make us feel guilty for intruding and stopping him getting down to his writing; or he could be making it because he likes us; or he could have run out of things to write and sees some potential material in this situation" (92). While the girl takes a shower, J.W.H. wants to know whether the girl or her sister is the pretty one. The narrator thinks that that's what is always the case, that the one you're not with is prettier than the one you are with. J.W.H. says, "That sounds like the rationalization of failure" (93). When the girl comes out of the shower, the narrator goes in and concludes in the last bit of this section: "No doubt his stories will tell me what they discussed while I was beneath it. Or maybe hers" (93). Once again everybody is a writer and everything can be written about, and most interestingly, the need to write prompts the creation of situations that can be written about. In Wilding's world the short story is progenitive.

In **Four** J. W. Holmes telephones the narrator to come to his office to help with spring-cleaning. J.W.H. is replacing old furniture with new and rearranging things, like putting the refrigerator in the bedroom. He's not going to be using the kitchen anymore because of the messiness it engenders. He wants the place to be like a motel, and the narrator thinks, "Now if you looked in from the Travelodge motel with a pair of binoculars you would think you were looking into an identical suite" (93). J.W.H. gets on the phone and orders liquor. Looking around, J.W.H. concludes that to keep the place really clean any sex in the future will have to be at the girl's place: "I don't want dirty girls coming in here and messing it all up.

Leaving hair and talcum powder everywhere. Staining the sheets. Clogging up the toilet" (94). "Dirty girls," Wilding has explained, is an allusion to Moorhouse's story "The Dirty Girl," which *Stand* magazine published. Wilding includes it in his story because "it could be construed as downright anti-women" (Email "comments and corrections," November 28, 2011). When the phone rings, J.W.H. announces that he has to leave, and the story ends: "We leave the beer cans for the maid to clean up" (94).

The last story in *Scenic Drive* brings all the major characters together: J.W. Holmes, the magazine lady, Dexter, the literary barmaid, and of course the narrator-writer. J.W. Holmes wants the narrator to go with him to the magazine lady's room, and there are literary precedents: "Jack Kerouac and Neal Cassady used to share their women in common" (95). The narrator comments on this idea: "He has been reading literary biography again. He sits in his office with his binoculars beside him, gazing out over the water to the Travelodge motel, reading about Balzac's mistresses, Dickens' second household, Swinburne at the flagellators, Raymond Chandler's cat" (95). The narrator continues with a summary of the deteriorating relationship between himself and J.W.H.:

> There is little trust between J.W. Holmes and me any more. No doubt there never was. We are geared to using these phrases implying process and change; such phrases as 'any more,' 'I have begun to.' We would be truer to our selves if we had only present tenses, we would not be able to express conditionals, we would not be able to speculate on the future, we would not be haunted by the past, we would not be deluded into believing that anything can ever be different. (95)

After musing on the resistance to the present tense by teachers and literary critics, the narrator returns to the unanswered question of J.W.H.'s relationship with the magazine lady; are they having sex or not? The two writers go to her room and the magazine lady is "dubious at J.W.H.'s proposal" (96). She says she is not the person he wants, but that her sister might be, although her sister is not here. J.W.H. tells her to "dress up in her clothes and pretend you're her" (97). She returns wearing a see-through negligee and J.W.H. has sex with her first because he doesn't want "to catch any diseases from" the narrator. The narrator watches, feeling like a wallflower; then Dexter pops up, coming out from behind a mirror. He's filming the whole thing, and things get wilder when J.W.H. finishes with the magazine lady: "Later, when it was my turn with the magazine lady, Dexter screwed J.W.H. He set the camera up on a tripod and triggered it by a remote control cable switch. He wanted to use the shots for the gay market, he said" (97).

In the next sequence the writer phones J.W.H. to talk about the episode. J.W.H. says "What episode?" (97) and all the while is typing: "He asks me to repeat one or two phrases in the course of my description" (97) but denies any knowledge of the event although, as he tells the narrator, the story he's working on is about "Group sex" (98). The narrator thinks this is proof, but J.W.H. goes into a long denial/attack on the narrator:

> All I can see is you've been climbing through my window at night again and reading my notes and staining my sheets. You seem to have lost both inspiration and integrity. Dexter tells me you've been pestering him for copies of his dirty picture books; the cheap series. I thought it was just to pull yourself off in front of, but now it seems you're stealing the ideas to write about. You can't get away with that. You steal my group sex material and I'll sue you for plagiarism. (98)

When the narrator replies, "But I was there," J.W.H. tells him he should go on holiday, "take a harbour cruise. Visit the zoo" (p. 98).

When he calls the magazine lady she too asks "What episode?" (98), and when he describes what happened, she thinks he's talking about an article and quickly says it's not appropriate for her magazine. Then she denies everything, and concludes, "It sounds like one of those horrid picture books of that seedy friend of yours" (98). The narrator says it's going to be and she tells him sarcastically that he can "give signed copies to young girls you're trying to impress" (99).

The last section takes place at the pub where the literary barmaid works. Instead of reading Kerouac, this time she is reading a magazine that the narrator believes is the magazine lady's magazine. The cover shows a "naked lady with two naked men" who "look like J.W. Holmes and Dexter" (99). The barmaid grows irritated at his looking at the cover of the magazine she's engrossed in. He says "Hello" and she signals for the bouncer (99). She tells the bouncer that he is "annoying" her, and the narrator says in defense, "But I know her" and she "shakes her head" (99). "And your sister," he adds, but the bouncer says, "She doesn't have a sister, buster" (99). When the narrator tries to explain, "He throws me out on to the concrete pavement gleaming in the harsh sun" (99). Thus ends the story and the book.

But Wilding was not through with the literary barmaid character, nor with Wendel. In "Yet Once More," collected in *Reading the Signs* (1984), the narrator receives a phone call from Wendel asking him if he wants to have a drink and meet his new "girl friend from the west" (108). The girl from the West was Fiona Giles, daughter of a West Australian Senator. Giles and Moorhouse had a relationship that he chronicled in *Forty-Seventeen*. She went on to become a feminist, author, and teacher. Her books include *Dick for a Day* and *Fresh Milk: The Secret Life of Breasts*. Wilding recalls the only time he met her: "Frank was on with her when he lived in Oxford in 1981. I never did get around to seeing them then. But we did have this one meeting in Sydney. Red-haired. He had a thing about red-heads" (Email "questions," November 14, 2010).

The rift between the two writers is much on the narrator's mind: "Wendel hasn't phoned me to have a drink for five years. For eighteen months there has been a slight demilitarization, a slow process, with cautious surveillance" (108). The narrator makes his way to Wendel's dwelling, a house (probably in Balmain) with a huge tree in front that "We used to climb up it when the parties required climbing up from" (109). Wendel and the girl are in "his lair" and they both have wet hair, signifying a shower, signifying recent sex. Wendel and the narrator drink beer, then Wendel fixes martinis, his signature drink. Then the three of them decamp for a jazz cellar to continue drinking, but first they stop by the narrator's dwelling so he "can roll a couple of smokes for the road and one for an emergency any emergency" (110). Wendel brings a beer, and neither he nor the girl from the west "smokes"—these are not cigarettes. As they walk several blocks towards their destination, they tell the girl the stories that adhere to each block, going back to the 1890s (Lawson's era), the 1920s, and the 1960s (their own personal historical time and space): "Everywhere is redolent with stories, they leap from windows and beckon from gratings. These are the bars, those the alleys... Stories settle on us like pigeons on a national monument" (110).

Apprehensive, they enter the jazz cellar where the next section begins: "One untold story to explain the apprehension, the true story of the girl at the bar is reading Jack Kerouac" (111). Here the reader feels a satisfying frisson, fulfilling the title "Yet Once More," the opening words of Milton's "Lycidas," so yet once more we are back in the tension-filled world of Wendel and the narrator and the literary barmaid. Wilding also intended the title to project a larger frame of reference: "The phrase 'Yet once more' has a revolutionary ring to it, I think it may come ultimately from Revelations in the Bible. It refers to the Lord throwing down the mighty from their seats of power" (Email "Re: catching up," April 18, 2005). The first paragraph is basically a reprise of the story in *Scenic Drive*. The narrator and the girl talk about books, prompted by the one she's reading, and she announces that she writes and needs advice on where to publish. In the original story, the narrator and the girl go to her apartment and reenact one sexual fantasy after another. In this version, Wendel interrupts the proceedings by coming into the pub and saying they could start a magazine "just to publish you" and "name it after you"—a not so subtle ploy to find out her name (111). Then Wendel moves away to a table, leaving the narrator in the awkward position of remaining at the bar and obviously trying to pick up the barmaid, so he joins Wendel at the table whereupon "Wendel's woman arrives" (112). This is going to be "one of those evenings," the narrator thinks (112). The woman disparages the barmaid, and the narrator defends her by calling her a writer: "'One of those,'" says Wendel's woman" (112).

Then Wendel announces that he is having dinner with "his magazine lady," reprising that recurring figure in the novel (112). This leaves both the narrator and Wendel's woman in a state of frustration. They are to have dinner together, although the woman would rather be with Wendel and the narrator with the literary barmaid or the magazine lady. Indeed, the narrator has to leave the restaurant they have gone to, to return to the bar to retrieve his wallet, and there an older woman protects the literary barmaid from any advances he might make. Now he convinces himself that it will be necessary for him to have sex with Wendel's woman and as he describes it, "We lie on the bed and she says, 'I expect to hear him come breaking through the door any minute.' I don't. Maybe some time in a few days' time. But not right this minute. He doesn't need to, his presence is already with us. We give up" (113).

The narrator adds, "There are other stories that could be told here too but the general point is clear enough without them" (113). And so the story ends with Wendel, the girl from the west, and the narrator leaving the jazz club and walking back to the car. But Wendel disrupts things again when he leaves them to get his mail from the general post office where they pick him up a bit later. The narrator's final summation is one of ambivalence and a muted hopefulness: "It is good that there are still some things unresolved. That will give us the energy to move forward through these times of the emotional plague. Unless they are the constituents of the emotional plague; in which case we will have located them and can begin changing them (114)."

"Yet Once More" attests to the seemingly endless variations upon the Moorhouse-Wilding relationship that Wilding had been exploring since the late 1960s. Structurally, the story is kind of a five-year-later postscript to the events occurring in *Scenic Drive*. After going through *Scenic Drive* story by story, it is useful to recall Wilding's description of the process of its composition quoted earlier in this chapter: "But it wasn't written sequentially. Though I put it into a sort of chronological order so it could read like a novel or a narrative...But in fact it doesn't matter which order the stories are read in. (Email "SD further," March 21, 2011). The novel gains by its arrangement, and a careful reading reveals far more narrative and thematic complexity than has yet been recognized in the meager critical responses to *Scenic Drive*.

## Chapter 6

# Sex and the Single Male

## The Phallic Forest

Published in 1978 by Wild & Woolley, *The Phallic Forest* was an end-of-the-decade response to the censorship struggles of the late 60's and early 70's. Earlier, Ron Smith, editor of the girlie mag *Squire*, had urged Wilding to put together a collection of "so-called Disgusting and Unacceptable Stories" ("Adventurous Spirits" 90), but the project never got off the ground. In 1972 Wilding and Moorhouse had created *Tabloid Story*, a packaged short story magazine to foster new writing, much of which had explicit sexual content and hot-button four-letter words. In retrospect, however, Wilding believes that the whole censorship controversy was something of a side show: "The libertarians focused on taboo words, while substantive issues of political and economic change were displaced from attention...At the time, however, I was swept along in the anti-censorship struggle along with many others ("Adventurous Spirits" 90).

In any event *The Phallic Forest* brought together fourteen stories, most of which had appeared earlier in venues such as the girlie mags, *Tabloid Story*, and other little magazines. All in all it was rather a mixed bag of controversial Australian stories and some English stories and a few that did not fit comfortably into any category. In a way, then, *The Phallic*

*Forest* is Wilding's final fictional word on the censorship wars of the seventies.

In "The Tabloid Story Story," his retrospective overview of the innovative fiction magazine that he and Moorhouse edited, Wilding cited four types of fiction published in *Tabloid Story*. All four, incidentally, were typical of the experimentation going on in Australia and elsewhere during the late 60's and 70's. One was stories by fabulists, represented in the magazine by writers such as Dal Stivens, Rudi Krausmann, and Peter Carey. Wilding himself turned to the fabulist mode on occasion. Second was "the literature of process, fiction interested in, self-conscious of, its own evolution, aware of its generative process..." (305). This category defines a large number of Wilding's stories. Third was "the confessional, revelatory mode—less defined by its manner than by its materials—sexuality, drugs, inner city bohemian life styles, despairs and ecstasies" (305). Here he cited Moorhouse and Vicki Viidikas—two obvious examples. The fourth category was the social realist story, with which he identified Carmel Kelly, Moorhouse, Brian Cole, and himself. In *The Phallic Forest* elements of all of these categories would find their way into the collection.

Promotionally, the book sought to capitalize on the sensational by collecting "stories about sex—the ones that could never be collected before." The cover text goes on to mention a number of incidents involving censorship, including the uproar over a film made of "The Phallic Forest" that led to raids and prosecutions in Melbourne. It concludes: "Banned, censored, cut and mutilated when they were first written, they are all collected here complete and unabridged" (cover text).

The cover of the book featured a color photograph by Wes Stacey, a quite significant photographer and designer on the girlie magazines and the new women's magazines. It depicted a nude male and female embracing each other, standing on a verandah in the midst of lush greenery. (The photo seems to have been inspired by the film made of the title story, though the couple in the photo are not the actors in the black & white film.)

Wilding dedicated the book "to Frank Moorhouse/for those days." By then the Wilding-Moorhouse friendship was over, but the intense rivalry certainly was not. Today Wilding recalls the purpose and intent of the dedication:

> I dedicated PF to Frank in the days when we were not speaking to each other.
>
> PF was a collection of bits and pieces left out of other collections for various reasons (censored, early stories, scraps)—so I thought a collection of scraps was all he deserved. And 'for those days' was meant acidly—just a few days—rather than the splendid years of my happy life now. All studiedly ambiguous of course.
>
> No one noticed.
>
> No reaction from Frank. (Email, August 30, 2010).

Moorhouse had earlier, in his first book, included Wilding in an acknowledgment: "I thank Don Anderson, Stephen Knight, Michael Wilding and Gillian Burnett for critical and emotional support." (*Futility and Other Animals*, dedicatory page). Wilding's name, however, was deleted in later editions.

The epigraph also pointed to a recurring preoccupation with the stories from the Balmain days: the real identities of the characters being written about. It reads:

> All these people that you mention
>
> Yes, I know them, they're quite lame
>
> I had to rearrange their faces

And give them all another name

The poet Robert Adamson recited these lines from a Bob Dylan song to Wilding following a reading at which Wilding had satirized some academics in the audience who didn't realize they were the target of his wit. In his memoir, *Inside Out,* Adamson wrote: "I didn't know that Dylan was regarded with skepticism at the Forth & Clyde, but it didn't surprise me when I did find out: they were down on pretty much everything. Michael, however, loved the quote and used it as an epigraph to his book *The Phallic Forest...* (301)."

The first three stories in the collection are among the most sexually explicit that Wilding has authored, and that is saying something. Two of them, "The Phallic Forest" and "The Image of a Sort of Death," had been withdrawn from *Aspects of the Dying Process*. Wilding recalls what happened: "The manager of UQP, Frank Thompson, submitted the MS to the Vice Chancellor Zelman Cowan, who objected. They both had problems with these two stories. Sexual explicitness. Queensland, of course, was at this point in time significantly less liberal in such matters, and politically too, than NSW. Rather than cut and mutilate them, high-minded as I was, I removed them altogether" (Email, December 8, 2010). In a 2008 essay Wilding recorded how he felt when he learned that the "offending material" was going to be cut from the two stories: "I was outraged. I often was in those days. My deathless prose to be mutilated! It was unthinkable, unacceptable. How could writing still be treated like this in the 1970s? This was the sort of thing that had driven Lawrence into exile fifty years earlier. I already was in exile" ("Adventurous Spirits" 88).

Denied publication in the book, "The Phallic Forest" appeared that same year, 1972, in *Tabloid Story I*. Peter Carey considered it Wilding's best story ("Adventurous Spirits" 88).

# Sex and the Single Male

"The Phallic Forest" employs lush Lawrentian-type imagery to depict an eroticized natural world. Thus it opens: "The phallic forest Julia walked in shot high soaring poplars to the damp soft clouds. Conifers grew in it groping upwards to the sky's convexity, each pine needle part of that vertical thrust. Palm trees sprang lithely, scaly but slender until they reached their clear height and then showered out in foliate triumph amongst ecstatic humming birds and honey eaters hovering there" (11). And this from *Lady Chatterley's Lover*: "Constance sat down with her back to a young pine-tree, that swayed against her with curious life, elastic and powerful, rising up. The erect, alive thing, with its top in the sun! And she watched the daffodils turn golden, in a burst of sun that was warm on her hands and lap" (92). The story proceeds along allegorical lines as in a fairy tale, and there are repeated allusions to "dwarfs, Pinnochio, Noddy and Big Ears" and Mr. Punch (19). They belong to the mythic forest outside the house where Julia lives with Oliver; both, we are told, are "intellectuals" (12) and they spend their time talking and observing the comings and goings of their bourgeois neighbors.

In the beginning when Oliver and Julia first moved into the house, they made love frequently, but now boredom and indifference have set in. Now Oliver is interested in another woman, named Pippa. While Oliver pursues Pippa, Julia entertains visitors, gathering sexual lore from their conversations. Meantime nature has turned malevolent; the trees soar too high, funguses have set in, spores get into her clothing. And a nearby neighbor whom they view from their balcony has begun masturbating in his backyard, and later, he shines a flashlight on Julia as she sits in the outside toilet. In response, Oliver seals up the house tighter, further cutting it off from natural energies. At one point Julia leaves the house, wandering through the streets of the city, while Oliver tries to go to bed with Pippa. The story reaches its climax, as it were, when Julia is watering the backyard garden and the masturbatory neighbor is spotted with his phallus going back and forth through a knothole in the fence. Instead of being frightened, Julia turns her hose on him, spraying the lusty neighbor whose phallus simultaneously sprays semen into the garden. The result is a Lawrentian transformation:

> And her forest thrived again. The trees bloomed once more, the lizards grew new tails, worms lay taut alongside each other, in bipolar ecstasy. It thrived and became now truly her forest. Noddy and Big Ears nestled up to her, Pinnochio kissed her fully on the lips and Mr. Punch laid his head in her lap. Snow White became a best friend and one of the dwarfs lent her a knife to use to carve her name on the stiff scaly bark of the trees. (19)

The fairy tale ending is crossed with Biblical imagery as well: "...as Moses struck the rock twice, so did she. And the water came out abundantly, and the congregation drank, and their beasts also" (19). Wilding has addressed this dimension of the story:

> There are mentions of Snow White and the Seven Dwarfs in the Phallic Forest—that's the only children's story I am conscious of. But I wasn't making any specific allusion or parody or anything of it. Just sort of, in passing, eroticizing the 7 dwarfs. I think there was an underground comic allegedly doing the same—a porno version of Snow White, but I don't think I ever saw it. Just part of the general context of the late 60s. Don't remember if I was conscious of Pinnochio—I never read it. Never read most of them (Email, October 3, 2010).

Like many of Wilding's stories, this one is also rooted in real experience:

> The story itself was based on a true story I was told by Kerin Cantrell (who was Julia), first wife of Leon Cantrell (who wrote on my early work). They were both grad students at Sydney in my early years there. Kerin observed the guy next door. Her husband was trying to have it off with some visiting girl friend of hers. My interest in it was that Kerin's telling of the story of her neighbor seemed to me to embody her own inexpressible frustrations and unhappinesses about their marriage. And her superior

reflections on the trapped lives of the neighbours was her inexpressible recognition of her own life" (Email, October 3, 2010).

Upon reading the story in the early 1970s Christina Stead wrote to Wilding expressing her admiration, "I think *TPF* is one of the best pictures of a woman's mind I have seen" (undated typescript).

"The Phallic Forest" enjoys a special place in the Wilding oeuvre because it was also the basis for a controversial film of the same title. The black & white film played at the Melbourne Film Co-op and created a stir. According to Wilding, the film followed the story closely (Email, October 3, 2010). This is not surprising, because Wilding himself worked on the film with director Kit Guyatt. Their film played on a double-bill with Phil Noyce's documentary *Good Afternoon*. (*Wild & Woolley* 114-115). Victoria Anoux starred in the film. Her married name is Victoria Thompson, and her brother-in-law is the movie actor Jack Thompson. In her memoir *Losing Alexandria* Thompson recalled the impact the film had on Patrick White, the old lion of Australian letters. She describes the film as a blue movie with plenty of nudity but enlivened by a talented writer, Michael Wilding. White, she says, was excited when he saw it and once sent her a post card of a Rousseau painting of a naked girl in a forest because it reminded him of the film.

The second story in the collection, "The Image of a Sort of Death," was also published in 1972, also in *Southerly*. This story has a complicated history. Wilding wrote it when he was in the UK in 1967-68, as part of a novel that included "Aspects of the Dying Process," "Bachelor Literature" (which appeared many years later in Wilding's memoir *Wildest Dreams*), and a MS in the Mitchell Library in Sydney that has never been published. When the novel failed to find a publisher, Wilding says that he "chopped up the sections into separate stories" (Email, December 8, 2010).

The explicit sexual imagery and content of "The Image of a Sort of Death" belie a widespread view of this period, which maintains that stories about sex could not find their way into well-established academic literary journals. According to this view, the stories that Wilding published in the girlie mags were the objectionable ones that would have been censored. But that is not at all the case. Wilding's girlie mag stories were nowhere near as four-letter-word explicit as a story like "The Image of a Sort of Death." Wilding agrees with this assessment: "The girlie magazines had to tread carefully here. So the more explicit material appeared in the respectable literary journals more easily, sometimes though not that often—and of course in *Tabloid Story*, which began that year, 1972" (Email, December 8, 2010).

In terms of characters and setting, "The Image of a Sort of Death" clearly belongs to the world of the Australian urban stories in *Aspects of the Dying Process*. The setting is Paddington, where Wilding lived in the late 1960s, before moving to Balmain. And several of the characters are familiar from other stories. David, for example, is David Murray, a boy in "The Altar of the Family" and a young man in "Aspects of the Dying Process." David was based on Peter King, a political scientist with whom Wilding was friends. King wrote film reviews during this period and later held a chair in New Guinea. Upon returning to Sydney he headed up Peace Studies. He and Wilding traveled together to the Philippines in 1966, on Wilding's way to the UK. Fowler and his girlfriend Jacquie from "Aspects of the Dying Process" are peripheral figures in "The Image of a Sort of Death." Fowler was a folksinger, now a clergyman, Garry Shearston. Jacquie was a model. Nina and Kate, who appear in the novel *Living Together*, were based on a couple of private school girls, friends of Peter King's (Email, December 8, 2010). The ubiquitous Dexter turns up as well. Dexter was an American, Ron Smith, who edited the girlie mag *Squire* (Email, December 8, 2010). The character Al, making his first appearance, was based on filmmaker Michael Thornhill (Email, December 8, 2010). The real identities and subsequent accomplishments of these figures offer eloquent testimony to the talented intellectual and artistic people who made up the actual and fictional world of Wilding's fiction.

Clearly, "The Image of a Sort of Death" is a part of Wilding's milieu of social and sexual relationships in the era of terrace houses and avant-garde attitudes and liberated behaviors in the inner suburbs of Sydney. But "Image" ups the sexual ante a good deal. It is interesting to speculate where "The Phallic Forest" and "Image" would have appeared in *Aspects of the Dying Process* if they had not been withdrawn. Wilding himself says that he can't remember and that the only thing he is sure of in that regard is that "Aspects of the Dying Process" would have been, as it is, the last story of the collection (Email, December 9, 2010). Wherever they appeared, "Phallic" and "Image" would have confirmed the movement from coming-into-the-country motifs to a full-on immersion in the sexual and cultural life of Push and Bohemian Australia in the late 60s and early 70s. They would have further dramatized Wilding's conversion from English reticence (relatively speaking) to Australian bacchanalia, from wintry repression to sun-burnt hedonism.

"Image" begins with a young man named Brook who as Wilding recalled was based loosely on Don Anderson, at the time a lecturer in English at the University of Sydney (Email, December 8, 2010). Anderson later became known for his prescient book reviews and his advocacy of avant-garde writing coming out of the U.S. Brook is attending a party at Nina's terrace house. Nina gives him a guided tour of the house while her boy friend David remains downstairs watching television. David's apathy regarding Nina and his interest in other women create an opening for Brook regarding Nina. The whole story, replete with anatomical details of sexual experience, concerns the ever-shifting play of desire and consummation among the twenty-somethings who make up the cast of Wilding's young Bohemians and artists. Nina's terrace house is a model of order, taste, and design according to the standards of the period. Thus the batik fabric and the Beardsley print, the books by Norman Mailer and Susan Sontag, darlings of the day, the correct magazines of the intellectual set—no science fiction, no girlie mags. Brook, on the other hand, resides in a rather different place: "The terrace he lived in was a ruin of decay and dilapidation and uncleanliness, his own room an oasis of elegant colours and culture, where music always played" (21). Living also in the house is Kate, a softer, rounder seductress than the rather highly burnished Nina. Brook is mutually attracted to both women but uncertain as to which one he should sleep with first. The animus driving the story is the control exerted by the two women. They possess the power to decide whom to sleep with and they know it. It is perhaps easy to read this story, and others of Wilding's as "sexist," but this would be an oversimplification because in point of fact, in this and in many of his stories women are empowered to a degree that later feminists have failed to recognize or admit. If not in the workplace and not in other respects, the female characters are empowered in bed, in sexual liberation, in the break with traditional social and sexual mores. But they were often empowered in artistic, intellectual, and literary endeavors as well. Wilding published their poems, their stories, their essays, their novels. And one has to remember, they were all in their twenties. And the women who have written of that time, like Kate Jennings and Elisabeth Wynhausen and Germaine Greer and a host of other 70s Feminists, have documented as well their own sexual appetites. Strangely, these are received with approbation, while those of male writers are not.

Torn between his simultaneous desire for Nina and Kate, both of whom are available although each must signal Brook before he dares act, Brook goes home after running into Kate at the pub with Al, an unreconstructed sexist ("You've been slipping it into Nina?" [25]), and attempts to resolve his dual desires by masturbating, "though it was like having to switch TV channels to watch two simultaneously programmed films" (28).

Picking up suggestive hints from both, Brook continues to vacillate between Nina and Kate, and the rhetoric of his predicament is both explicit and funny: "That Kate, too lazy to plan with foresight and aware of her propensity to forgetfulness and distraction, might decide to fuck him now while he was lodged firmly in her consciousness; which meant that Nina, who would have preferred him forever circling on the periphery, like airliners awaiting permission to land, felt she might be impelled to fuck him immediately to forestall Kate's likely impetuousness" (32). At the same time Brook feels threatened by such liberated female sexuality. The imagery is drawn from nature: "...Nina liked to have a store [of men] in reserve, as spiders encapsulate flies, leaving them alive but paralysed, ready and not decaying, not withering" (32). Imagery of a contest and entrapment conveys a similar fear in this key paragraph describing Nina's conquest of Brook:

> 'The prize? You're the prize. Whoever gets you keeps you,' she hugged him, 'till she's finished.' And moving gently in her at that, and the vision of Kate provoked a bitter-sweet excitement, but before he could decide whether it really was Nina he wanted to be got and kept by, her gentle movements and her warm nakedness and the vision of Kate hovering above him all combined and he was suddenly involuntarily convulsively drawn from himself, and she'd got him. (37)

The language also inverts the gender of a kept woman to that of a kept man. Subsequent passages emphasize the impingement of Kate's sexuality upon the physical intimacy of his couplings with Nina. An additional component is the frequent sounds of sexual congress coming from Kate's coituses with Al, emanating from an upstairs bedroom. Wilding makes the point both explicitly and obliquely: "And though he could not fuck them both simultaneously, he could draw as near as possible to that impossibility, an asymptote yearning for its infinity's conjunction" (39). This last phrase pushes the act of fornication into the zone of algebraic geometry, as an asymptote, from the Greek *asymptotos*, meaning "not falling together," means in the modern sense a line which is tangent to a curve of infinity. The asymptote is doomed to fail, and so is Brook.

So when Kate receives him into her bed, he has now apparently achieved his dream: to sleep with both women. Kate's voracious sexual appetite outpaces his, however, and he perceives her as draining him "like some wild-eyed smiling vampire" (41). Still, Brook wants more; he wants to have simultaneous sex with Nina and Kate. When he returns to Nina's bed, she casts him out and then the competition between the two women is not who will sleep with him first but who will relent first in readmitting him to their bed. The story ends with a summing up of the geometry of sexual desire and its possible consequences:

> ...and Brook had fucked them both as near as possible simultaneously more or less. So looked at that way, they all had more or less won and had their prizes. Perhaps it was the symmetrical perfection of it that troubled Brook, who did not really want to achieve a state in which there was nothing more to be gained. And except for a few refinements of detail, like mirrors or a bed for all three of them, there was little omitted from the circle's perfection. Which was the image of a sort of death. (43)

Here Wilding draws upon his studies in the Renaissance to reconfigure *le petit mort*, the little death that stood as a metaphor for orgasm and that in at least one modern scientific study of brain activity during orgasm, seems to be an apt metaphor for decreased blood flow at the crucial moment of said orgasm.

The third story in *The Phallic Forest* is probably the most notorious work in Wilding's panoply of sexual fiction. "The Nembutal Story," published in *Tabloid Story 2*, in *Nation Review* (1973), pp. 12-13, was a direct response to Frank Moorhouse's "The Oracular Story," which appeared the year before, in 1972, in *Tabloid Story*. Both are reprinted in *The Tabloid Story Pocket Book* (Wild & Woolley, 1978), a very useful anthology of *Tabloid Story* stories with an immensely helpful history of *Tabloid Story* by Wilding (with additional commentary by Moorhouse and Brian Kiernan). This volume offers the easiest access into that innovative and important experiment in censorship-busting. Already though, by 1978, *Tabloid Story* had acquired the remoteness of an historical artifact—an end of an era feeling.

Both "The Oracular Story" and "The Nembutal Story" were censored. The Brisbane Vice Squad, for example, seized all the copies of "The Oracular Story" on the University of Queensland campus, and distributors of *Tabloid Story* in Queensland and Western Australia demanded the removal of "The Nembutal Story" from *Tabloid Story 2*. Its removal was marked by a blank page and a half ("The Tabloid Story Story" 310-311). Wilding's views on censorship are laid out in 'The Tabloid Story Story" in the following remarks:

> New writing often deals with sex. Not always, not compulsively, not inevitably—but often; and this was getting us into problems with the straight papers that were potential host magazines. We had no intention of censoring or of rejecting material because of its sexual component—if you do that you don't have any new writing. (310)

Even today, however, it is easy to see why such stories provoked strong reactions.

"The Oracular Story" is a first-person account of the narrator's relationship with Hestia, who is upset over her recent breakup with Milton. Milton is of course Moorhouse's version of Wilding, based upon Wilding's standing as a Milton scholar. Hestia and the narrator discuss Milton a bit, then Hestia, increasingly depressed, pops ten Nembutals before the narrator can stop her. Then the narrator takes the drugged, unconscious Hestia to her house where he proceeds to strip her clothes off, examine her genitalia, and speculate as to the number of penises that have entered her. He thinks of Milton's penis, and then he enters her himself. A few days later Milton and three radical students come to Hestia's house where the narrator is staying. Hestia tells Milton what happened, that the narrator saved her life and then had sex with her when she was passed out. Milton's response: 'It was rape,' Milton said, enviously. 'The ultimate putdown of a woman. You're unsavoury.'" (29). Milton challenges the narrator regarding his beliefs and accuses him of lacking theory and a coherent critique. Instead the narrator embraces the idea of individualism and resists Milton's socialist-based philosophy.

The scene shifts to an inland lake where the narrator and Hestia are swimming. Hestia remarks that Milton has also accused her of not having a coherent critique. The narrator makes various remarks that are meant to be oracular: "'Everything is contained within us,' I said, 'in degrees—as every proposition contains the whole universe'" (30). Another time, she asks, "Do we like each other? Or is it that we like each other as parts of Milton?" to which the narrator replies, "Probably as parts of Milton" (31). They have sex on a motorcycle seat. Later, they continue their philosophical discourse back in bed. She asks him if he thinks of other men who have slept with her and specifically mentions Milton, and he replies, "Yes—you are the vessel from which we both drink'" (33). But probably the strangest thing is, he asks her to bring him some of Milton's sperm, and then he says, "Milton and I could have traveled a route unbelievably different to anything we will now do" (33). The story ends with Hestia praising the narrator as an "oracular bastard" (33). Obviously what some readers objected to was not the philosophizing and literary insider back and forth, but the rape of an unconscious woman. That was the sticking point.

When Wilding wrote his riposte to Moorhouse's story, he made the rape central to the narrative, starting with the title, "The Nembutal Story." And he was quite certain about its intent: "The Nembutal Story was written at Frank. At, not for" (Email "Re: a couple of quick items," December 12, 2004). He meant it to be just as provocative as Moorhouse's. Of those days, Wilding remembers, "I think Frank and I were editing Tabloid Story when he presented 'The Oracular Story' to me. Around 1972 I think. I found it somewhat distasteful. I wrote 'The Nembutal Story' in response. Christina Stead found that distasteful, too. I suspect she was right" (Email, November 24, 2010). So these years later Wilding himself seems to be distancing himself from this story.

Regardless of the sensational content, Wilding's story is amazingly complex as a first person narrative structure. It's probably the single most complex narrative in the Wilding oeuvre. The narrator calls into question whether the rape in Moorhouse's story is factually rendered or not. He states early on: "Had I simply read that page [of the rape], not knowing there was any incident it was based on, I would have thought it just another of his decreasingly pleasant stories with their fading distinction between fictional creation and compulsive fantasy" (44). His criticism here of Moorhouse's fictional technique recalls a charge of over-explicitness directed at Joe/Moorhouse in the first story Wilding wrote about Moorhouse, "Joe's Absence."

To complicate the narrative further, we learn that the narrator knows about another Nembutal rape because he is currently having an affair with "another girl," unnamed, who tells him that she was drug-raped by a third party, Henry Bosco. Instead of Hestia, however, Wilding's name for the girl raped in Moorhouse's story is Wesley, a deliberately gender-ambiguous name, one might add. Without retelling the story narrated by Moorhouse, Wilding's narrator believes the story is authentic because Wesley had tried to commit suicide—an authenticated fact, he assures us. But what he wonders about is whether he himself had sex with Wesley that same night, after the Nembutal rape. It has been three years and he can't remember. He concludes of this whole possibility: "I cannot deal with her emotions, they are for her to write about, that option is always open to her" (p. 46). This is what one might call a masculinist feminist construction. The sentence absolves him, in a way, and empowers her as a writer, in a way.

Wilding's narrator cannot discern what is true and what is not in Moorhouse's story, but he can spot the authenticating detail, such as the KY jelly that the narrator in "The Oracular Story" used in the rape. Lying in Moorhouse's bed one night with another girl, named Faith, Wilding's narrator and Faith discuss the presence of KY jelly on the bedside table. To Wilding's narrator the appearance of this object in the story is the "residual detail of truth, not the careful construction of a literary artifact" (46).

In another paragraph of incredible metafictional and intertextual complexity, Wilding's narrator says that Wesley "is not her real name nor have I seen it in other stories of his" (47). He continues, "In his story she is unhappy because a character called Milton has fucked her brother" (47). Wilding's narrator comments on Milton's relationship with Wesley: "Milton having been fucking her, that of course is the point I almost left out, though its presence is obvious enough" (47). But he denies having had sex with her brother, just as he states that she did not have a brother. Then he speculates that perhaps the word "brother" is meant metaphorically to mean a "racial sister, Faith" (the girl he is on with now). The complexity continues: "Whereas, going back for a moment, I am pretty certain that the character he calls Milton is me; from a paragraph from another story he read to me once about this Milton" (47). This is not the only time in the Wilding-Moorhouse back-and-forth stories that a fictional character confronts his fictionality. Wilding's narrator further clarifies/complicates matters when he writes: "My point is his mixture of 'truth' if you like, things that seem close to how they were, and complete untruth—my fucking her hypothetical brother whom he calls Frank—and uncertainty—his fucking Wesley" (47).

Wilding's narrator then goes on to probe the purpose and motivation behind, beneath, inside Moorhouse's "writing the story of that for me" (48). The narrator fully acknowledges what any reader of the two stories must confront: "His story he gives me is an impossible object, one of those irresolvable seemingly three, two, four dimensional objects drawn. That can never be pinned down, constructed, settled" (48). The narrator feels that the story has targeted him, and identifies one self-characteristic that Moorhouse would be familiar with: "My obsessiveness: that is something having shared that house with me, of which he is certainly aware..." (48). After more analysis of possible facts and motives, Wilding's narrator recalls a statement of literary methods and goals that the Moorhouse narrator articulated "not long ago":

> I am thinking of writing stories no longer for publication, no longer to give magazine editors and publishers' readers the pleasure of rejecting me, but stories designed for editors and publishers' readers, stories that will psychologically torment them, that will make them uneasy and destroy their nerve, that will do psychic damage to them, stories designed not for publication but for the destruction of those in literary office. (49)

This brilliant riff, a Wilding homage to Moorhouse, shows, I believe, the intense literary relationship that the two writers enjoyed in those halcyon days of their early careers. Wilding's narrator imagines two possibilities: that Moorhouse's doctrine of psychic damage through the medium of short stories is directed at him and meant to initiate Wilding's "psychic destruction" (50). A second possibility is that Moorhouse is offering "a gift from him, providing material for me to write about, a gift like his giving himself to Wesley, unsolicited, unexpected, imposed" (50). Since that gift to Wesley occurred in the form of a rape, one is reminded here of the "rape" of Joe's manuscripts in "Joe's Absence," the first stone, as it were, cast at Moorhouse by Wilding. In 2010 Wilding recalled their mutual pleasure at the outset of the stories written at one another: "Frank and I thought the idea of writing stories in response to each others' stories quite exciting" (Email, Suzanne Falkiner to Michael Wilding. November 24, 2010.)

One other reference in the story points to the editorial collaboration between the two writers that resulted in the writing and publication of both in *Tabloid Story*: "When I finished reading his story and he came back with the beer ready to discuss the magazine with our designer, I said, I'll tell the true account of the nembutal incident, at which we both laughed, at those private meanings of the word true" (50). Not surprisingly, the story ends on an unresolved note. Wesley tells the narrator not to make trouble about when she and he slept together, and the narrator ends the story with a question of his own: "Doesn't he know Henry Bosco's rape of this other girl upsets me more?" (50).

In their critical study *The New Diversity: Australian Fiction 1970-88*, Ken Gelder and Paul Salzman in a chapter titled "Sex" offer commentary on the two related stories. In their analysis of "sex, anxiety, and analysis" (174) they mention the bisexuality of the narrator of "The Oracular Story," adding that Wilding's story "answers (and questions) the other, entering the dialogue: "Is his story an attempt...to provoke me into answering for him?" (175). They also point out that since Wilding republished both stories in *The Tabloid Story Pocket Book* (1978) the two were obviously meant to be read together. Laurie Clancy labels Wilding's story "notorious" but says nothing of its precursor, Moorhouse's "The Oracular Story" (339), nor does Clancy mention Moorhouse's story in his section on the author in *A Reader's Guide to Australian Fiction.*

These two sexual hall-of-mirrors stories provoked other literary responses from other writers. First was Amy Witting's "A Piece of This Puzzle is Missing," published in *Tabloid Story* in 1974 and reprinted in *The Tabloid Story Pocket Book.* Amy Witting was the pen name of Joan Austral Fraser (1918-2001), a poet, fiction writer, and teacher. According to another writer, Barbara Jefferis, Witting wrote her story because of her anger at "the sexism of Frank Moorhouse/Michael Wilding *Tabloid Story* tales of sex with an unconscious drugged girl at a party" (35). In "The Tabloid Story Story" Wilding recounted the uproar attendant upon the publication of Witting's story: "There was an outcry about obscenity —in particular about Amy Witting's story, which ironically had been a reaction to the sexual note of some of the earlier stories. The next two issues of *Education* ran selections from the 200 letters from teachers complaining about the shocking filth etc. of the stories" (313).

There was also something of a hoax involved in Witting's sending in her story to the editors of *Tabloid Story.* She enclosed a picture of an attractive young woman (Witting was fifty-six at the time). According to Wilding, "We didn't know Amy Witting was a pseudonym, or that she was middle-aged. I guess we thought it was a real name and she was our age—though we also published older male writers like Dal Stivens.

But the photo might have influenced Frank, if he was in a hetero phase at the time. Who knows?" (Email "Fw: Wittig" November 23, 2010). Thinking back to that event, Wilding concludes: "The Witting story was an annoying episode. She sent it in as a hoax from some sort of dislike of previous stories…I didn't much like it, thought it tacky, but Frank wanted to run it" (Email to Suzanne Falkiner, November 22, 2010). He also recalls the outcome of the public reaction to the story: "The issue—her story in part—got denounced in state parliament for obscenity, and the editor of *Education* got sacked as a result. So all in all very unsatisfying" (MW email to Suzanne Falkiner, November 24, 2010). His final word on the subject: "I was so annoyed about the Amy Witting episode in Tabloid Story—which got the editor of the host journal sacked—that I could never bring myself to read anything of hers" (Email "witting," November 24, 2010).

In Witting's story a female narrator mounts a verbal resistance campaign against the male-dominated voices of Wilding and Moorhouse. She wants to find the language to say no when the male's desires are not ones she wishes to reciprocate. The two males appear to be versions of Wilding and Moorhouse. Of Alan, her lover, she states:

> I don't like what Alan writes. I think it's utterly filthy. It's always about sex—not that he calls it that. That word he uses! Mind you, though he writes it all the time, he has trouble saying it. You can see it coming a mile off. Steady now, relax, bring it out easy. And here it comes. Alan will never get over his background (and neither will that word, in my opinion. (159)

The offensive word, no doubt, is "cunt."

She goes on to talk about what she wants, which is to be cuddled, rather than what the male in this case wants, which is "anal penetration, the last straw" (160). She also returns to the fact that Alan is a writer: "Sometimes I think he does things so as to write about them. I mean, if what he writes about is sex and he's the one that makes it happen, and he makes it happen so as to write about it, he's painting himself into a corner" (160). She has another thought, brought on my Alan's relationship/rivalry with another writer, Breen: "The arsehole having no gender, it occurred to me that he might be thinking of Breen" (161). She continues: "He always is thinking of Breen, one way or another. Usually he is wondering whether Breen writes better than he does. He points out that writing comes very easily to Breen, as if that mattered" (161). Later Alan, giving up on his sexual agenda, takes her round to Breen's, where Breen entertains them by talking about three rejection slips he received that day. Breen is in a homosexual relationship with his boyfriend Ken, another complicating matter in the sexual content of this story.

The story ends with Alan and the narrator returning to her room. As Alan plans to have sex with the narrator, she asks him to cuddle her and tells him she only wants to be loved, and then, a bit later, she trots out her own "dirty words" and one of them (unnamed) embarrasses Alan so much that he leaves abruptly. In his absence she practices the words she intends to use in the future against male advances: "Piss off. Piss off. Piss off" (163). Witting had chosen her pseudonym because it put a positive meaning to a word and condition that she wanted to reject entirely in the future: she never wanted to be unwitting.

Years later, Louise Dow offered another fictional rejoinder to the Nembutal stories of Moorhouse and Wilding, in her story "Written Off," published in *Meanjin* in 1987. It's somewhat ironic that the once conservative Melbourne quarterly so hostile to the sexual realism in the early works of Moorhouse and Wilding would now, under the editorship of Jenny Lee, publish a story replete with the *f* word and the *c* word, the old bugaboos of the censorship era, along with a little masturbation thrown in for good measure. Dow's narrator begins straight off connecting her experience with the Moorhouse/Wilding stories: "It's me they've been talking about all this time, as though I didn't exist...I'm mentioned all right, but only because there wouldn't be a story without me" (219). She designates one character as Frank, a tutor in English at the university, and tells of his "mind-fucking" and of the other kind: "We spent a lot of time in bars and cafes, fucked a bit, it was heady in a way. And this 'incident', which Milton, or Percy, or Michael as I shall call him (just for this story) recalled, did actually occur. This 'incident' was actually an event of major significance in my life" (219). She continues, "I did take ten nembutals that night. And then it got written down and became a story event and I became a character in it" (219).

The narrator continues in a bit of witty self-reflexivity: "...sooner or later it's going to be written up in the next wave of let's-dig-up-Australia's-literary-traditions books, and I'll be forever footnoted as the girl who swallowed the nembutal and got fucked unconscious by Frank or Michael or both, or their characters or both" (220). At this point it is perhaps redundant to report that we are in the midst of a "let's-dig-up-Australia's-literary-traditions" book. The narrator continues to comment on the sexist behavior of Frank and Michael and seems to be mixing elements of each real-life author to the point where the identities are both scrambled and merged. (For example, Frank teaches at the university, and the real Frank did not.) And she winds up making the same point that appears directly in Amy Witting's story and more or less directly in such stories as Moorhouse's "The True Story of The Jack Kerouac Wake": "He [Frank] got me to titillate him with details in cafes, showing intense interest in Michael's prick, what it felt like to be fucked by Michael's prick, what it felt like to be fucked by Michael, postulating that he probably wanted to fuck Michael himself but never daring it" (221). Dow's story ends thus:

> I remember nothing except Frank taking me home, a warm body dragging me, someone to cry to. Then I was unconscious. Five years later I read about it in Michael's story, and then found Frank's original story and it all jelled into a horrible realisation. That was when I remembered the scene in between waking up the first time and waking up the second time. I remembered the semen and the shower.
>
> Remembering was like being punched in the gullet. (p. 222)

Considering the importance of KY jelly in the two male stories, "jelled" seems like a Freudian-slip verb in the passage quoted. In any event the rhetorical shift is remarkable. In the early days of Feminism, only the boys, in the main, talked dirty. But the girls learned fast, they caught up; emboldened by their newfound freedoms, they could talk just as dirty as the boys. And so a true linguistic equality of the sexes emerged and everyone was happy.

"From His Apperception of the Terribleness of Things, " another entry in the Wilding-Moorhouse writing-at sequence of stories, appeared originally in Special Literary Supplement, ed. Frank Moorhouse, *Tharunka*, 16, 1970, p. 3. Wilding has interestingly explained the title's origin: "Terence Spencer, my professor and head of department at Birmingham (as portrayed in 'Campus Novel' in *Under Saturn*) was always sighing at departmental matters and saying 'The Terribleness of things.' It is from Horace, I think—sunt lacrimae rerum, these are the things of tears" (Email, October 3, 2010). In fact, the best gloss on the passage appears in "Campus Novel": "'The terribleness of things,' he said. '*Sunt lachrimae rerum et mentem mortalia tangunt.* The things of tears.'" ("Campus Novel" 103).

The characters Graham and Joe are immediately familiar, and so is the milieu of competitive writers in a state of anxiety both literary and sexual. The third major character is Joe's girl friend Angie, based on Jenny Roberts, a girlfriend of Moorhouse's. Later Jenny Roberts married David Rankin, an artist who now lives in New York with Lily Brett, an Australian writer. Wilding and Adamson later published a volume of Brett's poems with Paper Bark Press in the 1990s. Jenny Rankin became a poet and had an affair with Ted Hughes in England. (She appears under some other name in Emma Tennant's memoir *Burnt Diaries*). Judy, Graham's girl friend, is only alluded to, but she was based on Wilding's "long suffering girl friend Margaret Clancy" (Email, October 3, 2010).

The plot situation is relatively simple. Angie has just quit her job, and since Joe's only job is writing, he is keenly depressed at the prospect of no income. Graham is hanging out and we first see him thus: "Graham wandered round the room and found a copy of *Sire* with his story in it" (101). Angie seizes upon this detail to launch an attack at both writers:

> "What I don't understand about you and Joe," said Angie, bringing glasses in from the kitchen, "is your feeble egomania. I can understand someone looking at his name in print; but when it's something in *Sire* it's so pathetic." She stood behind him, looking down contemptuously,
>
> "Who're you talking to?" Joe asked.
>
> "Both of you; but I might as well not be. Graham's just perving over his own name." (p. 101).

In a superb rendering of dialogue Angie goes after Graham for never bringing his girl friend Judy to the pub, and moves from that topic to a question asked in several of the Wilding/Moorhouse stories and in those written by others about the two: "Just what is it between you and Graham?" (102). Then she mentions Helen and Pat (recurring character names in Wilding's stories of this period) as ones who have speculated about the relationship between the two writers. Angie rephrases the question: "What is it you can't face, what are you covering up? What is it between you and Graham. Or is it Helen?" (102-103).

Questions about Wilding and Moorhouse's friendship/rivalry keep surfacing in their stories and in stories about them by women authors, without there ever being a final answer except that the friendship ended though the rivalry never has.

Every time Joe goes into another room, Graham and Angie "would snatch kisses and contact from each other" (103). When Joe returns, Angie makes verbal "sorties" against first one, then the other. Then she makes a sustained assault on Joe, for Graham's benefit, as she launches into a long stream-of-consciousness narration of her adolescent sexual adventures with an older man. This experience marked her sexual coming of age, but when she is done, old, familiar anxieties surface in Graham's reception of the story:

> And it became suddenly important for Graham that she should have remained through that, still a virgin, and nothing that she said denied that she had so remained; but nor had she been specific. And it was important for him that he should know. But he could not ask, he could not inquisition her with Joe there any more than Joe could with him there, neither dared probe the depth of fantasy and the depth of truth, for fear of the answers. (105)

Aroused by the erotic story of Angie's early though finally ambiguous adventure, the two friends and rivals express their frustration in their reactions to a completely different kind of event. A mouse enters the room, and Joe throws beer bottle tops to chase it away. Graham, who "opened windows to let flies escape rather than crush them," is appalled at Joe's aggressiveness but fears revealing himself as a "frail liberal" (106). Angie finally tells Joe to stop, and the story ends with Joe aligning himself with the most macho writer he can invoke: 'Hemingway once said that the greatest practice in concentration a writer could have was big game hunting,' Joe said, aiming again. 'This is my practice' (106). Wilding had used this same passage in *The Short Story Embassy*, one will recall.

One of the most familiar stories in the collection is "Dexter intrudes into The Short Story Embassy but is deleted from the book of the same name." Familiar, that is, if one has read *The Short Story Embassy*, or if one has read other of the stories about Dexter, a recurring figure. The story certainly could have been included in *The Short Story Embassy*. If so, it would have appeared in the last third of the book. The narrative voice is first person (which means it's probably Laszlo/Wilding), and all the major figures are present. The narrator begins by commenting on the beginning of Tichborne's "alienation" (51). The "I" has been transcribing epitaphs—which places the story late in the narrative of the novel—when Dexter shows up, gathering material for his vampire book. Specifically he is "looking for vampires" (51). But upon seeing Valda, he wants to photograph her "naked on the altar being defiled by a priest" (51). But the narrator "has no wish to see Valda further defiled" or photographs of "her nakedness exposed to further people through the medium of picture books" (51). Valda herself offers no comment but merely smiles. But the most excited among the three writers is Wendel, who announces, "We have to have a priest for the church of the short story. To celebrate its rites" (51). Meantime, Tichborne's propensity to ask questions, to believe in "a world of answers," gets him in trouble again. He asks Wendel what the rites would be.

First of all, they need a priest, and the narrator believes that there is something priestly about Tichborne. When Dexter suggests that the priest must be defrocked, Tichborne resists both the idea of entering a theological college and of being defrocked. In the meantime Wendel lays out his vision of what should happen: Valda, dragged out of bed at dawn, will be "whipped for secretly practicing rites to poetry instead of to the short story" (52). Then she will be taken to the altar and desecrated by the priest, an action in which she is purified even as the priest "takes on her evil" (52). Upon hearing this, Tichborne asks what will happen next to the priest and Wendel replies that he hasn't "worked that out yet" (53). The story ends: "It is from around this point that I date Tichborne's alienation" (53).

Wilding has recently speculated about the origins of the Dexter story: "I think the Dexter story was originally written in the batch of pieces I wrote that became Scenic Drive. Then I decided it didn't fit there. It had the Scenic Drive stuff of Dexter and vampires, but the Valda and Tichborne material was a continuation of the SSE and didn't really fit (Email, August 30, 2010)." He also recalls where the purging by fire came from:

> Then there was the stuff about purging by fire. Somewhere along the line after this Vicki got burned in a caravan when a gas cooking stove exploded or something, so it seemed too close to

events—having been written before them, in fact—so I left it out. I think she may have harangued me about it. Often did. Then when I was collecting the uncollected bits and pieces for PF, I decided to salvage it (Email, August 30, 2010).

The whole episode suggests the fluid, improvisational sketchiness characteristic of the writing of that era and the many interactions among Wilding, Valda, and Moorhouse in the producing of stories to, at, and about each other.

"Laundrom*t Person," previously unpublished and never reprinted, explores another of Wilding's favorite topics, a story about a possible story. The title, otherwise puzzling, becomes clear as Wilding remembers the context and reason for the asterick: "Moorhouse had a column in The Bulletin called Around the Laundromats. Laundromat then complained the word was copyright and a trademark, so he changed it to Laundrom*t. So, to avoid infringing a copyrighted trademark..." (Email, January 4, 2011). Wilding has elaborated on the fuller implications of the asterick: "The sub-text of course is in those days, and again now in the press, f*ck was the way r*de words were printed. So it had a modish, anti-censorship obscene smart-arse sort of note to it. Reminding readers some of the stories had suffered in some way from censorship in their original attempts to get published" (Email, January 4, 2011). The unnamed narrator is a writer who lives alone, having broken up with his girlfriend. Since it was she who did the laundry, now that task falls to him, and much of the story is an interior monologue in Kerouac-like prose, in looping paragraph-long sentences concerning the possibility of romantic overtures to the sexy woman in the laundrom*t as well as the possibility of finding enough material in the laundrom*t for a story. At the same time he's thinking about her, about how to approach her, he's thinking about the possibility of a story coming from the experience.

And fascinatingly, Moorhouse's presence is felt in this story, though only an insider, someone closely attuned to the Sydney literary scene, would pick it up. Here is the narrator reporting on the present absence of the unnamed Moorhouse: "I could've said: I have a friend, well now I guess he's more of an acquaintance, an ex-acquaintance, really" (113). Here Wilding clearly marks the end of the friendship between him and Moorhouse, though again a casual reader would never be able to recognize the factual basis underlying the statement. And the narrator continues to pursue the laundrom*t connection:

> I could've said: I used to know this person who writes about laundrom*ts, he has a sort of column in an underground paper, and it's sort of a conversation piece, a dialogue, you know how they used to write dialogues in the nineteenth century...and so these dialogues are set in laundrom*ts, he, anyway, disapproves of people just dropping in their laundry to the laundrom*t and not washing it themselves but leaving it for someone else to wash and picking it up later. I think he feels this represents alienation, man's attempted separation from his own body, his own effluents, excreta, emissions, sweats, the denial of the body, the separation from the natural functions and processes, and an economic argument could be put up, I could put up an economic argument, though he probably wouldn't, that it represents the harmful separation of aspects of one's life, fragmentation, exploitation, cutting off from the realities of labour and production, compartmentalizing for ease of capitalist modes of organization, no longer the whole man, you do my washing while I go away and listen to some music and write a story about someone having to do the washing (113-114).

The reference to "underground paper" points to the original publication of Moorhouse's column in the underground *Thor* before it was picked up by The Bulletin (Email "some further minor corrections," July 31, 2012). Here, again fascinatingly, Wilding seems to be having a dialogue with his former friend, the kind of discussion that might well have taken place in actuality many times in their relationship. And Wilding seeks to refute Moorhouse's psychological interpretation of the meaning of laundromats by arguing, as Wilding often does, a Marxist economic interpretation that indicts capitalism. At the same time Wilding is aware of his own distance from an actual economic solution, as he imagines himself enjoying the leisure time to do pleasurable, and possibly profitable things, like writing a story, which act in itself would presumably be exploitative at a second or third remove.

The dialogue with the ex-friend (Moorhouse the laundrom*t writer) continues later in the story, a narrative like many of Wilding's, of unresolved ambiguities:

> This acquaintance I used to have I mentioned earlier, he held his laundrom*t conservations with his cat, we have all had our periods of isolation, and they deal with, these conversations, sexual emancipation and liberation. Those sort of things as the clothes whirled around. I asked him if he'd put in more technical detail about laundrom*ts as I wanted to use it in a novel I was writing in which two people spend an amount of time in the laundrom*ts. But he never put in that much technical information. So that part of the novel got reduced. Maybe I should've researched it more. Maybe I could ask you [the laundrom*t woman] for the information—vocabulary, really, proper terms, the appropriate vocabulary. (116-117)

The passage grants the legitimacy of "laundrom*t conversations," though at the same time it critiques Moorhouse's emphasis on personal psychological issues without a full understanding of the technical and economic facts regarding laundrom*ts. It also suggests the constant involvement in each other's work by the two former friends, at least during the period of their friendship and eventual estrangement.

The stream of consciousness manner is also on view in a long riff on Dexter, that familiar figure from many stories. Dexter is staying with the narrator while he, Dexter, works on a soft porn collection of photographs titled *Vampire Vamp*. The house is the same one that appears in "The Vampire's Assistant at the 157 Steps."

In one key passage the narrator brings everything together regarding life/sex and fiction/experience:

> Trouble with laundrom*ts you can't keep going back to them every day if she worked in a coffee bar, keeping the fantasies in tune with the days of wanting to screw the dentist's receptionist, then I could go and drink coffee every day and die of caffeine poisoning like Balzac, a biography of him is amongst those little magazines by the bed and I've been reading it for months but don't seem to get to my bed often enough in peace to read it and when I am there I get asked to vacate the house, but coffee bars, the first fuck I was ever offered in my life and I was too frightened to take it, got a bad unpublished novel out of it later, that was the result of hanging out in coffee bars. (117-118)

This sequence reminds one of the story "The Girl Behind the Bar is Reading Jack Kerouac," though that story only alludes to Kerouac but does not mimic/echo his manner.

In "Laundrom*t Person" no sexual congress is achieved, though the last paragraph suggests a possible sexual future based upon the story itself. But let Wilding spin out the implications:

> Should I give her this? This blue print, this daydream, this whatever it is that has gone as far as it can go without giving it to her. How it goes now depends on her reaction. If I showed her this would she freak out at the palpable interest I have in fucking her. But what's the point of not saying it if that is the palpable point, and if she does freak out, well that's what I need to know, to get to anyway so why be duplicitous about more than is necessary, what is this anyway, a story or a shoehorning fucking device, a way in or a way out, what it is depends on what she sees it as, it can always be a story if it doesn't get a fuck, isn't that what it's all about, or a lot of it anyway? (119)

Wilding often writes about the art of fiction but also just as frequently about the purpose or reception/outcome of fiction, of the short story form in particular. Thus "Laundrom*t Person" is a notable addition to that discourse on the purpose of fiction that informs many of his stories and especially *The Short Story Embassy*.

"Buying Jeans in Balmain," published in *Bottom Line*, 4 (July-August 1977), 24-5, is something of a companion piece to "Laundrom*t Person" in that it's about a casual commercial encounter between a young writer (unnamed) and a young girl (unnamed). Only four pages long, it can be summarized in one sentence: The narrator goes into a small storefront shop in Balmain to buy a pair of jeans, and the girl behind the counter, as it were, comes into the small cubical where he is undressing and performs oral sex and then copulation in the kind of short-circuit seduction that inhabited the dream lives of young men in those days and doubtless now. The end brings together the two central preoccupations of the narrator: sex and writing:

> ...though the legs are an unshortened length I can tuck them into my cowboy boots so I don't have to fuck around with needle and thread and when I need to send them to the laundrom*t I can go up and try on the Jag pair or the Roxy pair, it's a nice place to buy jeans and the other good thing is now I feel comfortable and I can get back to the typewriter and I've got that whole day's quota of new words ready to write right down, and a pair of jeans, and a suck and a fuck and an exhibitionistic buzz and it's still only 12:30 and all I've got to worry about now is where to get lunch. (123)

Wilding has explained the origin of the story thus: "Buying Jeans in Balmain was a spontaneous piece I jotted down, after trying to buy jeans in Balmain, though without the erotic excitement actually happening at the time, except what was going on unexpressed in my head, which had a life of its own, and still does, no other life being available these days" (Email, January 7, 2011). The Belgrade Film School made a film of it, though Wilding himself has never seen the film.

The somewhat grab-bag aspect of the collection—Wilding's own term —includes two fable-like tales, "The Fossil Evidence Re-Run" (published originally in *Sydney Morning Herald* (March 19, 1977), p. 18), "A Month in the Country" (published originally in *Alta*, University of Birmingham, 5 (1968), 297-8), and the satirical "Tittert*n" (published originally in

*National Review*, 1978). Of the latter and that asterisk, Wilding has stated: "I then put the * in Tittert*n as a way of sort of not being defamatory about Sir Ernest Titterton who proposed firing nuclear waste into space. And to give a bit of typographic coherence and theme to the volume" (Email, January 4, 2011). He also included four English stories. "Don't Go Having Kittens" and "Like Rat Turds to Me" appeared originally in the girlie mags. A pastiche, "Emma: Memoirs of a Woman of Pleasure" (published originally in *Makar*, 8 (1972), 5-12), twinned Jane Austin with John Cleland and was also, of course, set in England.

Far and away the most interesting of the English stories in the collection is "Come Down to the Cottage for the Weekend" (first published in the *Nation Review*, 24-30 August 1973, p. 1413). Although an English story, it is written in Wilding's emerging Australian sexual vernacular. It is also notable for its ribald plaintive lover motif, a Wilding specialty. A young man down from Oxford is spending a few days at the home of the girl Caroline with whom he is sexually infatuated. The first paragraph is a kind of authorial guide to writing about sex:

> He wrote in his notebook, 'He sat amongst them at the dinner table and wanted to say, I have had my finger up your daughter's cunt.' He looked at it. The entry. The satisfaction of putting it down. Though the difficulties too. What if she ever saw the notebook? Well, she knew he had had his finger up her cunt. Presumably. But still might not like it recorded. For use in a story some day. Or a novel. Or even simply as a remembrance of things past. To put it down required the breaking of some sort of taboo, a sort of demi-vierge's defloration. Demi-vierge, a word he'd puzzled at since he came across it, and had never been able to rediscover. But it was, anyway, hard to put it down: a word, cunt, he hadn't written before; nor said to her. Oh my. The assault of language, what just using the word meant about what he thought about them, her. (71)

The Proustian echo is evocative, and the "assault of language" is an excellent descriptor for a number of the stories in the collection. But this story also has a familiar class-consciousness as well, characteristic of almost all of Wilding's English stories. At the dinner table he imagines telling the parents in the most emphatic and explicit vernacular language he can think of, exactly what he has done sexually with their daughter. But class feeling and class resentment break into the sexual fantasy:

> ...eating your juicy red roast beef and drinking, not even sipping like I thought people sipped wine, bulk swallowing your glasses of red wine, eating more meat at a sitting than my father eats in a week and drinking more wine at a sitting than he's probably drunk in his life, being not only a working man and needing the protein of meat in a way you effete inactive chair-sitting bourgeoisie simply don't so you waste it all out straight away through your kidneys, but abstemious too. (72)

In another mark of class consciousness the narrator, after trying unsuccessfully to repair the bicycle of Caroline's little brother, "felt like Jimmy Porter, covered in bicycle oil and ineffectualness" (75). Jimmy Porter, the hero of John Osborne's famous play, *Look Back in Anger*, was the seminal Angry Young Man in post-war British literature. Wilding saw the play staged at Kidderminster around 1957, where Osborne had once worked as an actor.

There is a very funny sequence in which the suitor, in a state of high anxiety, is ushered into the parental bedroom where Caroline's parents "gave audience." At one point the father says, "'I think we're going to be having a bit of the old jig jig tonight.' Did his ears hear right, jig jig to naughty ears, what nightingale song was this at their closed window? He was suffused with shame" (76). While he's thinking of Eliot's language in *The Waste Land* and its explicit sexual context, Caroline explains to him what her father really meant: "Daddy has this twitching nerve in his leg and when it starts it keeps her [the mother] awake all night, sometimes she comes and sleeps in my bed" (76).

Sleeping arrangements for the narrator are another source of anxiety, and the story ends with him consigned to a lilo [an inflatable air mattress] where he lies awake wondering: "what oh what oh Caroline am I doing here alone in this room in this countryside I do not know, bicycle oil ingrained in the lines and nails of my fingers when will you ever come to me?" (77). Again, as is often the case in the English stories, anxiety about class collides with sexual desire. As Wilding became more and more Australian, the class factor dropped away, and the movement towards the appropriation of immediate (often sexual) experience began to dominate his short fiction.

It is clear that Wilding gained much from his expatriation to Australia. In an interview with Peter Lewis for *Stand*, he summed up his literary situation thus: "Like the people I was working with at this time, such as Frank Moorhouse and Vicki Viidikas in fiction and Robert Adamson in poetry, I was learning new ways of seeing things from the various innovatory approaches coming principally from America" (3). Wilding's work in the decades to come would take him in new directions.

# Chapter 7

# Renovated Realism

In 1982, Wilding published the last of his postmodern novels, *Pacific Highway*. Formally it looked like *Scenic Drive*, but whereas almost all of that novel took place indoors, *Pacific Highway* was a true road novel, with much of its action occurring in the outdoors, along the Pacific Highway, Route I, running from Sydney to Brisbane, a long haul by truck or automobile. But *Pacific Highway* had one other difference as well; it was much more politically explicit than any of Wilding's previous novels, and much less tied to Sydney. It was an up-up-and-away novel, with riffs that bespoke a more radicalized view of the world. According to Wilding, *Pacific Highway* "was bringing the political, utopian themes into that postmodern mode—and dealing with all the problems that that involved" ("After Libertarianism" 286). In the novel itself such rhetoric is quite explicit: "The evils of capitalism, the endless production of products that have no other use than to generate profit which is used to capitalize further production for further profit, the worthless products building up geometrically like a cancer, as the earth is hollowed and the vegetation stripped and the seas scooped to build these products (142)." What would prevail against this internationalist exploitation—once called imperialism—was uncertain; all one could do, it seemed, was continue the personal utopian quests for self-discovery and self-development through sex, drugs, and Kerouac-like flight into the raw heart of the Australian coastline with its little towns and communes along the off-roads where small communities of like-minded seekers from the Sixties and Seventies still searched for the groove laced with mushroom-induced visions. The sense of a modern Paradise Lost hovers over *Pacific Highway*.

Or what one could do, as Wilding did, was to reverse direction and reject postmodernism in favor of older, more traditional forms, namely social realism. Thus in *The Paraguayan Experiment,* published in 1984, Wilding projected about as complete a turnaround in favor of social realism as one could imagine. The book grew out of his interest in the Australian writer and labor activist, William Lane, author of *The Workingman's Paradise*, published in 1892 and reprinted in 1982 with a long introduction by Wilding. In that introduction he called attention to the socialist policies underpinning the novel's naturalistic portrait of urban poverty and labor strife in the 1890s, a period of great economic turmoil in Australia. In a later essay about Lane's method, Wilding might well have been echoing a pattern in his own work and career: "At the moment that Henry James was laying total stress on the dramatization of consciousness within highly stringent formal conventions, Lane insisted on retaining content, on the communicative, social role of literature" (*Studies in Classic Australian Fiction* 105).

At any rate, Wilding's novelistic account of William Lane's New Australia Movement hews straightforwardly to a linear plot based upon a close study of the aims, actions, and outcomes of the band of socialists who set out to create their own utopia in a South American nation. With this book, Wilding reflected a new commitment to a realist/naturalist base that differed sharply from the precepts and anti-realism of the postmodernist mode. In fact, he has called the novel "a dialectical response to *Pacific Highway,* a necessary development" ("After Libertarianism" 287). Returning to traditional narrative and the documents that charted the rise and fall of the New Australia Movement, Wilding committed himself to a fully developed and defined sense of plot. In his reading of the historical record, the colonizing effort in Paraguay failed not because of anything inherent in utopian schemes, but because of police and government agents who infiltrated the movement and conspired to undermine its success. Looking back on the process, Wilding has observed: "Establishing this [conspiracy] took me into documentary detail, into narrative sequence—into a version of traditional realism, though handled with the experience of postmodernism. It was also an 'historical' novel that was designedly relevant to contemporary experience. Renovated realism I called it" ("After Libertarianism" 287).

These new directions in Wilding's fiction in the 1980s were necessary ones, he felt. He has accounted for this shift towards political content in his fiction by pointing to the new realities of what he might, after Auden, have termed a low, dishonest decade:

> The 1980s I found a horrible decade. Having shifted to a more explicit political position and in having developed an increasingly politicized fiction I found, as a consequence, I was not getting published as readily, not getting invited to do anything, I was no longer on the circuit. I found it very hard to be positive during those years. The materials at hand were observations of the defeat of the progressive spirit. It was hard to treat that in a positive way. ("After Libertarianism" 287).

In addition to writing new stories, he continued to bring out collections that incorporated earlier pieces with newer ones more inflected with political content. *Reading the Signs* (1984) was typical: it included recent responses to the Eighties such as "Welcome O Foreign Writer," a monologue rant against American political and cultural imperialism, and "In the Penal Colony," a long road-trip story recounting a drunken visit to Tasmania with a pack of feckless poets and filled with the intensity of instant experience that characterized so many of the early stories. *The Man of Slow Feeling: Selected Short Stories,* a kind of Wilding's greatest hits, appeared in 1985. Then there was something entirely different, *Under Saturn* (1988), which consisted of four long stories of about fifty pages each, three set in England, and one in Greece. Perhaps the most important was "Campus Novel," a dead-on realist/satirical account of a tyrannical chairman of an English Department (University of Birmingham). Years to come, Wilding would turn once again to the campus novel genre for new inspiration. Despite Wilding's gloomy assessment of the 1980s his publishing activity in those years showed no slackening, what with two novels and three collections of stories. In addition he produced two volumes of criticism, *Political Fictions* (1980) and *Dragons Teeth: Literature in the English Revolution* (1987). Each reflected his long-standing interest in the social and political themes underpinning works that formalist criticism tended to ignore or erase in favor of aesthetics and structural elements. *Political Fictions* was particularly important. It kicked off Wilding's turn towards social realism at the beginning of the new decade. It offered brilliant readings of *Huckleberry Finn* and William Morris' *News from Nowhere*, Jack London's *The Iron Heel*, D. H. Lawrence's *The Rainbow* and *Kangaroo*, and two modern classics, Arthur Koestler's *Darkness at Noon* and George Orwell's *1984*.

The next decade continued much in the same vein. There were four collections of stories, three of which recycled earlier work with new stories: *Great Climate*, published in London in 1990, and in America the next year under the title *Her Most Bizarre Sexual Experience*, republished earlier stories along with new ones. Then *Somewhere New: New & Selected Stories* in 1996 followed the same pattern of old and new stories. The aim was to keep the oeuvre current and to maintain the profile. In the meantime in 1994 he published a volume of all new stories, *This Is For You*. Christina Stead called Wilding: "good on women...good on obsession." A major work, it contained several stories set in America, including "NY 1969," "For Trees," and "Pioneers." In another story, "Red Rock," Wilding evoked the model of Jack Kerouac once again: "And this morning I started to read Jack Kerouac and like every time I read Kerouac I put down the book, whichever book, and want to write, always his note is the note of memory and search and wanting to write it as close to as it was as you can dare, as at this stage you can try..." (66). In an earlier story, "Writing a Life," Wilding had alluded to the other pole of his literary imagination, Henry James. The male viewpoint character, named Michael, observes that "...[he] introduced alien idioms into its texture for the stridencies of contrast, for discordant counterpoints; much as dear old HJ had done..." (*Under Saturn* 164).

By now multinationals had taken over the publishing industry and their goal was mass-market titles. The lively era of experimentalism and avant-garde publishing of the 1960s and '70s seemed remote indeed. The multinationals selected certain writers to market heavily and the local book reviewers went along willingly. Almost as a ghostly reminder of the past, Wilding in 1994 published *Book of the Reading*, a compilation of his most oft-read stories from days gone by and presented in a limited edition by Paper Bark Press, which Wilding had formed with poet Robert Adamson. It contained ten stories, including "The Words She Types," ones dealing with "Joe" and "Valda" (Moorhouse and Viidikas), and the scathing satire "Welcome O Foreign Writer."

As usual, Wilding's energies found expression in multiple directions. He continued to produce literary criticism of a high quality based upon restoring classic texts as well as neglected writers to the social/political sphere in which their works were conceived. *Social Visions* appeared in 1993. It contained political readings of texts ranging from *Gulliver's Travels* to such works as those of Joseph Conrad (*Heart of Darkness* and *Nostromo*), Alan Sillitoe's political novels, and Isaac Singer's stories. In 1997 Wilding published *Studies in Classic Australian Fiction*, a title that deliberately echoed D. H. Lawrence's *Studies in Classic American Literature* (1923), a far-reaching book in which Lawrence sought to peel back American writing—and the culture it presumed to represent—like an onion, exposing the strong inner core. Wilding has a different purpose, a different agenda. Instead of Lawrence's probing impressionism, Wilding adopts a more measured tone and couches his essays in the methodology (though not the dreary language) of critical scholarly discourse, complete with learned footnotes. On the surface his volume looks like a piece of criticism familiar enough to anybody in the global academy. But Wilding's book is no less daring than Lawrence's, for Wilding means to recover that which has been lost. He seeks to bring about the return of the repressed; only what is repressed is what, in some cases, is transparently on the surface. Wilding sought to refocus criticism on political and economic themes, often overt, of a tradition of Australian writers whose works, to suit the purposes of "apolitical" New Critics or complicit ideologues of the Cold War, had had the politics read out or erased, deleted, suppressed.

The case of Joseph Furphy is most instructive. The censorship of the political in Furphy was direct, emphatic, and effective. In order to get his long book *Such is Life* (1903) published, Furphy agreed to the excision of a lengthy chapter espousing socialism. Wilding rightly calls this "one of the great scandals of Australian publishing," but what is equally surprising is how long it took to get the cancelled section restored—forty-three years. And even so, plenty of critics have been happy enough to go on reading the book as though it contained no socialist material at all. Without the explicit socialist analysis, political and economic themes threaded through the book were easier to ignore.

Henry Lawson's work illustrates another suppression of the political. Long acclaimed as a canonical Australian writer, Lawson has been declawed, depoliticized, by an insistence upon viewing his work as emblematic local color fiction dealing with the bush and the Australian archetype of the drover. And that is certainly a strong dimension of his work, not to mention the Drover's wife. But as Wilding meticulously discloses, Lawson was also a dedicated political-unionist writer whose work embodied a comprehensive view of the working class, both its exploitation by capital and its own internal coherence and group solidarity. Wilding analyzes a passage from the story "'Two Boys at Grinder Bros'" to show its overt leftist political stance. Then he deftly summarizes how Lawson's stories have systematically been depoliticized: "These stories have generally been labelled Dickensian and sentimental by Lawson's commentators; as if infant mortality, the exploitation of child labour, and slum life were somehow literary tropes and not all too common, everyday realities" (40-41). Wilding's whole book might be seen as an attempt to return tropes to their realistic base. Among other things, his book offers a lucid and powerful argument on behalf of realism.

His concluding essay on Patrick White is especially strong in identifying what is missing in White and what is present. In White's commitment to modernism, the Nobel Prize recipient found a way to address an international insider audience while debasing the currency of materially grounded and closely observed social reality of the kind discredited by the new formalism. Wilding reveals how a novel about an artist, such as *The Vivisector*, is set in a rarified—and unreal context—when compared with Balzac's *Lost Illusions*, in which the artist hero is thoroughly defined amidst the economic realities of publishing, authorship, reviewing, the nexus of ambition and advancement, the management of fame and reputation, of everything that goes into the making of that capital A artist so beloved by modernism. The problem with *The Vivisector* is the problem with modernism: "Art is not presented in any social context; the novel celebrates the artist's anti-social qualities—the destructiveness, the alienation, the isolation." In a 1991 video interview Wilding spoke of White's work as the result of "a vast effort of will" and called it "very nihilistic." For Wilding's generation, he said, White "wasn't a living force. None of us learned anything from him." Wilding preferred instead the more organic, loosely structured work of Christina Stead, because she "drew from the life" (*Writer's Talk: Michael Wilding*).

In chapters on Marcus Clarke, Jack Lindsay, and Christina Stead (to whom he devotes two chapters) Wilding engages in a similar repositioning of their work in a social-realist context. Wilding makes it all seem so simple, drawing our attention to both the obvious and the subtle renderings of political and economic material, that one wonders how generations of critics could have been so blind. Like Lawrence, Wilding defamiliarizes the known and sends us back to the classics with fresh vision. With this work Wilding demonstrated once again that he is one of Australia's leading literary critics. At the end of the decade Wilding published a book going back to Renaissance England for its sources and story line. *Raising Spirits, Making Gold, and Swapping Wives: The True Adventures of Dr John Dee and Sir Edward Kelly* (1999) reflected Wilding's long-standing interest in alchemy. He updated Dee's diaries to bring the famous alchemist's writings into a modernized English style while maintaining the flavor of 16$^{th}$ century English. Wilding's creative excavation of Dee has drawn praise from the cognoscenti and illuminati who study alchemy.

The book of Wilding's in the 1990s, however, that made the biggest splash was the memoir *Wildest Dreams*, published in 1998. The book had a long gestation. In a 1991 video interview Wilding commented at some length on its origins:

> What I most recently wrote was my version of Balzac's *Illusions Perdus, Lost Illusions*, the definitive novel about the literary life. I'd always wanted to write such a book even before I'd begun writing. I'd read all these books about the young writer goes to Paris, to London, whatever. Now I've done that; it's called 'The Literary Pages." It's focused on postmodernism, on writing about writing. It focuses on reviewing, publishing, movie-making, and writing. Other things come into it, but at the same time it has that realist basis and tries to record what happened, what were the costs, what were the debts. It took me about five years to write. At the time I didn't know what I was doing. I'd start a book called "Farewell to Bohemia" and it would peter out after thirty pages. I'd start an epic and it would peter out. And then a stroke of inspiration came one day and I realized that all of these failed bits were actually part of the same book, which was this memoir of thirty years of writing. I realized that unknown to myself I'd

written 2/3rds of this saga and so then I had the direction and could complete it. (*Writer's Talk: Michael Wilding*)

The archetype underlying both books is, of course, that of the young man from the provinces. "It's always the same story, every year the same enthusiastic inrush of beardless ambition from the provinces to Paris," says Loustreau, one of the many failed artists turned journalists in Balzac's novel. Wilding writes thus of his own hopeful artist self at the outset of his career in the city: "But he knew what it was to be the young writer arrived in a metropolis, unknown yet there to be known, the writer's growth the discovery of the metropolis, objective correlative, homology, or only subject" (4).

What Balzac and Wilding have to say about fiction, about literature, is that it begins and ends in a materialist base. Both Balzac's and Wilding's protagonists are of humble birth: the father of Lucien Chardon (whose last name means thistle) is a chemist who "sold pills to cure flatulence"; the father of Wilding's protagonist is an iron-moulder, a subject Wilding has written movingly about in several stories. In Balzac, Paris is the mecca of modernity, of sophistication, wealth, beauty, success, fame, all that the ambitious provincial yearns for. Early in the novel Lucien's hopes and illusions about Paris are summed up in one rhapsodic passage:

> He had a vision of Paris in all its splendour: Paris, an Eldorado to the imagination of every provincial; clad in gold, wearing a diadem of precious stones, holding its arms out to talent. He would receive a fraternal accolade from illustrious men. There genius was welcomed. There would be found no envious little gentry to humiliate writers with their cutting sarcasms and no parade of stupid indifference to poetry. There the works of poets gushed forth, were paid for and offered to the world. After reading the first few pages of *The Archer of Charles the Ninth* the publishers would open their coffers and ask him: "How much do you want?"

A brief summary of Lucien Chardon's career in Paris is useful in light of the progress of Wilding's protagonist, named Graham. Balzac's young writer leaves his provincial town and goes to Paris where he is certain that his "genius" will be instantly recognized. It is not. Instead he enjoys some success because of his good looks and because he buys the most fashionable clothes in order to transcend his bumpkin beginnings. He quickly plunges into debt and acquires a loyal, pretty, and stupid chorus girl for a mistress. Instead of attending to the craft of writing, Lucien schemes to get his already completed manuscripts published and earns money by becoming a journalist, a reviewer, instead of a real artist. There is a very funny passage in which a publisher finally agrees to publish Lucien Chardon's novel, *The Archer of Charles the Ninth*. The publisher explains: "We don't like *The Archer of Charles the Ninth*; it isn't enough to excite the reader's curiosity. There were several kings named Charles and so many archers in the Middle Ages! Why now, if you said *A Soldier of Napoleon*! But *The Archer of Charles the Ninth*? Cavalier would have to give a course of lectures on French history in order to sell a single copy in the provinces." In a final irony, it does not matter what Lucien's novel is called because by the time it is published he is the object of a rival political/journalistic cabal and his novel dies without ever being reviewed. This is one of many illusions about literature that are dashed in Balzac's novel. Eventually things come apart for Lucien, the chorus girl dies, and he returns to the provinces.

Wilding's Paris, of course, is Sydney, not London or Paris—a far-flung outpost quite remote from Wilding's English origins, but increasingly home as the years passed and Wilding became, among other things, an Australian writer.

The opening pages of *Wildest Dreams* are attentive to every detail of the new experience, from the "romance of the rooming house" (2) to the recognition of the siren lure of the indolent climate: "You did not need to be wealthy to be warm in Sydney" (3). The young writer-to-be, we are told, "fell in love with the city, not initially, not with some sudden immediate recognition. It took much longer than that, it was a matter of discovery, of gradual revelation, of slow familiarity. The harbour welcoming there in the golden sun, blue as the clear sky" (2). A year or so later, upon returning from a trip back to England, Graham thinks about the differences between old England and new Australia: "Here the sun and the distance away from the old world had bleached away sexual inhibitions. Here people drank and made love and felt the sun on their pores with a freedom that he could never imagine could ever be attempted in England" (54-55).

Wilding paints himself, in the guise of Graham, as a double provincial: someone born of proletarian circumstances in a marginalized space, in the Midlands, near the Welsh border. Although Wilding won a scholarship to Oxford, he never forgot his class origins. So this is one degree of provinciality. The second is that he was in a sense "exiled" to the colonies, to Australia. In a chapter of *Wildest Dreams* called "American Poets in London," Wilding speaks of exactly this doubleness: of being a visiting colonial, which is preferable to being a visiting provincial proletarian from the Midlands. When Wilding read *Lost Illusions*, he doubtless saw in Lucien Chardon's experiences in Paris confirmation of his own experiences in the literary and publishing worlds of Sydney. Lucien discovers that to most publishers "books were like cotton bonnets to haberdashers, a commodity to be bought cheap and sold dear." The more Lucien learns about the real nature of literature, the more he is shocked at the "brutally materialistic aspect that literature could assume." In Balzac's France the great enemy of Literature is Journalism, defined by one character as "an inferno, [a] bottomless pit of iniquity, falsehood and treachery." Opposed to this view is the idealism of a group of poor, dedicated intellectuals and writers with whom Lucien comes into contact. One poet assures him that to become a real writer will require ten years of hard work, but Lucien, caught up in the pleasures of Bohemian Paris, becomes a reviewer instead. But reviewing, he learns to his dismay, is simply a matter of literary politics. He learns how to review a book without reading it first, and how to attack a book that he admires and, conversely, how to praise a book that he doesn't admire. Nothing is real in the world of book publication and promotion. Lucien's idealism is constantly tested and undercut. Poetry, he learns, is discounted by publishers as a minor, economically unfeasible form of authorship. What is wanted is historical novels in the manner of Sir Walter Scott. But journalism and economic necessity are the biggest impediments to the production of literature. Literature is always constrained by the marketplace. As Lucien realizes, "It's hard to keep one's illusions about anything in Paris. Everything is taxed, everything is sold, everything is manufactured, even success."

Similarly, Wilding's young hero goes through a series of initiations into the real conditions of literary production. At first he believes the problem is simply which tradition to emulate: "Graham was torn between Lawrence and Sillitoe and the proletarian tradition, and the conscious artifice of Henry James. Or between the provincial celebrations of George Eliot and the exotic expatriation of Durrell" (20-21).

But he soon learns that other possibilities intrude upon the purest commitments. There is, for example, the lure of reviewing, the same form of journalism that helped undo Balzac's *naif*. Wilding identifies the problem: "And writing about writing, writing reviews, writing lectures, all that was always ready to intervene, the fiction dreamed, delayed" (43). One of Wilding's solutions, of course, was to write fiction about writing fiction.

Another salient connection between Balzac's world of writing and that of Wilding's is politics. In Balzac the young writer is willing to change his political alignment to enhance his career. In the case of Wilding, Graham remains true to his political convictions, but not without a price. The cost is years of doubt, suspicion, and neglect. From the beginning Graham aligns himself with the Left; his faith in the Left is a mark of his idealism.

Graham's experiences in publishing take him behind the scenes into the world of distribution and marketing. Balzac's fascination with all aspects of book making, from the manufacture of paper itself to the sale of the finished product printed on that paper, is certainly shared by Wilding's Graham. The chapter "Publish and Perish" details Graham's experience with a businesswoman named Bobbie (obviously drawn from Wilding's association with Pat Woolley in the 1970s). From this insider perspective Graham acquires new knowledge of the economic forces driving every aspect of publishing. None of this knowledge is consoling. He learns, for example, to suspect the reported sales figures of certain literary authors. He believes that for various undisclosed reasons, certain writers are "propped up." Who does the propping? Revelations about CIA funding of periodicals and authors suggest one answer—a depressingly political one.

In short, Graham's adventures in the publishing trade expose the same sort of systems of control and manipulation that Balzac analyzes in monumental detail in *Lost Illusions*: "... the play of wheels within wheels in Parisian life, the machinery behind it all." Despite such glimpses into the darkness of market forces, Graham resists the "real danger" of "irrevocable pessimism." Irony and humor help a great deal in carrying Graham through periods of despondency, and *Wildest Dreams* is laced with the mordant awareness that the novel today can scarce risk the audacity of nineteenth century realism which sought to understand the entire world: "In an atomised, isolated existence, each individual locked in a specialised role, social relationships fragmented and reduced, it was hard to see any overall picture, it was hard to get the overview of a Balzac or a Dickens" (248).

Overall, Wilding's Graham succeeds in his embrace of Sydney as a literary landscape in a way that Balzac's Lucien never does. Early in *Wildest Dreams* we read this of Graham: "As he grew into the literary present, he became conscious of the literary past. The flat, dusty walls of the brick city in the dusty sun filled out, developed the depth of a past, emanated the resonances of former hopes, lost futures, offered sites for all those imaginary possibilities, backdrops of desire, settings for anecdotes in its eating houses, pubs, streets" (41).

*Wildest Dreams* ends with Graham teaching creative writing at a university in California (Santa Barbara). In his office he can look at his bookshelf, "His oeuvre stacked there, multiples, overstocks, remainders, canceled editions, waiting for good homes to go to, better than letting them be pulped into egg cartons." In the story's last sentence Graham imagines his own ending to a story that one of his students is trying to write: "'Or maybe he swims out across the Pacific to an island and escapes,' said Graham. 'And survives and writes a book'" (310). The island is Australia, or alternatively, the island in Australia where Michael Wilding lives—and writes.

In 2006 he published a second memoir, *Wild Amazement*, and in 2011 a shorter but essential memoir focused on his adventures in small press publishing, *Wild & Woolley: A Publishing Memoir.*

*Wild Amazement* continues the project launched with *Wildest Dreams* and according to an authorial note, is part of the ongoing work "Literary Pages." A principal difference between the two books is that *Wild Amazement* is narrated in first person, though it maintains its distance from its actual subjects by means of character names familiar from earlier stories. Like the first volume, *Wild Amazement* explores the lively literary scene of Sydney in the Sixties, and Sydney thereafter, as careers soared and careers plummeted, as the literary world changed from hope, experimentation, and protest to various forms of success, failure, accommodation, and cooption. It also goes into much richer detail in the depiction of Valda (Vicki Viidikas), the lost angel of the period, an uncompromising talent bordering on genius. In the case of Joe, it adds several more chapters to the ongoing saga of the always lively Wilding/Moorhouse relationship. *Wild Amazement* also contains some compelling chapters dealing with England, with Wilding's native Worcester. Like many an expatriate before and afterwards, Wilding revisits the scene of his early life and gives us once again a moving account of the protocols of class, which he labels "the English disease" (47): "In Australia the democratic veneer was such that you did not feel endlessly judged in every restaurant, at every bar, with every purchase. No doubt judging went on, but it was more covert. It was not like the offensiveness and insolence of England where every phoneme of your accent, every thread of your garment was being pored over, microscopic examination of education, region, blood line, family connections" (47-48). His commentary on that topic makes a fine gloss on all those moments in his fiction when the English disease obtrudes. A later chapter brings Wilding face to face with his past, as he takes part in making a documentary film based upon his fictionalized (but factually based) stories about learning, humiliation, and the registers of snobbery in the grammar school in Worcester where he began the road to Oxford. The resultant documentary *Reading the Signs* makes for very good viewing, with Wilding on camera talking about his grammar school, his stories, and the Midlands.

To Wilding, Australia, especially Sydney, offered freedom, love, possibility, escape, and many other good things as well. Here is how he puts it: "Living in Sydney was what in England you would save up for a year to experience in a week" (102). It was, he writes, the "endless tropical escape" (102). But for Wilding that world was profoundly changed in a single political act. In a manner not told before in his work, the idea of a revitalized Australia ended on November 11, 1975, with the overturning of Whitlam's Labour government. Though Wilding is too ironical to identify wholly with Labour, still, that moment spelled a certain end of innocence. It was, in his words, "one of those significant days. The day they hanged Ned Kelly. Armistice Day...This time our innocence was destroyed, our naivety" (169). It also inaugurated, for Wilding anyway, a long period of retreat, paranoia fueled by the spirit of the times (and some prolonged marijuana use, about which he is quite candid), and a general sense that, as Virginia Woolf put it, echoing Tennyson, someone had blundered. From the late seventies onward, Wilding views the world apocalyptically, then post-apocalyptically, resulting in an increasingly pessimistic assessment of modern life propelled always, it seems, by his dismay at capitalism's next stage.

Besides memoirs, Wilding continued to edit various collections as had long been his practice. He and David Myers of Central Queensland University Press edited three volumes of short stories: *Best Stories Under the Sun* (2004), *Best Stories Under the Sun 2: Traveller's Tales* (2005); and *Confessions and Memoirs: Best Stories Under the Sun 3* (2006). Each of these volumes had a strong internationalist flavor, with stories from many parts of the globe. Other editing projects included *Cyril Hopkins' Marcus Clarke* (2009), edited by Laurie Hergenhan, Ken Stewart, and Wilding; and *Heart Matters* (2010), edited by Peter Corris and Wilding.

But Wilding was also writing a good deal of fiction during those years and earlier. In 2002 he returned to the novel form, and brought out *Academia Nuts*, a title that sounds more like a Marx Brothers comedy than what it is, a dead-on analysis, in comic terms, of everything that's wrong with university education today in Australia, and by easy cross-referencing, America as well. In fact, many of the recent reforms in Australian universities derive from the American model: thus more hours of classroom instruction, more imposition of theory, more attempts to turn education into a mode of industrialized production. The death of literature, of reading, of the literary life are all by-products of an emphasis upon bureaucratic procedures and an insistence upon theoretical criticism based on endless ponderings of racism, feminism, gender, and ethnicity.

Wilding locates, naturally enough, the site of his novel at ground zero of his professional life, the Department of English at the University of Sydney, where he spent his academic career. Now retired as Professor Emeritus, Wilding relives the years of the discipline's decline, when the study of literature and history became something else, something, to use a favorite Wilding word, "appalling."

The analysis arises from conversations among three University of Sydney professors. Henry Lancaster, a novelist and short story writer closely modeled upon Wilding himself, Dr. Bee, a cynical professor of literature, and Dr. Pawley, a Marxist critic who offers powerful insights into the nature of capitalism and its twin motives of competition and greed. (Dr. Pawley embodies the political aspect of Wilding's career, a Leftist critique of capitalism and globalism.) For anyone familiar with Wilding's circle of friends, it is tempting to speculate about one character or another being based on actual people, but Wilding has pointed out, "With Aca Nuts I was careful not to have recognizable characters generally. The materials were all based on actual academic episodes and incidents, in the main, but I fictionalized the characters into generic types." Then he continues: "Pawley and Henry are different aspects of myself. Dr Bee drew on aspects of Christopher Bentley, to whom the book is dedicated" ((MW email "Re: oh," March 30, 2012). Bentley was a colleague of Wilding's at the University of Sydney who one day in the middle of the semester simply walked away from the job and never returned (MW email "Re: who," March 31, 2012).

From their vantage point in favored restaurants scattered around the city and inner suburbs, the three men watch the world stumble into absurdity. They spend a great deal of time remarking upon the erosion of traditional learning. At one point Henry muses upon the triumph of the new: "The vanguard now was 'Cross-dressing in History,' 'The Development of the Gay Mardi Gras' in the 1990s,' 'Women Travellers since 1968,' 'Time, Space and the Body.'" Such titles, and far more more extreme ones, will be familiar to academics in English departments everywhere.

In Henry's own career, as a writer of fiction, the legions of political correctness threaten at every hand. In a scene late in the novel Henry meets two young women, both hilariously named Fiona, who work for a multinational publisher. The Fionas gleefully tell Henry that they've pulped all the dead white male list into egg cartons. What they want instead is fiction by women native peoples. The only thing left for Henry, aging white male, is to go to lunch, where he joins Dr. Bee and Pawley. They have the rest of the day to discuss the decline and fall of just about everything. There is hardly any aspect of modern university life that is not inimical. Dr. Bee observes at one point, for example, that the $200 fee for parking on campus is actually "just a licence to hunt for parking." Administrators are in the saddle and ride the faculty. In the end the novel holds out a bit of hope. Dr. Pawley (the scholarly radical side of Wilding) finds in Dr. Dee, the Elizabethan Magus, an image of magic that transcends the mundane: "There was another reality. Somewhere. He had to believe that. Otherwise it was all insupportable." Thus Wilding finds in magic, intellect, and resistance a form of heroism, a hopeful note indeed. In a mordantly funny coda, Wilding added a new chapter to the novel and reissued it in 2003. The new chapter grew out of the fact that the Chair of the English Department refused franking privileges for mailing review copies. Such administrative repression fulfilled the wildest dreams that the retired professors could have imagined over lunch at The Golden Bowl (La Botte D'oro in Leichhardt).

Henry and his gang return in *Superfluous Men* (2006). The stylized photograph on the book cover, incidentally, was based on a photo from La Botte D'oro depicting playwright David Williamson, biographer Brian Kiernan, book critic Don Anderson, Dale Atrens, author of *Don't Diet*, and Michael Wilding (MW email "Re: beats," April 1, 2012). The retired ones gather as always at their favorite restaurants to bemoan the wrack-and-ruin of academic life and to reflect upon the idiocies of university bureaucracies and the rise of new ideologies in criticism based on the new mantra of Cultural Studies. Beneath the sardonic commentary are large heapings of truth laced with the fears attendant upon superannuation—of being forgotten, of being forever irrelevant, of moving closer and closer to the great void. But amidst the negativism and pessimism, Wilding's protagonist, Henry Lancaster, finds a way to recover and move forward. The novel follows obliquely but rather closely the trajectory of Wilding's life following his retirement: health problems, hints of marital discord, and some uncertainty about how to extend his literary career. Henry's appointment as columnist for a newsletter published by the Writers' Centre at Rozelle (a post Wilding held for a number of years) stimulates his return to writing fiction. In a bit of self-reflective analysis, Henry's description of his working habits matches exactly what Wilding has said many times:

> It fitted in with his fantasies of the Higher Journalism. No more Lit. Crit. But in between the bouts of fiction he liked to write something different. It had always been the way he had worked, turning to Lit. Crit. when the fiction dried up, returning refreshed to fiction when the Lit. Crit. bogged down. Perhaps this was what he needed to get the fiction flowing again. He'd been slowing down, despite the freedom of early retirement. He had expected to write more with all that time on hand. But perhaps he needed the stimulus of the other, the reflective literary opinions to balance the creative moments, the variety, the alternatives. (131)

The novel ends on a hopeful note. Henry leaves the Writers' Centre, which is being taken over by the University, and he completes a new novel. The novel's last words are triumphant: "Renascent men" (337).

*National Treasure* in 2007 marked another genre move, as Wilding pivoted from what one might call the post-academic novel to an intellectualized crime/thriller genre. The novel introduces a new focal character, Plant, who specializes in "research assistance, investigative reporting" and who is hired to shepherd a "national treasure," Scobie, a popular Australian author who is losing his grip on sanity and his ability to churn out the best-selling pap that has made him a national treasure. The comedy runs from intellectual irony to zany farce, with the climax taking place at the iconic Sydney Opera House where the crazed author unveils a sudden but most timely discovery of his Aboriginality, a sure fire means in politically correct circles of recapturing and re-energizing the vast national love that he has long enjoyed. Wilding explains that he "took actual episodes and events—but fictionalized the characters. So events like the old ladies booing Scobie, Scobie stripping off, the book launch with no beer, the plagiarizing novelist, the novelist with a research assistant—all these are well enough known episodes in the literary life, I just bundled them together from gossip I'd heard or events I'd observed" (MW email "Re: oh," March 30, 2012). One character, however, is a very familiar one from Wilding's early work: Valda reappears as Nada—"Vicki Viidikas at her worst," as Wilding has commented in an email (March 30, 2012). When Scobie proclaims that Nada was the best writer of them all, she takes a $50 bill out of her nose where she has been inhaling coke, and says, "What's this 'was'?" (*National Treasure* 136). Still glamorous in that 60s' hippie-chick style, Nada no longer allows her writings to be published; she is too pure an artist to make any compromise.

Ross Fitzgerald, an author and newspaper columnist, has described the publishing situation in Australia in the second decade of the 21$^{st}$ century in terms similar to what Wilding has been saying for thirty years:

> What does the Australian publishing scene look like? Lots of product, but much good material is not getting out. The global publishers dominating the Australian book trade now work on a strict managerial model. Each book stands alone. Gone are the days when best-selling cookbooks subsidized small-run new fiction and poetry. Indeed, gone are the days when large publishers could justify doing small runs at all. ("Small Publishers Press On Regardless with Short Runs of Novels," December 3, 2011)

Taking advantage of the new digital technology, Wilding re-entered the small press publishing scene with a new imprint, Press On, in partnership with Nick Walker's Arcadia, based in Melbourne. Press On publishes fiction that might not otherwise appear, just as in the days of Wild & Woolley. Press-On has published fiction by well-known authors, including Inez Baranay (*With the Tiger*), Peter Corris (*Wishart's Quest*), Morris Lurie (*Hergesheimer Hangs In*), Phillip Edmonds (*Leaving Home with Henry*), Garry Disher (*Play Abandoned*), and Wilding himself. His two most recent novels, *The Prisoner of Mount Warning* (2010) and *The Magic of It* (2011), are Press On titles.

Plant is the viewpoint character in both novels. *The Prisoner of Mount Warning*, which is something of a reprise of the road-tripping of *Pacific Highway*, takes Plant on a wild ride up the coast from Sydney to Byron Bay. His goal is to find Charles Dorritt, who plans to publish his memoirs of torture and sex-slavery during the time when he fell into the hands of the security services. The connections with *Pacific Highway* are obvious: "Plant drove north, out on the freeway towards Newcastle and, after the freeway ended, up the Pacific Highway" (76). "This was the Pacific Highway. The road to the state's dope-growing source. One of the sources. One of the many. That didn't take away the point. There might be many roads to kif. But this was certainly one of them" (76). Plant's cleverness plays upon familiar Australian tropes: "I love a fun-burnt country" (32). And there are fond memories and descriptions of Balmain as well as evocations of "Hippyville...Byron Bay. Nimbin. Mushroom country" (70). One character remembers, "These were the good times. People just got stoned and got laid and got wiped out. There was too much happening to remember any of it. If you can remember it you weren't there" (71). Back in Sydney at one point, Plant recalls the kind of feeling for the North that informs *Pacific Highway*: "There was something about up north. The feeling was lighter, less oppressive. Maybe it was just the urban oppression of Sydney that was getting him down. Too many people" (205).

In *The Magic of It* Plant goes to Oxford as part of another conspiracy/surveillance plot, thus allowing Wilding to revisit once again the town and university where he once lived and studied, sites that he has written about in earlier works such as "Writing a Life" in *Under Saturn*. The novel involves other familiar Wilding interests, including black magic, dope-smoking, and sinister government conspiracies. As in the previous novels, Plant is a likeable paranoid narrator with a quick wit and wry sense of humor. It is likely that with Plant, Wilding will continue to turn out his version of spy novels.

During this same period of intense literary activity--writing, publishing, and editing--Wilding researched and wrote a substantial work on 19$^{th}$ century Australian literature. *Wild Bleak Bohemia: Marcus Clarke, Adam Lindsay Gordan and Henry Kendall: A Documentary* will be published by Australian Scholarly Publishing, Melbourne, 2013.

Certainly the 21$^{st}$ century has seen no slackening in the output or quality of Wilding's writing, editing, and publishing. The year 2013 will mark fifty years of Wilding's preeminence in Australian letters.

# References

## Works Cited

### Introduction: Water Glimpses

Davis, Mark. *Gangland: Cultural Elites and the New Generationalism.* St. Leonards, NSW: Allen & Unwin, 1997.

Hergenhan, Laurie. Review of *Studies in Classic Australian Fiction* in *Australian Literary Studies*, 18.2 (1997): 205-207.

Jose, Nicholas, ed. *The Literature of Australia.* New York: W. W. Norton, 2010.

Pierce, Peter. "Just Wild About the Book Business,'" *Canberra Times*, December 3, 2011, p. 28.

Richardson, Owen. "Wild and Woolley: A Publishing Memoir," *The Saturday Age,* November 26, 2011, p. 30.

Syson, Ian. "Michael Wilding's Three Centres of Value," *Australian Literary Studies*, 18.3 (1998): 269-279.

Wilding, Michael. "Writing Humour" in *Serious Frolic: Essays on Australian Humour*, eds. Fran De Groen and Peter Kirkpatrick. St Lucia, Qld.: University of Queensland Press, 2009.

Williamson, David. "Wild & Woolley: A Publishing Memoir," November, 2011, typescript, p. 4.

*Writer's Talk: Michael Wilding.* Video, 32 min. Interviewed by Don Graham. The University of Sidney Television Service, 1991.

### Chapter 1: The Undergrowth of Literary Production: England, Editing, Early Stories

Bennett, Bruce. *Australian Short Fiction: A History.* St Lucia, Qld.: University of Queensland Press, 2002.

Graham, Don. "The Rhetoric of Personal Address in Michael Wilding's Short Fiction," *Antipodes* (June 2012), 77-79.

Lawrence, D. H. *Lady Chatterley's Lover.* New York: Barnes & Noble Classics, 2005.

Lewis, Peter. "Interview with Michael Wilding," *Stand*, 33.1 (1991): 44-47. (Quotations are from an undated typescript).

Syson, Ian. "After Libertarianism: An Interview with Michael Wilding," *Australian Literary Studies*, 18.3 (May 1998): 280-292.

Tennant, Emma. *Burnt Diaries.* London: Cannongate Press, 1999.

Wilding, Michael, ed. *Three Tales* by Henry James. Sydney: Hicks Smith, 1967.

- - -. *The West Midland Underground.* St. Lucia: University of Queensland Press, 1975.

- - -. *Wild Amazement.* Rockhampton: Central Queensland University Press, 2006.

- - -. "Writing Humour" in *Serious Frolic: Essays on Australian Humour.* Eds. Fran De Groen and Peter Kirkpatrick. St Lucia, Qld.: University of Queensland Press, 2009.

Yeo, Robert. "Michael Wilding's Short Stories: A Speculative Note," in *Running Wild: Essays, Fictions and Memoirs Presented to Michael Wilding.* Eds. David Brooks and Brian Kiernan. *Sydney Studies in Society and Culture, no. 22.* New Delhi: Manohar. Sydney: Sydney Association for Studies in Society and Culture, 2004.

## Chapter 2: Varieties of Jamesian Experience: *Aspects of the Dying Process*

Borges, Jorge Luis. *Ficciones.* New York: Alfred A. Knopf, 1993.

Davidson, Jim. "Interview with A.A. Phillips," *Meanjin* 36. 3 (October 1977): 286-297.

Gerrand, Rob, ed. *The Best Australian Science Fiction Writing: A Fifty Year Collection.* Melbourne: Black, Inc., 2004.

Harrison-Ford, Carl. "The Short Stories of Wilding and Moorhouse," *Southerly* 33. 2 (1973): 167-178.

Moorhouse, Frank. *The Americans, Baby.* Sydney: Angus and Robertson, 1972.

- - -. "There's No Such Thing as a Gay Novel," interview with Frank Moorhouse by Martin Smith, *Campaign* (Sydney), 21 (1977): 19.

Smith, C. P. "Night Flight to Amsterdam," *Man* (July 1970): 18, 20, 94-96.

Tennant, Emma. *Burnt Diaries.* London: Cannongate Press, 1999.

Webster, Owen. "The Literary Life of Australia," *Overland*, 45 (Autumn 1970): 27-32.

Wilding, Michael. "Adventurous Spirits" in *The Writer's Press—UQP's First Fifty Years.*Ed. Craig Munro.St Lucia: University of Queensland Press, 1988.

- - -. *Aspects of the Dying Process.* St Lucia: University of Queensland Press, 1972.

- - -. "Don't Go Having Kittens," *Man*, 75.1 (January 1974): 64-66, 115.

- - -. "Like Rat Turds to Me," *Chance International*, 2.10 (1970): 57-61.

- - -. *Reading the Signs.* Sydney: Hale & Iremonger, 1984.

- - -. "They Might Have Been Brother and Sister," *Squire*, 3. 3 (November 1966): 8-10, 31, 34

- - -. "A Survey," *Australian Literary Studies*, VIII (1977): 115-126.

- - -. *Somewhere New: New & Selected Stories.* Rockhampton, Qld.: Central Queensland University Press, 1996.

- - -. "The Fir Trees," *Casual*, 1.2 (1970), 17-19.

- - - , ed. *The Tabloid Story Pocketbook.* Sydney: Wild & Woolley, 1978.

- - -. *Wild & Woolley: A Publishing Memoir.* Artamon NSW: Giramondo Publishing Company, 2011.

- - -. "Writing Humour" in *Serious Frolic: Essays on Australian Humour.* eds. Fran De Groen and Peter Kirkpatrick. St. Lucia, Qld.: University of Queensland Press, 2009.

## Chapter 3: Varieties of Kerouackian Experience: The West Midland Underground

Doyle, Arthur Conan. *The Complete Sherlock Holmes*, II. Introduction and Notes by Kyle Freeman. New York: Barnes & Noble Classics, 2003.

Kiernan, Brian, ed. *The Most Beautiful Lies: A Collection of Stories by Five Major Contemporary Fiction Writers: Bail, Carey, Lurie, Moorhouse and Wilding*. Sydney: Angus & Robertson Publishers, 1977.

- - -. "Notes on Frank Moorhouse," *Overland*, 56 (Spring 1973): 9-11.

Lawrence, Larry. "Don't Knock Zen," *Man International*, 9. 1 (1970): 43.

Moorhouse, Frank. *The Americans, Baby*. Sydney: Angus and Robertson, 1972.

- - -. *Tales of Mystery and Romance*. North Ryde, N.S.W: Angus & Robertson, 1980 [1977].

Roberts, Nigel. "Untitled" in *We Took Their Orders and Are Dead: An Anti-war Anthology*, eds. Shirley Cass, Ros Cheney, David Malouf and Michael Wilding. Sydney: Ure Smith, 1971.

Syson, Ian. "After Libertarianism: An Interview with Michael Wilding," *Australian Literary Studies*, 18. 3 (May 1998): 280-292.

Trika, Pradeep. *Frank Moorhouse: The Writer as an Artist*. Shipra, India, 2000.

Viidikas, Vicki. *New and Rediscovered: Vicki Viidikas*, ed. Barry Scott. Transit Lounge Publishing. Yarraville, Australia, 2010.

- - -. *Wrappings*. Sydney: Wild & Woolley, 1974.

Waller, Louise. "To Be Worded Again, To Be Answered" [review of *New and Rediscovered: Vicki Viidikas*]. www.foame.org/Issue8/reviews1.html/Cached.

Wilding, Michael. "Cars in My Life" in *Car Lovers: Twelve Australian Writers on Four Wheels*. Ed. John Dale. Sydney: ABC Books, 2008.

- - -. "The Man of Slow Feeling," *Man*, 68 (July 1970): 30-33, 38.

- - -. *This is For You*. Sydney: Angus & Robertson, 1994.

- - -. *Wild Amazement*. Rockhampton: Central Queensland University Press, 2006.

- - -. *Wild & Woolley: A Publishing Memoir*. Artamon, NSW: Giramondo Publishing Company, 2011.

- - -. *Wildest Dreams*. St Lucia: The University of Queensland Press, 1998.

- - -. "Writing Humour" in *Serious Frolic: Essays on Australian Humour*. Eds. Fran De Groen and Peter Kirkpatrick. St. Lucia: University of Queensland Press, 2009.

## Chapter 4: Writers Living Together: *The Short Story Embassy: A Novel*

Amis, Kingsley. *Jake's Thing*. Harmondsworth, Middlesex, England: Penguin, 1979.

Brooks, David, and Brian Kiernan, eds. *Running Wild: Essays, Fictions and Memoirs Presented to Michael Wilding. Sydney Studies in Society and Culture, no. 22.* New Delhi: Manohar. Sydney: Sydney Association for Studies in Society and Culture, 2004.

Clunies Ross, Bruce A. "Laszlo's Testament or Structuring the Past and Sketching the Present in Contemporary Short Fiction, Mainly Australian," *Kunapipi* 1.2 (1979): 110-23.

- - -. "Paradise, Politics and Fiction: The Writing of Michael Wilding," *Meanjin* 46. 1 (1986): 19-27.

Graham, Don. "Koka-Kola Kulture: Reflections Upon Things American Down Under," *Southwest Review*, 78. 2 (Spring 1993): 231-244.

Kiernan, Brian, ed. *The Most Beautiful Lies: A Collection of Stories by Five Major Contemporary Fiction Writers Bail, Carey, Lurie, Moorhouse and Wilding*. Sydney: Angus & Robertson, 1977.

- - -. "Recent Developments in Australian Writing with Particular Reference to Short Fiction." *Caliban* (Tolouse), 14 (1977): 123-134.

Leves, Kerry. "Foreword" to *New and Rediscovered: Vicki Viidikas*. Ed. Barry Scott. Yarraville, Australia: Transit Lounge Publishing, 2010.

McLaren, John, "Harvest of Stories," *Overland*, 44 (Winter 1970): 52-53.

Moorhouse, Frank, ed. *Days of Wine and Rage*. Ringwood, Victoria: Penguin Books, 1980.

Wilding, Michael. "Characters," *Newswrite*, 117 (July 2002): 3.

- - -. *Living Together*. St Lucia: University of Queensland Press, 1974.

- - -. *The Phallic Forest*. Sydney: Wild & Woolley. Dunedin, John McIndoe, 1978.

- - -. *The Short Story Embassy: A Novel*. Sydney: Wild & Woolley, 1975.

- - -. "A Survey." *Australian Literary Studies*, 8 (1977): 115-26.

- - -. "Trenchant Writer Blitzed Bohemia." *The Australian*, (December 11, 1998): 16.

- - -. Vivid Sketches from an Age of Liberation," *Sydney Morning Herald*, May 15-16, 2010: 36.

- - -. *Wild & Woolley: A Publishing Memoir*. Artamon NSW: Giramondo Publishing Company, 2011.

- - -. "Writing Humour" in *Serious Frolic: Essays on Australian Humour*. Eds. Fran De Groen and Peter Kirkpatrick. St. Lucia: University of Queensland Press, 2009.

Wynhausen, Elisabeth. *Manly Girls*. Ringwood, Victoria: Penguin, 1989.

**Chapter 5: Post-Modernism in High Gear: *Scenic Drive***

Gelder, Ken and Paul Salzman. *The New Diversity: Australian Fiction 1970-1988*. Melbourne: McPhee Gribble Publishers, 1989.

Hergenhan, Laurie. "Brian Kiernan, Critic and Editor: Some Reminiscences," *Antipodes* 22. 1 (June 2008): 12-13.

McLaren, John. "Recent Fiction," *Overland* 149 (1976): 64-66.

Wilding, Michael. *Scenic Drive*. Sydney: Wild & Woolley, 1976.

- - -."The Importance of Rewriting," *Newswrite*, 90 (February 2000): 3.

- - -. *Wild & Woolley: A Publishing Memoir*. Artamon N.SW.: Giramondo Publishing Company, 2011.

- - -. *Wildest Dreams*. St Lucia: University of Queensland Press, 1998.

## Chapter 6: Sex and the Single Male: *The Phallic Forest*

Clancy, Laurie. *A Reader's Guide to Australian Fiction*. Melbourne: Oxford Universitiy Press, 1992.

Dow, Louise. "Written Off," *Meanjin* 46. 2 (June 1987): 219-222.

Jefferis, Barbara. "Late Bloomer, Shining Light: Amy Witting, Writer, 1918-2001," *Sydney Morning Herald*, September 25, 2001, p. 35.

Lawrence, D. H. *Lady Chatterley's Lover*. New York: Barnes & Noble Classics, 2005.

Moorhouse, Frank. *Futility and Other Animals*. Sydney: Gareth Powell Associates, 1969.

Wilding, Michael. "Adventurous Spirits" in *The Writer's Press—UQP's First Fifty Years*. Ed. Craig Munro. St Lucia: University of Queensland Press, 1988.

- - -. ed. *The Tabloid Story Pocketbook*. Sydney: Wild & Woolley, 1978.

- - -. *Under Saturn*. Australia: Black Swan, 1988.

- - -. *Wild & Woolley: A Publishing Memoir*. Artamon NSW: Giramondo, 2011.

## Chapter 7: Renovated Realism

Balzac, Honoré. *Lost Illusions*. Trans. by Kathleen Raine. Introduction by James Madden. New York: The Modern Library, 2001.

Bennett, Bruce. *The Spying Game: An Australian Angle*. Melbourne: Australian Scholarly Publishing, 2012.

Fitzgerald, Ross. "Small Publishers Press On Regardless with Short Runs of Novels," *The Australian*, December 3, 2011.

Syson, Ian. "After Libertarianism: An Interview with Michael Wilding," *Australian Literary Studies,* 18.3 (May 1998): 280-292.

Wilding, Michael. *Pacific Highway*. Sydney: Hale & Iremonger, 1982.

- - -. *The Paraguayan Experiment* Ringwood, Victoria: Penguin, 1984.

- - -. *Studies in Classic Australian Fiction. Sydney Studies in Society and Culture, no. 16.* Sydney: Sydney Studies. Nottingham, U.K.: Shoestring Press, 1997.

- - -. *This Is For You.* Sydney: Angus & Robertson, 1994.

- - -. *The Prisoner of Mount Warning.* Melbourne: Arcadia/Press On, 2010.

- - -. *Under Saturn: Four Stories.* Moorebank, N.S.W: Black Swan, 1988.

- - -. *Wild Amazement.* Rockhampton: Central Queensland University Press, 2006.

- - -. *Wildest Dreams.* St Lucia: University of Queensland Press, 1998.

*Writer's Talk: Michael Wilding.* Video, 32 min. Interviewed by Don Graham. The University of Sydney Television Service, 1991.

## Bibliography

Albahari, David. "Interview with Michael Wilding," *Australian Literary Studies*, 9 (1980): 321-327.

Amis, Kingsley. *Jake's Thing.* Harmondsworth, Middlesex, England: Penguin, 1979.

Anderson, Don. *Hot Copy: Reading & Writing Now.* Ringwood: Penguin, 1986. Pp. 46-48.

- - -. *Text & Sex.* Sydney: Random House Vintage, 1995. Pp. 123, 139-140, 145.

Balzac, Honorè. *Lost Illusions.* Trans. by Kathleen Raine. Introduction by James Madden. New York: The Modern Library, 2001.

Bennett, Bruce. *Australian Short Fiction: A History.* St. Lucia: University of Queensland Press, 2002.

- - -. "Michael Wilding" in James Vinson, ed., *Contemporary Novelists.* 4th edition. London: Macmillan, 1987.

- - -. *The Spying Game: An Australian Angle.* Melbourne: Australian Scholarly Publishing, 2012. Pp. 29-32, 35

Borges, Jorge Luis. *Ficciones.* New York: Alfred A. Knopf, 1993.

Burns, Teresa. "Interview with Michael Wilding," *Journal of the Western Mystery Tradition*, vol. 3, no. 24, (March 2013).

Caesar, Adrian. "Pursuing Wild Dreams," in *Running Wild: Essays, Fictions and Memoirs Presented to Michael Wilding*, ed. David Brooks and Brian Kiernan. *Sydney Studies in Society and Culture, no. 22.* Sydney: Sydney Association for Studies in Society and Culture. New Delhi: Manohar, 2004. Pp. 259-266.

Cantrell, Leon. "The New Novel" in K. G. Hamilton, ed., *Studies in the Recent Australian Novel.* St. Lucia: University of Queensland Press, 1978. Pp. 225-57.

Clancy, Laurie. *A Readers' Guide to Australian Fiction.* Melbourne: Oxford University Press, 1992.

Clunies Ross, Bruce, "A New Version of Pastoral: the Fiction of Michael Wilding," *Australian Literary Studies,* XI (1983): 182-194.

- - -. "Laszlo's Testament or Structuring the Past and Sketching the Present in Contemporary Short Fiction, Mainly Australian," *Kunapipi*, 1.2 (1979): 110-123.

- - -. "Paradise, Politics and Fiction: The Writing of Michael Wilding," *Meanjin* 1.2 (1979): 110-123.

- - -. "Stories of Things Happening,' in *Running Wild*, pp. 233-246.

Conlon, Stephen. "The New Idea of the University as an Academic Theme Park: *Academia Nuts,*" *Asian Journal of Literature, Culture and Society* 1.1 (February 2007): 1-22.

Davidson, Jim. "Interview with A.A. Phillips," *Meanjin* 36.3 (October 1977): 286-297.

Davidson, Robyn. *Tracks.* New York: Random House, 1995.

Davis, Mark. *Gangland: Cultural Elites and the New Generationalism.* St. Leonards, NSW: Allen & Unwin, 1997.

Dow, Louise. "Written Off," *Meanjin* 46.2 (June 1987): 219-222.

Doyle, Arthur Conan. *The Complete Sherlock Holmes, II.* Introduction and Notes by Kyle Freeman. New York: Barnes & Noble Classics, 2003.

Dunn, Irina. "Tribute to Michael Wilding," *Newswrite*, 122 (December 2002): 5.

Fitzgerald, Ross. "Small Publishers Press On Regardless with Short Runs of Novels," *The Australian*, December 3, 2011.

- - -. "That Odd Notion of Throwing a Party for People Who Prefer To Be Alone, Writing," *The Weekend Australian*, (1), May 5-6, 2012.

Gelder, Ken. "Character and Environment in Some Recent Australian Fiction," *Waves* (York University, Ontario), VII (1979), 437-444.

- - -. "Uncertainty and Subversion in the Australian Novel," *Pacific (Moana) Quarterly* (Hamilton, New Zealand), IV (1979): 437-444.

- - - and Paul Salzman. *The New Diversity: Australian Fiction 1970-88*. Melbourne: McPhee Gribble, 1989.

Gerrand, Rob, ed. *The Best Australian Science Fiction Writing: A Fifty Year Collection*. Melbourne: Black Ink, Inc., 2004.

Gillard, G. M. "The New Writing: Whodunnit?" *Meanjin*, XL (1981): 167-174.

Giuffre, Giulia, "Interview with Michael Wilding," *Southerly*, 46 (1986): 313-321.

Graham, Don. "Koka-Kola Kulture: Reflections Upon Things American Down Under," *Southwest Review*, 78.2 (Spring 1993): 231-244.

- - -. "Michael Wilding's 'Lost Illusions': The Balzacian Underpinnnings of *Wildest Dreams*," in Francis de Groen and Ken Stewart, eds., *Australian Writing and the City: Refereed Proceedings of the 1999 Conference*. Sydney: ASAL, 2000. Pp. 138-143.

- - -. "Review of *Academia Nuts*," *JAS Review of Books*, 20 (November 2003).

- - -. "Review of *Her Most Bizarre Sexual Experience*," *Antipodes*, 6.1 (June 1993): 89.

- - -. "Review of *Somewhere New: New & Selected Stories*," *Studies in Short Fiction*, 34.4 (Fall 1997): 528-530.

- - -. "Review of *Studies in Classic Australian Fiction*," *Journal of English and Germanic Philology* (April 1999): 273-275.

- - -. "Review of *Wildest Dreams: A Selective Memoir*," *Antipodes*, 13.1 (June 1999): 45-46.

- - -. "The Rhetoric of Personal Address in Michael Wilding's Short Fiction," *Antipodes* (June 2012): 77-79.

- - -. "The Voice on the Verandah," in *Running Wild*, pp. 247-258.

Harrison-Ford, Carl. "The Short Stories of Wilding and Moorhouse," *Southerly*,33.2 (1973): 167-178.

Harrison-Ford, Carl, Tim Thorne, Don Anderson, Andrew Riemer, Bill Ashcroft and Helen Daniel in Helen Daniel, ed., *The Good Reading Guide*. Melbourne: McPhee Gribble, 1989. Pp. 273-76.

Hauge, Hans. "Post-Modernism and the Australian Literary Heritage," *Overland*, 96 (1984): 50-51.

Hergenhan, Laurie. "Brian Kiernan, Critic and Editor: Some Reminiscences," *Antipodes*, 22.1 (June 2008): 12-13.

- - -. "Literary New Chums: Michael Wilding and Marcus Clarke," in *Running Wild*, 223-232.

- - -. "Re-Fashioning the Campus Novel: Michael Wilding's *Academia Nuts*," in Confluenze *Intertstuali. In onore de Angelo Righetti*, eds. Annalisa Pes and Susanna Zinato. Liguori, Naples, 2012. Pp. 131-9.

- - -. "Review of *Studies in Classic Australian Fiction*," *Australian Literary Studies*, 18.2 (1997): 205-07.

Holt, Patricia, ed. *A City in the Mind: Sydney--Imagined by Its Writers*. Sydney: Angus & Robertson, 1972.

Jefferis, Barbara. "Late Bloomer, Shining Light: Amy Witting, Writer, 1918-2001," *Sydney Morning Herald*, September 25, 2001, p. 35.

Jose, Nicholas, ed. *The Literature of Australia*. New York: W.W. Norton, 2010.

Kiernan, Brian. "Literary Sydney" in *Twentieth Century Sydney*, ed. Jill Roe. Sydney: Hale & Iremonger, 1980.

- - -. "Notes on Frank Moorhouse," *Overland*, 56 (Spring 1973): 9-11.

- - -. "Recent Developments in Australian Writing with Particular Reference to Short Fiction," *Caliban*, 14 (1977): 123-124.

- - -. *Studies in Australian Literary History. Sydney Studies* in Society and Culture, no. 17. *Sydney:* Sydney Association for Studies in Society and Culture. Nottingham, U.K.: Shoestring Press, 1997.

- - -. ed. *The Most Beautiful Lies: A Collection of Stories by Five Major Contemporary Fiction Writers: Bail, Carey, Lurie, Moorhouse and Wilding.* Australia: Angus & Robertson, 1977.

- - -. "Tichborne Redivivus: Re-viewing Michael Wilding's Fiction," in *Running Wild*, pp. 197-208.

Kusnir, Jaroslav. "Michael Wilding, Murray Bail, Rodney Hall and Frank Moorhouse, in Nicholas Burns and Rebecca McNeer, eds., *A Companion to Australian Literature Since 1900*. Rochester, NY: Camden House, 2007. Pp. 359-374.

Lawrence, D. H. *Lady Chatterley's Lover.* New York: Barnes & Noble Classics, 2005.

Lawrence, Larry. "Don't Knock Zen," *Man International*, 9.1 (1970): 43.

Lewis, Peter. "Interview with Michael Wilding," *Stand* (Newcastle upon Tyne, U.K.), 33.1 (1991): 44-47.

McLaren, John. "Harvest of Stories," *Overland*, 44 (Winter 1970): 52-53.

Matchett, Stephen. "Well-Schooled Eye for Scandal," *Australian*, Higher Education, August 31, 2011, p. 37.

Maver. Igor. "'My Beloved Mississippi River': Michael Wilding's *Somewhere New*," *Antipodes*, 12, ii (December 1998): 83-89.

- - -. "Non-Australian Settings in Michael Wilding's Selected and New Short Stories in *Somewhere New*," in Igor Maver, *Contemporary Australian Literature Between Europe and Australia. Sydney Studies in Society and Culture*, no. 18. Sydney: Sydney Association for Studies in Society and Culture. Nottingham, U.K.: Shoestring Press, 1999. Pp. 17-41.

- - -. "Oh My America, My Newfoundland, Australia...", *Acta Neophilogica* (Ljubljana), XXVIII (1995): 75-80.

Moorhouse, Frank. ed. *Days of Wine and Rage*. Ringwood, Victoria: Penguin Books, 1980.

- - -. *Futility and Other Animals*. Sydney: Gareth Powell Associates, 1969.

- - -. "Girls Galore," *Dissent* (Winter 1967): 13-16

- - -. *The Americans, Baby*. Sydney: Angus & Robertson, 1972.

- - -. *Tales of Mystery and Romance*. North Ryde, NSW: Angus & Robertson, 1980.

- - -. "There's No Such Thing as a Gay Novel," Interview with Frank Moorhouse by Martin Smith, Sydney *Campaign*, 21 (1977): 19.

Obradovic, Nadezda, "A Return to Narrative: Talking with Michael Wilding," *Antipodes*, 8.ii (June 1994): 9-13.

Parigi, Frank. "Frank Moorhouse and Michael Wilding--and Internationalsm," *Antipodes*, 8.ii (June 1994): 15-20.

Pierce, Peter. "Just Wild About the Book Business," *Canberra Times*, December 3, 2011, p. 28.

- - -. "Michael Wilding," *Dictionary of Literary Biography,* ed. Selina Samuels. Thomson Gale, 2007.

Pym, Anthony. "How Much of Australia Fits into Spain?" *Meanjin*, 3 (1989): 663-670.

*Reading the Signs* (Documentary on the Writing of Michael Wilding). David Dunn, director, J.B.J. Berrow, producer. Central Independent Television, Birmingham, U.K. 1988. 30 min.

Reid, Ian. "The Social Semiotic of Narrative Exchange," in Terry Threadgold, E.A. Grosz, G. Kress and M.A.K. Halliday, ed., *Semiotics, Ideology, Language. Sydney Studies in Society & Culture, no. 3,* Sydney Association for Studies in Society and Culture,1986.

Richardson, Owen. "Wild & Woolley: A Publishing Memoir," *The Saturday Age*, November 26, 2011, p. 30.

Riemenschneider, Dieter. "The Triangle of Art and Life: Michael Wilding, Short Story Writer" in Jacqueline Bardolph, ed., *Telling Stories: Post-Colonial Short Fiction in English*. Amsterdam and Atlanta: Rodopi, 2001. Pp. 427-38.

Sallah, Adrienne. "Virgin Sock-Washers and Tweed Jackets: The Short Story in the 1970s," *Southerly*, 68.2 (November 2008): 181-196.

Sallah, ben Joned. "Interview with Michael Wilding," *New Straits Times* (Kuala Lumpur), January 20, 1999: 6.

Sarzin, Anne. "Wildng Chronicles the Decline of Literary Life in Sydney," *University of Sydney News* (May 1998): 280-292.

Smith, C. P. "Night Flight to Amsterdam," *Man* (July 1970): 18, 20, 94-96.

Syson, Ian. "After Libertarianism: An Interview with Michael Wilding," *Australian Literary Studies*, 18.3 (May 1998), 280-292.

- - -. "Michael Wilding's Three Centres of Value," *Australian Literary Studies*, 18.3 (May 1998): 269-272.

Tennant, Emma. *Burnt Diaries.* London: Cannongate Press, 1999.

Trika, Pradeep. "Australian Short Fiction—The Last Thirty Years," *Commonwealth Studies*, 4.i & ii (1996): 144-149.

- - -. *Frank Moorhouse: The Writer as Artist.* Shipra, India, 2000.

- - -. "Michael Wilding's Short Stories with Magnitude," *The Literary Criterion*, 30.i & ii (1995): 141-144.

- - -. "The New Wave in Australian Fiction: 1965-1995," *Occasional Papers* (March 1999): 43-51.

Vauthier, Simone. "Reading the Signs of Michael Wilding's 'Knock Knock'" in Giovanna Capone, ed., *European Perspectives: Contemporary Essays on Australian Literature.* St. Lucia: University of Queensland Press, 1991. Pp. 128-139.

- - -. "Lost and Found: Narrative and Description in Michael Wilding's "What It Was Like, Sometimes," *Journal of the Short Story in English, Les Cahiers de la Nouvelle* (University of Angers), 12 (1989): 63-76.

Viidikas, Vicki. *Condition Red.* St. Lucia: University of Queensland Press, 1973.

- - -. *New and Rediscovered: Vicki Viidikas*. Ed. Barry Scott. "Foreword" by Kerry Leves. Yarraville, Australia: Transit Lounge Publishing, 2010.

- - -. *Wrappings.* Sydney: Wild & Woolley, 1974.

Waller, Louise. "To Be Worded Again, To Be Answered" [review of *New and Rediscovered Vicki Viidikas*], www.foame.org/Issue8/reviews1.htnl/Cached

Webster, Owen. "The Literary Life of Australia," *Overland*, 45 (Autumn 1970): 27-32.

Wilde, W. H., Barry Andrews and Joy Hooton, ed., *The Oxford Companion to Australian Literature*. Melbourne: Oxford University Press, 1985. 2$^{nd}$ edition., 1994. Pp. 815-816.

Wilding, Michael. *Academia Nuts*. Glebe, NSW: Wild & Woolley, 2002. Rev. edition, 2003.

- - -. "Adventurous Spirits" in *The Writer's Press--UQP's First Fifty Years*. Ed. Craig Munro. St Lucia: University of Queensland Press, 1988.

---. "Among Leavisites," *Southerly*, 59, iii-iv (Spring and Summer, 1999): 67-93.

- - -. *Aspects of the Dying Process*. St Lucia: University of Queensland Press, 1972.

- - - and Charles Higham, eds. *Australians Abroad: An Anthology*. Melbourne: Cheshire, 1967.

- - -. "A Survey," *Australian Literary Studies*, VIII (1977): 115-126.

- - - and David Myers, eds. *Best Stories Under the Sun*. Rockhampton: Central Queensland University, 2004.

- - - and David Myers, eds. *Best Stories Under the Sun 2: Traveller's Tales*. Rockhampton: Central Queensland University, 2005.

- - -. *Book of the Reading*. Brooklyn, NSW: Paper Bark Press, 1994.

- - - and David Myers, eds. *Confessions and Memoirs: Best Stories Under the Sun 3*. Rockhampton: Central Queensland University, 2006.

- - -. "Cars in My Life," in *Car Lovers: Twelve Australian Writers on Four Wheels*. Ed. John Dale. Sydney: ABC Books, 2008.

- - - and Michael Green. *Cultural Policy in Great Britain*. Paris: UNESCO, 1970.

- - -. Laurie Hergenhan, and Ken Stewart, eds. *Cyril Hopkins' Marcus Clarke*. Melbourne: Australian Scholarly Publishing, 2009.

- - -. "Don't Go Having Kittens," *Man*, 75.1 (January 1974): 64-66, 115.

- - -. *Dragon's Teeth: Literature in the English Revolution*. Oxford: Clarendon Press/New York: Oxford University Press, 1987.

- - -. *Great Climate*. London: Faber & Faber, 1990; in U.S., *Her Most Bizarre Sexual Experience* New York: Norton, 1991.

- - - and Peter Corris, eds., *Heart Matters*. Melbourne: Viking, 2010.

- - -. "Like Rat Turds to Me," *Chance International*, 2.10 (1970): 57-61.

- - -. *Living Together*. St Lucia: University of Queensland Press, 1974.

- - -. *Milton's Paradise Lost*. Sydney: Sydney University Press, 1969.

- - -. *Marcus Clarke*. Australian Writers and Their Work. Melbourne: Oxford University Press, 1977.

- - -, ed. *Marcus Clarke: For the Term of His Natural Life, Short Stories,*

*Critical Essays and Journalism*. St Lucia: University of Queensland Press, 1976.

- - -, ed. *Marvell: Modern Judgments*. London: Macmillan, 1969. Nashville: Aurora, 1970.

- - -. *National Treasure*. Rockhampton: Central Queensland University Press, 2007.

- - -. *Pacific Highway*. Sydney: Hale & Iremonger, 1982.

- - -. *Political Fictions*. London: Routledge & Kegan Paul, 1980.

- - -. *Raising Spirits, Making Gold and Swapping Wives: The True Adventures of Dr John Dee and Sir Edward Kelly* Nottingham, U.K.: Shoestring Press. Sydney: Abbott Bentley, 1999.

- - -. *Reading the Signs*. Sydney: Hale & Iremonger, 1984.

- - -. *Scenic Drive*. Sydney: Wild & Woolley, 1976.

- - -. *Social Visions*. Sydney Studies in Society and Culture, no. 8. Sydney: Sydney Association for Studies in Society and Culture, 1994.

- - -. *Somewhere New: New & Selected Stories*. Rockhampton: Central Queensland University Press, 1996.

- - -. *The Magic of It*. Melbourne: Arcadia/Press On, 2011.

- - -. "The Man of Slow Feeling," *Man*, 68 (July 1970): 30-33, 38.

- - -. *The Man of Slow Feeling: Selected Short Stories*. Ringwood, Victoria: Penguin, 1985.

- - -. *The Paraguayan Experiment*. Ringwood and Harmondsworth: Penguin, 1984.

- - -. *The Phallic Forest*. Sydney: Wild & Woolley. Dunedin: John McIndoe, 1978.

- - -. *The Prisoner of Mount Warning*. Melbourne: Arcadia/Press On, 2010.

- - -, ed. *The Tragedy of Julius Caesar* and *The Tragedy of Marcus Brutus* by John Sheffied. London: Cornmarket, 1970.

- - -. *The Short Story Embassy: A Novel*. Sydney: Wild & Woolley, 1975.

- - -. "They Might Have Been Brother and Sister," *Squire*, 3.3 (November 1966), 8-10, 31, 34.

- - -. *Studies in Classic Australian Fiction. Sydney Studies* in Society and Culture, no. 16. Sydney: Sydney Association for Studies in Society and Culture. Nottingham, U.K.: Shoestring Press, 1997.

- - -. *Superfluous Men*. Melbourne: Arcadia/Press On, 2009.

- - -, ed. *The Tabloid Story Pocketbook*. Sydney: Wild & Woolley, 1978.

- - -. *This is for You*. Sydney: Angus & Robertson, 1994.

- - -, ed. *The Oxford Book of Australian Short Stories*. Melbourne: Oxford University Press, 1994.

- - - and Stephen Knight, eds. *The Radical Reader*. Sydney: Wild & Woolley, 1977.

- - -, ed. *Three Tales by Henry James*. Sydney: Hicks Smith, 1967.

- - -. "Trenchant Writer Blitzed Bohemia," *The Australian* (December 11, 1978): 16.

- - -. *Under Saturn: Four Stories*. Moorebank, NSW: Black Swan, 1988.

- - -. "Vivid Sketches from an Age of Liberation," *Sydney Morning Herald*, May 15-16, 2010: 36.

- - -. *The West Midland Underground*. St Lucia: University of Queensland Press, 1975.

- - - and Shirley Cass, Ros Cheney, and David Malouf, eds. *We Took Their Orders and Are Dead: An Anti-war Anthology.* Sydney: Ure Smith, 1971.

- - -. *Wild Amazement.* Rockhampton: Central Queensland University Press, 2006.

- - -. *Wild & Woolley: A Publishing Memoir.* Artamon NSW: Giramondo Publishing Company, 2011,

- - -. *Wildest Dreams.* St. Lucia: The University of Queensland Press, 1998.

- - -. "Writing Humour" in *Serious Frolic: Essays on Australian Humour*, eds. Fran De Groen and Peter Kirkpatrick. St Lucia: University of Queensland Press, 2009.

Williamson, David. "Wild & Woolley: A Publishing Memoir," November, 2011, typescript, p. 4.

*Writer's Talk: Michael Wilding.* Video, 32 min. Interviewed by Don Graham. The University of Sidney Television Service, 1991.

Wynhausen, Elisabeth. *Manly Girls.* Ringwood, Victoria: Penguin, 1989.

Yeo, Robert. "Michael Wilding's Short Stories: A Speculative Note," in *Running Wild*, 187-196.

# INDEX

Abraham, Lyndy, xi
*Academia Nuts*, xv, 74, 228
"Across the Plains, Over the Mountains, and Down to the Sea," 42, 110
Adamson, Robert, 4, 31, 89, 91, 100–101, 107, 157, 182, 211, 217
"Adventure of the Empty House, The," 109
"Adventurous Spirits," 127, 179, 182
"After Libertarianism," 213–215
Alice in Wonderland, 73
*Alta*, 208
"Altar of the Family, The," 31, 186
*Ambassadors, The*, 58
"American Poet's Visit, The," 168
Amis, Kingsley, 17, 127
"And Did Henry Miller Walk in Our Tropical Garden," 57, 79
Anderson, Don, xiv, 106, 120, 181, 187, 230
Anoux, Victoria, 185
*Anglo-Saxon Chronicle*, 159
*Antipodes*, 24, 100
*Antique Children*, 23
"Around the Laundromats," 204
"As Boys to Wanton Flies," 31
*As I Lay Dying*, 135
"Aspects of the Dying Process," 4, 12–14, 23–24, 30, 38, 44–45, 54, 57, 65, 79, 84, 126, 182, 185–187
*Aspects of the Dying Process*, 4, 12, 14, 23–24, 30, 38, 44–45, 54, 57, 79, 84, 126, 182, 186–187
*Assembling*, 24

*Atlantic, The*, 22
Atrens, Dale, 230
"Australia," 34
*Australian Highway*, 122
*Australian Short Fiction: A History*, 5
*Australian Ugliness, The*, 28
*Australians Abroad*, 4, 15, 37

Bach, Johann Sebastian, 104
"Bachelor Literature," 185
*Bachy*, 23
"Ballad of the Lonely Masturbator, The," 109
Balzac, Honoré de, 142, 173, 207, 219–225
*Bananas*, 51
*Bande á Part*, 68
Bail, Murray, xiv
Baranay, Inez, 142, 232
Barth, John, 116
Barthelme, Donald, 116
Beardsley, Aubrey, 187
Beckett, Samuel, 8
Bennett, Bruce, 5
Bentley, Christopher, 229
Berry, Betsy, xi, 24
*Best Australian Science Fiction Writing: A Fifty Year Collection, The*, 83
*Best Stories Under the Sun*, 228
*Best Stories Under the Sun 2: Traveller's Tales*, 228
*Big Sur & the Oranges of Hieronymus Bosch*, 36

Birns, Nicholas, 100
Blake, William, 58
Blockley, Mary, 159
*Book of the Reading*, 217
Borges, Jorge Luis, 83
*Bottom Line*, 208
Bowles, Paul, 116
Boyd, Robin, 28
Brautigan, Richard, 115–116, 156
*Breakfast at Tiffany's*, 60
Brett, Lily, 200
"Brian Kiernan, Critic and Editor: Some Reminiscences," 118
Brophy, Brigid, 17
"They Might Have Been Brother and Sister," 147
Browne, Sir Thomas, 161
Bryson, Bill, 19
Bukowski, Charles, 13–14, 116
*Bulletin, The*, 4
Burgess, Anthony, 21
Burnett, Gillian, 33, 181
Burns, Tim, 156
*Burnt Diaries*, 51, 200
Burroughs, William, 89, 116
"Buying Jeans in Balmain," 208
"Bye Bye Jack. See You Soon," 100–101, 113, 148, 154, 164

*Caliban*, 130
"Campus Novel," 200, 216
"Canal Run," 5, 7
*Cannery Row*, 119
Cantrell, Karin, 184
Cantrell, Leon, 184
Captain Cook, 161
Carey, Peter, xiv, 180, 182
*Car Lovers*, 100
"Cars in My Life," 3, 71
Cass, Shirley, 4

Cassady, Neal, 109, 151, 173
Cataldi, Lee, 55
Chairman Mao, 69
*Chance International*, 57
Cheney, Ros, 4
Chesterton, G.K., 122
*Chidiock Tichbourne*, 118
Christensen, Clem, 122
*Cimarron Review*, 23
Clancy, Laurie, 196
Clancy, Margaret, 23, 119, 200
Clarke, Marcus, xv, 32–34, 117–118, 219, 228, 234
"Class Feeling," 5–8, 12, 45
*Cleo*, 143
Cleland, John, 209
*Coast to Coast*, 44
Cohen, Leonard, 115
Cole, Brian, 180
"Come Down to the Cottage for a Weekend," 209
"Coming to an End," 81
*Condition Red*, 128
*Confessions and Memoirs: Best Stories Under the Sun 3*, 228
Conrad, Joseph, 217
*Contemporary Literary Criticism*, 100
Corris, Peter, 228, 232
*Cosmopolitan*, 143
Cowan, Zelman, 182
Cream, 102, 142
"Creative Writing," xi, xv, 120, 146, 226
Cunningham, Alison, 55
*Cultural Policy in Great Britain*, 4
*Cyril Hopkins' Marcus Clarke*, 228

*Daisy Miller*, 64, 78
Danko, Alex, 155–156

*Darkness at Noon*, 216
Davidson, Jim, 17, 61
Davidson, Robyn, 61
Davis, Mark, xii
Dawson, Paddy, 108
*Days of Wine and Rage*, 119
"Day to Day," 156
*Dead Father, The*, 116
"Death and the Compass," 45
Delacour, John, 141
*Dharma Bums, The*, 102
Dickens, Charles, 156, 173, 225
Dickey, James, 19
*Dick for a Day*, 175
"Dirty Girl, The," xi–xv, 1–79, 81–113, 115–211, 213–234
"Disgusting and Unacceptable Stories," 179
Disher, Garry, 232
*Dissent*, 37
Donavan, 142
*Don't Diet*, 230
"Don't Go Having Kittens," 209
"Don't Knock Zen," 103
Dow, Louise, 198
Doyle, Arthur Conan, 109
*Dragons Teeth: Literature in the English Revolution*, 20, 216
Dryden, John, 20
Duncan, Isodora, 90, 123
Duncan, Robert, 123
Dûrer, Albrecht, 161
Durrell, Lawrence, 3, 224
Dylan, Bob, 22, 91, 142, 182

*Ear in a Wheatfield, The*, 90, 96
Edmonds, Phillip, 232
*Education*, 196–197
Elgar, Edward, 104
Eliot, George, 156, 224

Eliot, T.S., 99, 156, 210, 224
Ellis, Bret Easton, 171
Ellwood, Thomas, 134
"Emma: Memoirs of a Woman of Pleasure," 209
*Esquire*, 65
"Expatriation, Location and Creativity," 2
"Europe," 8

Fabinyi, Andrew, 37
"Falling," 19
Falkiner, Suzanne, 195, 197
Faulkner, William, 13, 135
Fellowship of Australian Writers, 73
Ferlinghetti, Lawrence, 36, 59
Ferraro, Alison, 25
Ferraro, David, 25
*Ficciones*, 45
Fitzgerald, F. Scott, 61, 122, 232
Fitzgerald, Ross, 232
"Foreword," 133
*For the Term of His Natural Life*, 118
*Forty-Seventeen*, 175
"For Trees," 216
*Forum*, 143
"Fossil Evidence Re-Run, The," 208
Fowler, Henry Watson, 64–68, 71–78, 94, 186
*Framed*, 8
Fraser, Joan Austral, 196
*Fresh Milk: The Secret Life of Breasts*, 175
Freud, Sigmund, 61
"From His Apperception of the Terribleness of Things," 135, 200
Fromm, Erich, 60
"Frrrried Potatoes," 2
Fulton, Elizabeth, 154

Furphy, Joseph, 218
*Futility and Other Animals*, 42, 123, 181

Gable, Clark, 168
*Gangland*, xii
*Gargoyle*, 23
Garner, Helen, xiii
Gass, William, 116
Gelder, Ken, 147, 196
Gerrand, Rob, 83
Gent, Peter, 61, 65
Giles, Fiona, 175
Ginsberg, Allen, 59, 106
"Girl Behind the Bar is Reading Jack Kerouac, The," 150, 165, 207
Godard, Jean-Luc, 68
Goldberg, Samuel, 13
Goldblum, Jeff, 8
Gordon, Adam Lindsay, xv, 33, 106
Graham, Don, 24
*Great Gatsby, The*, 61
*Great Climate*, 23, 83, 216
Green, Michael, 4
Greer, Germaine, xiii, 25, 61, 188
Gregory, Sue, 81
Grimes, Sandra, 33
*Guernica*, 171
*Gulliver's Travels*, 217
Guyatt, Kit, 185

*Handbook of Renaissance Rhetoric, A*, 25
*Harpers*, 23
Harrison-Ford, Carl, 54, 79, 115
*Heart Matters*, 228
*Heart of Darkness*, 22, 217
"Hector and Freddie," 81

Hemingway, Ernest, 89, 111, 135, 202
Hendrix, Jimi, 142
Hergenhan, Laurie, xiii, 118, 228
*Hergesheimer Hangs In*, 232
"Her Most Bizarre Sexual Experience," 151, 169
*Her Most Bizarre Sexual Experience*, 23, 83, 151, 216
Hewett, Dorothy, 101
Higham, Charles, 4, 15, 23, 37
*History of the Life of Thomas Ellwood, The*, 134
*Holiday Peak*, 32
Holly, Buddy, 102, 104
Holmes, Sherlock, 104, 109
Holmes, Oliver Wendel, 32
Hope, A.D., 4
Horace, 200
Houghton, Des, xiv
*Huckleberry Finn*, 216
Hughes, Robert, xiii
Hughes, Ted, 200

"I am Monarch of All I Survey," 37
"Image of a Sort of Death, The," 182, 185–187
*In a Sunburnt Country*, 19
"In the Penal Colony," 101, 215
*Inside Out*, 182
*Invitation to a Marxist Lesbian Party*, 25
*Iron Heel, The*, 216
Isherwood, Christopher, 3, 140

"Jack Kerouac Wake, The," 111
"Jack Kerouac Wake—The True Story, The," 112
*Jake's Thing*, 127

James, Henry, xii, 4, 15, 32, 44–45, 51, 79, 101, 104, 112, 115, 122, 214, 217, 224
"Jealous of Ali," 5, 81
Jefferis, Barbara, 196
Jennings, Kate, 61, 148, 188
"Jerusalem," 58
"Joe's Absence," 31–33, 36, 42, 44, 54, 63–64, 79, 104, 110, 124, 193, 195
Joplin, Janis, 90
Jose, Nicholas, xiv
Joyce, James, 86, 112
*Julius Caesar*, 4, 20
"Just Wild about the Book Business," xv

Kali, 90
*Kangaroo*, 46, 139, 216
Karina, Anna, 68
Keesing, Nancy, 24
Kelly, Carmel, 180
Kendall, Henry, xv, 234
Keneally, Thomas, 4
Kerouac, Jack, xii, 60, 100, 103, 105–106, 110–112, 115, 150–151, 165, 168, 173, 176, 199, 207, 216
Kierkegaard, Soren, 60
Kiernan, Brian, 100, 111, 118, 130, 140, 155, 190, 230
King, Peter, 186
Knight, Stephen, 24, 55, 120, 181
Koestler, Arthur, 216
Krausmann, Rudi, 180
Kristofferson, Kris, 107

*Lady Chatterley's Lover*, 7, 59, 183
"Laundrom*t Person," 204, 207–208
Lane, William, 214
Lawrence, D. H., 45, 90, 216–217

Lawrence, Larry, 103
Lawson, Henry, 15, 218
*Leather World*, 66
*Leaving Home with Henry*, 232
Leavis, F.R., 45
Leves, Kerry, 133
Levy, Sandra, 61, 112
Lewis, Peter, 211
"Like Rat Turds to Me," 209
Lilith, 90
Lindsay, Jack, 4, 219
*Literature of Australia, The*, xiv
*Living Together*, 25, 58, 135, 143, 186
London, Jack, 216
*London Magazine, The*, 21
*Look Back in Anger*, 210
*Losing Alexandria*, 185
*Lost Illusions*, 142, 219–220, 223, 225
Lurie, Morris, 232
"Lycidas," 176

"MacFlecknoe," 20
McGann, Bernie, 35
McKellar, Dorothea, 19
Mackenzie, Henry, 83
McInerney, Jay, 31
McLaren, John, 144
*Magic of It, The*, 233
Maiden, Jennifer, 133
Mailer, Norman, 89, 187
*Makar*, 209
*Making It*, 21
Malouf, David, 4
*Man*, 44, 83–85, 215
*Manly Girls*, 119, 121
*Man of Feeling, The*, 84, 215
"Man of Slow Feeling, The," 83–84, 87

*Man of Slow Feeling, The: Selected Short Stories*, 215
Mansfield, Katherine, 122
*Marcus Brutus*, 4, 20
Marvell, Andrew, 20, 52
*Marvell: Modern Judgements*, 4, 20
Mason, Bobbie Ann, 171
"Mass Media and Literary Criticism," 37
"Mateship," 153
Maugham, Somerset, xi
*Meanjin Quarterly*, 17
Medusa, 90
Meek, Jan, 143
Mendelson, Phyllis Carmel, 100
Michelangelo, 117
"Midnight Readings," 101
Miller, Henry, 36, 57–60, 64, 79, 103, 160–161
Milton, John, 134
*Milton's Paradise Lost*, 4, 20
*Modern Auto*, 165
*Modern English Usage*, 94
Modigliani, Amedeo, 171
Monroe, Marilyn, 90
"Month in the Country, A," 208
Moorhouse, Frank, xii–xiv, 4, 11, 14, 31–32, 89, 98, 111, 117, 139, 181, 190, 196, 200, 211
Morris, William, 216
*Most Beautiful Lies––The: A Collection of Stories by Five Major Contemporary Fiction Writers: Bail, Carey, Lurie, Moorhouse and Wilding*, 100, 111, 130, 155
Murdoch, Iris, 21
Murray, Les, xiii
"My Country," 19
Myers, David, 228

*National Times*, 143
*National Treasure*, 231–232
*Nation Review*, 148, 190, 209
"Nembutal Story, The," 124, 171, 190–192
Neville, Richard, xiii–xiv, 37
*New and Rediscovered*, 139
*New Directions*, 94
*New Diversity: Australian Fiction 1970-88, The*, 147, 196
*New Poetry*, 96
*News from Nowhere*, 216
*Newswrite*, 35, 116
*New Yorker, The*, 22
"Night Flight to Amsterdam," 85
*1984*, 216
*Nimrod*, 23
*Nostromo*, 217
"Notes on Frank Moorhouse," 111
Noyce, Phillip, 185
"NY 1969," 216

Oakley, Barry, xiii
"Odour of Chrysanthemums," 45
"Odour of Eucalyptus," 44, 54
O. Henry, 122
*On the Road*, 59, 101–102, 104–106, 109–110
"Oracular Story, The," 124, 171, 190–191, 193, 196
Orton, Arthur, 118
Orwell, George, 216
Osborne, John, 210
*Ovdje*, 54, 57
Ovid, 20
*Oxford Book of Australian Short Stories, The*, 24
*Oz*, 37, 142

*Pacific Highway*, 213–214, 233

*Pamela*, 9
*Paradise Lost*, 4, 20, 134
*Paradise Regained*, 135
*Paraguayan Experiment, The*, 214
Paterson, A.B., 15
"Path of Poetry, The," 156
*Penguin Book of Comics*, 69
*Penguin Italian Cookbook, The*, 69
"Phallic Forest, The," 162, 180, 182–183, 185, 187
"Phallic Forest, The," 7, 15, 22, 36, 64, 68, 74, 108, 142, 155–156, 162–164, 180–181, 185–186, 208, 227
*Phallic Forest, The*, 116, 135, 179–180, 182, 190
Phillip, Arthur, 49
Phillips, A.A., 17
"Piece of This Puzzle is Missing, A," 196
Pierce, Peter, xv
Pinnochio, 183–184
"Pioneers," 216
*Play Abandoned*, 232
Podhoretz, Norman, 21
Poe, Edgar Allan, 122, 137
*Poetry Australia*, 37
*Political Fictions*, 216
*Portable Marcus Clarke, The*, 34
Porter, Cole, 65
*Portnoy's Complaint*, 18
Pound, Ezra, 63
Powell, Gareth, 42
*Prisoner of Mount Warning, The*, 233
Proust, Marcel, 209
"Punishment and Cures," 128

*Radical Reader, The*, 24
*Rainbow, The*, 216

*Raising Spirits, Making Gold, and Swapping Wives: The True Adventures of Dr John Dee and Sir Edward Kelly*, 220
Rand, Ayn, 60
Rankin, David, 200
Ravlich, Robyn, 156
*Reader's Guide to Australian Fiction, A*, 196
"Reading the Signs," 5–6
*Reading the Signs*, 5–7, 101, 150, 175, 215, 227
*Reading the Signs* (documentary film), 5–7, 101, 150, 175, 215, 227
"Recent Developments in Australian Writing with Particular Reference to Short Fiction," 130
"Red Rock," 110, 216
Reich, Wilhelm, 60–61
*Review of Contemporary Fiction*, 23
Rexroth, Kenneth, 21, 168
Reynolds, Jacquie, 68
Richardson, Owen, xv
Riley, Carolyn, 100
Robbe-Grillet, Alain, 156
Roberts, Jenny, 200
Roberts, Nigel, 4, 107
Robson, Wallace, 2
Rogers, Leslie, 108
Roth, Philip, 18
Rubens, Peter Paul, 171
*Running Wild: Essays, Fictions and Memoirs*, 140

"Sailing to Byzantium," 20
Salzman, Paul, 147, 196
Sanders, Ed, 116
*San Francisco Review of Books*, 116

*Scenic Drive*, 141–142, 144, 146–148, 150, 155, 161, 165, 167, 173, 176–178, 213
"See You Later," 82
Segal, Lynne, 61
Semmler, Clement, 44
"Sex in Australia From the Man's Point of View," 51
Sexton, Anne, 144
Shakespeare, William, xiii, 60, 99
Sharp, Martin, 141
Shearston, Garry, 64, 186
Sheffield, John, 4, 20
*Short Story Embassy, The*, 82, 115–117, 122–123, 135, 139–141, 143, 148, 202, 207
*Silence du Mer, Le*, 34
"Silence of the Seer, The," 4
Sillitoe, Alan, 217
*Simpsons, The*, 118
Singer, Isaac, 217
*Slow Motion: Changing Masculinities, Changing Men*, 61
"Small Publishers Press On Regardless with Short Runs of Novels," 232
Smith, C.P., 85
Smith, Ron, 147, 179, 186
Snowden, Lord, 69
Snow White and the Seven Dwarfs, 184
*Social Visions*, 217
"Somewhere New," 15–18, 22–24, 26–27, 29, 32, 54, 79
*Somewhere New*, 5, 24, 83, 216
Sonnino, Lee, 25
Sontag, Susan, 187
*Southerly*, 31, 123, 185
Spencer, Terence, 200
*Squire*, 65, 147, 179, 186

Stacey, Wes, 180
*Stand*, 5, 16, 57, 92, 100, 173, 211
Stead, Christina, 4, 26, 95, 116, 185, 192, 216, 219
Steinbeck, John, 119
Stewart, Ken, 228
Stivens, Dal, 180, 196
*Story of My Life*, 31
Stow, Randolph, 4
*Straight Sex: The Politics of Pleasure*, 61
Strauss, Richard, 104
*Studies in Classic American Literature*, 217
*Studies in Classic Australian Fiction*, xiii, 214, 217
*Such is Life*, 218
Sullivan, Erroll, 36
*Sun Also Rises, The*, 28, 111
*Superfluous Men*, 230
"Sybarites, The," 18, 24, 32–33, 38, 54, 56, 79
*Sydney Morning Herald*, 70, 116, 142, 155, 208
Syson, Ian, xii, 112

*Tabloid Stories*, 14
"Tabloid Story Story, The," 180, 191, 196
*Tabloid Story 2*, 190–191
*Tabloid Story Pocket Book, The*, 190, 196
Talbot, Colin, 142
*Tales of Mystery and Romance*, 112
"Tales of the Brave Ulysses," 142
Taylor, Jacquie, 69
Tchaikovsky, 102
"Tell No More," 82
*Tempest, The*, 99
Tennant, Emma, 51, 200

# Index

*Texas Quarterly*, 21
*Tharunka*, 200
"Their Minds Keeping on Working," 87, 92
"There's No Such Thing as a Gay Novel," 14
"Thing for the Tentacle Ladies," 87, 93, 96
*This Is For You*, 37, 101, 110, 216
Thomas, Dylan, 22
Thomas, Kristin Scott, 8
Thompson, Deborah, 7–9, 12
Thompson, Frank, 167, 182
Thompson, Jack, 185
Thompson, Victoria, 185
Thornhill, Michael, 186
*Thor*, 31, 205
*Three Tales*, 4
"Tichborne's Elegy, Written in the Tower before His Execution," 138
"Tichborne Redivivus: Re-Viewing Michael Wilding's Fiction," 140
Tichborne, Sir Roger, 118
Tichbourne, Chidiock, 118, 138
*Times Literary Supplement*, 116
Tiny Tim, 142
Titterton, Sir Ernest, 209
"Tittert*n," 208
"To His Coy Mistress," 52
Toth, Laszlo, 117
*Transatlantic*, 16
*Transition*, 24
Tranter, John, 4
"Trenchant Writer Blitzed Bohemia," 139
Trikha, Pradeep, 119
*Tropic of Cancer*, 59, 160
*Trout Fishing in America*, 116

"True Story of the Jack Kerouac Wake, The," xi–xv, 1–79, 81–113, 115–211, 213–234
*Turn of the Screw, The*, 122–123
"Two Boys at Grinder Bros," 218

*Ulysses*, 60
*Under Saturn*, 200, 216–217, 233

Valentino, Rudolph, 161, 168
"Vampire's Assistant at the 157 Steps, The," 142, 153, 206
*Vanity of Dulouz*, 101
Vedia, Mandie Molina, 45
Vercors (Jean Brullen), 34
"Vicki Viidikas Born 1945," 120
Viidikas, Vicki, 4, 11, 31, 61, 87, 99, 103, 117, 120, 128, 133, 139, 157, 180, 211, 226, 232
*Vivisector, The*, 219
*Vogue Australia*, 143

Walker, Nick, 232
*Waste Land, The*, 99, 210
"Watertight VW, The," 54
Webster, Owen, 13
"Welcome O Foreign Writer," 215, 217
*We Took Their Orders and Are Dead: An Anti-war Anthology*, 4
*West Midland Underground, The*, 4, 7–8, 81, 129, 141
*Westerly*, 54
West, Morris, 156
White, Patrick, 4, 31, 118, 185, 219
*Wild Amazement*, xi, 95–96, 99, 106, 121, 226
*Wild and Woolley: A Publishing Memoir*, xv, 100, 112–113, 226

*Wild Bleak Bohemia: Marcus Clarke, Adam Lindsay Gordon and Henry Kendall*, xv
*Wildest Dreams*, 4, 32, 112, 145, 153, 185, 220, 222–223, 225–226
Wilding, Dorothy Mary (Bull), xi–xv, 1–17, 19–26, 28, 30–37, 41–42, 44–51, 54–55, 57–60, 62–65, 67–76, 78–79, 81–91, 93–101, 103–113, 115–131, 133–135, 137, 139–160, 162–164, 166–167, 169, 171–173, 175–177, 179–182, 184–198, 200–211, 213–234
Wilding, Michael, xi, xiv, 1, 4, 89, 111, 118, 120, 133, 139–140, 181, 185, 195–196, 219, 221, 226, 230
Wilding, Richard "Wild Man of Letters," xi–xv, 1–17, 19–26, 28, 30–37, 41–42, 44–51, 54–55, 57–60, 62–65, 67–76, 78–79, 81–91, 93–101, 103–113, 115–131, 133–135, 137, 139–160, 162–164, 166–167, 169, 171–173, 175–177, 179–182, 184–198, 200–211, 213–234
Wilkes, Gerald, 31
Williamson, David, xiii, xv, 230
Wiltshire, John, 45
*Wishart's Quest*, 232
*With the Tiger*, 232
Witting, Amy, 196–197, 199
Woolley, Pat, 36, 112, 115, 142, 155–156, 225
"Words She Types, The," 217
Wordsworth, William, 86, 164
*Workingman's Paradise, The*, 214
*Wrappings*, 87
Wright, Judith, 4
*Writer's Talk: Michael Wilding*, 219, 221
"Writing Again After a While," 87, 90, 92–93
"Writing a Life," 217, 233
"Writing Humour," 1, 14, 115
"Written Off," 198
Wynette, Tammy, 88
Wynhausen, Elisabeth, 61, 119, 139, 143, 188

Yeats, W.B., 20
Yeo, Robert, 5
"Yet Once More," 150, 175–177
Yevtuschenko, Yevgeny, 73

*Zimmer's Essay*, 91

www.ingramcontent.com/pod-product-compliance
Lightning Source LLC
Chambersburg PA
CBHW050132170426
43197CB00011B/1809